M000266805

FROM Passion TO Leadership

INSPIRING STORIES OF THOSE WHO LEAD FROM THE HEART

Ali Schneider
Barb Kunst
Bob & Sue Burdick
Curt & Lori Beavers
Dany & Debbie Martin
Dougie Barlow
Harriet Sulcer
Ilona Morrison
Janice Neigum
Jeff Roberti

Jennifer Myers
Kerry & Mickey Daigle
Loren Lahav
Melissa Hyde
Nicole Scott
Nila Mason
Radka Prusha
Shelly Mackey
Wendy Campbell
Wendy Stewart

Compiled, edited, and published by

 CHANGE EMPIRE BOOKS

Published by Change Empire Books
www.changeempire.com

All rights reserved

Edited & designed by Change Empire Books

This book is sold subject to the condition that it shall not, by way of trade or otherwise, be lent, resold, hired out, or otherwise circulated without the publisher's prior consent in any form of binding or cover other than that in which it is published and without a similar condition including this condition being imposed on the subsequent purchaser.

The scanning, uploading, and distribution of this book via the internet or via any other means without the permission of the publisher is illegal and punishable by law. Please purchase only authorised electronic editions and do not participate in or encourage electronic piracy of copyrightable materials. Your support of the authors' rights is appreciated.

While the authors have made every effort to provide accurate internet addresses at the time of publication, neither the publisher nor the authors assume any responsibility for errors or for changes that occur after publication. Furthermore, the publisher does not have any control over and does not assume any responsibility for author or third-party websites or their content.

Legal disclaimer:

This book is designed to provide information and motivation to our readers. It is sold with the understanding that the publisher is not engaged to render any type of psychological, legal, or any other kind of professional advice. The content of each article is the sole expression and opinion of its author, and not necessarily that of the publisher. No warranties or guarantees are expressed or implied by the publisher's choice to include any of the content in this volume. Neither the publisher nor the individual author(s) shall be liable for any physical, psychological, emotional, financial, or commercial damages, including, but not limited to, special, incidental, consequential or other damages. Our views and rights are the same: You are responsible for your own choices, actions, and results.

Authors have tried to recreate events, locales and conversations from their memories of them. In order to maintain their anonymity in some instances, authors have changed the names of individuals and places, and may have changed some identifying characteristics and details such as physical properties, occupations and places of residence.

Letter from Jay Martin

I started this company to help as many people as possible realize their dreams.

I recently wrote a little pamphlet titled "Like a Bridge Over Troubled Waters", as a marketing piece to give people my insights into the Juice Plus+ Company, the products we offer, and how joining our mission can offer people more choices in their life, especially during the difficult times that so many are facing today. This book is a great accompaniment to my booklet. This is because these stories give you, the reader, a glimpse into how people from all walks of life took advantage of a partnership with the Juice Plus+ Company to create meaningful choices, and build their dreams.

I know each of these people, and they are not just telling their stories. They are sharing what is possible when you partner with us. The Juice Plus+ Company and our Partners teach one another. Our success is like a team sport.

I hope that these stories spark something within you. I am the luckiest man in the world because I have been able to work alongside people like the authors in this book, get to know them and their families, and their own personal quirks. I have laughed with them, and I have celebrated with them. This is a rich bunch of authors – rich in humor, heart, and a desire to help humanity. And if you do get inspired, then read my pamphlet "Like a Bridge Over Troubled Waters".

Jay Martin, Founder
The Juice Plus+ Company

Contents

Desperation to inspiration ~ 1
Jeff Roberti

Set the world on fire ~ 15
Shelly Mackey

Promises made, promises kept ~ 29
Harriet Sulcer

Meant for more ~ 43
Nila Mason

Make the bed or make a fortune ~ 57
Bob & Sue Burdick

I am enough ~ 71
Wendy Campbell

Becoming me ~ 83
Janice Neigum

Make a life, not just a living ~ 95
Curt & Lori Beavers

The best is yet to come ~ 107
Melissa Hyde

There are no excuses, only priorities ~ 121
Dany & Debbie Martin

Keep punching ~ 133
Kerry & Mickey Daigle

What if? ~ 147
Jennifer Myers

Believe ~ 159
Barb Kunst

What if? How one little question can change the
world ~ 173
Loren Lahav

Finding purpose ~ 183
Ali Schneider

Holding the space for good, to turn to great ~ 191
Dougie Barlow

You have to give up something ~ 205
Ilona Morrison

100 dollars in my shoe ~ 215
Radka Prusha

Surviving to thriving ~ 229
Nicole Scott

Love lifted me ~ 241
Wendy Stewart

Authors ~ 251
Write Your Own Book ~ 273

CHAPTER 1

Jeff Roberti

The distant hum of early morning traffic permeates the thin walls of my one-bedroom apartment. Sparsely furnished on a young bachelor budget, the open space is an echo chamber, sounds reverberating and bouncing from wall to wall with gleeful abandon.

I rub the sleep from my eyes as I hear my answering machine beep and click on repeat and glance at the clock radio. *Who is calling at 4am?*

I pull myself out of bed, my feet hitting the floor with a thud, and shuffle into the living room. The red light blinks furiously on the machine, and a corresponding feeling of panic rises in my throat. Nobody calls with good news at this time of the day. Hitting *play* reveals a voice trying to be heard through strangled sobs, but I can't understand a word my mother is saying.

The fact that my mother is crying hysterically is not a good sign.

About to rewind the tape, I pause when the phone rings and pick up the receiver, tentatively holding it to my ear and bracing myself for bad news.

"Jeff Roberti?" an unfamiliar voice asks.

"Yes," I say, swallowing loudly, my throat dry.

"This is Pastor Diaz at the regional hospital in Orlando." His voice is quiet, gentle, almost paralyzing as I wait for him to drop the bad news. "I'm afraid to tell you that your father has just died," he continues, adding, "I'm sorry, son."

The room starts to spin, my world is thrown into chaos. I drop the receiver to run to the bathroom and purge from both ends.

How can Dad be gone? He's only 46.

I sit on the floor and weep until the morning sun burns through the windows and I am weak with exhaustion.

Mom and Dad and my younger brother Jonathan were only in Orlando, two hours away, in order to see our other brother Paul graduate his diploma with the navy. Knowing they were together is some small comfort, though it doesn't ease my grief.

As the hours press on, and phone calls fly back and forth across the state, I learn that Dad died of a massive heart attack that nobody saw coming. They went out to dinner and then returned to the motel, and in the early hours of the morning, he got up, grabbed his chest, and died. No second chance.

I waved them off a few days ago—Mom behind the wheel of her rusty old Plymouth—and said a brief goodbye, never imagining it would be the last time I saw Dad alive.

What will Mom do now? Dad sold encyclopedias to support the family, and despite his incredible work ethic, there has always been more month than money. He was talking about them moving back to West Virginia, about buying Mom a new car, for years. I suppose neither of those will happen now.

Images of my childhood clamor for attention in my head. I remember getting up late at night to get a drink of water or go to the bathroom, and I'd see my dad sitting up in the living room—smoking, thinking, his face drawn into taut lines of worry. My parents have struggled financially for years, and now, at 22 and as the oldest of three boys, I want to step up and help. I just don't know how. I've waited tables, mowed lawns, cleaned pools, worked construction—anything and everything to make ends meet. But it will never be enough.

I am soon convinced that stress killed my father, and it shapes my model of the world.

This inspires me to take a more philosophical approach to life than my friends and family anticipate – I decide to make my father's death mean something. It's not what happens in life; it's what you do with what happens. It's the meaning you give it.

I don't want my dad's death to be just some tragic event that happens to our family—I want to take the pain and turn it into purpose. This becomes what drives me, fueled by a yearning hunger for more. I don't want to end up like him, stressed, almost broke, and dead before I'm 50.

My burning desire to succeed is backed by an incredibly strong work ethic. I just need the right path to get there. I try a network marketing company that delivers decent results, but I want *greatness*. So, I keep looking. I need an opportunity to go into business for myself, to be my own boss, and to earn what I'm worth. There's no point in simply trading time for money.

I listen to tapes of every speaker I can get my hands on, and am fortunate enough to meet and be mentored by prodigious sales pros like Jim Rohn, Larry Thompson, and Mark Hughes.

I'm invited to a convention in North Carolina that I'm assured will change my life. It's a ten-hour drive from Sarasota, and I don't have money for flights or a hotel, but that's not about to stop me. I jump into my car and start driving… Rolling Stones and Zeppelin playing as loud as the crackly car stereo will allow—which, to be honest, isn't very loud, given my car is a dinosaur limping towards extinction.

After a long drive, with more than a few pitstops for coffee and naps, the signs welcome me to Asheville. I sleep in the car, shower at the nearest gym to the venue, and put on my one suit. When I arrive in the crowded parking lot of the Grove Park Inn,

I pull my hair back into a ponytail, adjust my skinny tie, and walk into the conference with the most confidence I can muster.

The energy in the room is palpable, electric, and I pull my jacket tighter around my middle as excitement courses through my body. Speakers are positive, encouraging, inspiring, and every new person who steps on the stage fills me with the confidence to take the next step towards my own business. The adrenaline courses through my body—I'm ready.

This is it. This is what I'm meant to do.

God has answered my prayers. This is my chance to do something great.

I fill out an application to become a partner and walk away from the event, confident that this is my path. I don't have a higher education, and I don't have contacts, connections, or a dollar to burn, but I have a strong vision and a work ethic to match. I tear up my list of excuses, borrow some money against my car and buy a box of inventory, ready to start putting my dreams into action.

As Jim Rohn once told me, "Jeff, if it's to be, it's up to me."

Jay Martin and the Juice Plus+ Company are about to change my life. *I have just officially become the business owner of my own health product distributorship!*

*

Zig Ziglar is known for saying, "You will get all you want in life if you help enough other people get what they want."

I create the mindset that I am going to go out and meet people, come from a position of strength, a voice of authority, and support it with all the passion and enthusiasm I have burning within. I want to lead by example and be the best distributor and best partner on my team. I'm going to acquire the most new customers and most new partners, hold myself accountable, and build safety in numbers.

I create a 90-day plan and put it into immediate action. I go into a market, camp out for three months, and run ads in the newspaper to invite people to my presentations. I become very good at getting the phone to ring and while I don't have the money for an office, I use hotel lobbies to meet people and present to them from my presentation book, sharing the company story, the product story, and the opportunity story. I speak to 20 or 30 people every day for a year; in other words, close to 10,000 people a year see me speak as I introduce them to the Juice Plus+ whole food based nutrition in a capsule as well as to the business opportunity.

My drive and ambition are burning bright, but I also have a servant's heart and people can tell that I really care. I add to my team at lightning speed and am honored to meet so many incredible people.

One day over lunch, I flick through the magazine of another network marketing company and see an article about a couple named Bob and Sue. I call Bob and arrange to meet them in Fort Lauderdale for a presentation. Bob has a long beard and tattoos peeking out of his shirt—he looks a little like Charles Manson and I'm a little intimated, unsure if he will respond to my energy.

After the presentation is finished, I ask, "Did you see an opportunity and are you prepared to get started?"

Wordlessly, he shuffles over to Sue and talks to her quietly, nodding every so often, before coming back and looking me square in the eye. "Jeff, we're going to borrow the money from our rent money and get started here tonight," he says. "But if this is a scam, I'm gonna chase you to the frickin' ends of the earth."

And with that I sign the first power couple on my team—and then everything changes for all of us.

I just keep building one leader after another. In one year, I become the number one income earner, at just 24 years old. Corporate invite me to Memphis to see if I am a two-headed monster. They can't believe that somebody is building this fast, but I studied the best guys in sales to get to this point. I believe in the company, I believe in the product, and I believe in the opportunity. Most importantly, I believe in myself. What I lack in money, education, experience, and background, I make up for with work ethic.

"Nobody can lift your weight for you," I tell the guys at head office. "You get out of this what you put into it."

They all smile and nod in agreement.

Expansion feels good and I won't stop until there is nothing left to reach for.

Soon, the day arrives. I have worked hard, reinvested into the business, burned the midnight oil, and put in that extra 10% effort above everybody else. And it has paid off. My bank balance shows the goal I had in mind and I know exactly what I want to do with it. I drive down to the new car dealership, puffs of smoke exiting my exhaust when I accelerate. Today I get to fulfil a dream I've had since I was a kid, sitting in the back of my mom's rusty, dinged car, dreaming of a sleek new car in the driveway.

I'm so proud when I hand over the cheque to the sales guy, who seems a little taken aback by someone of my age buying a shiny, top model automobile with all the bells and whistles.

Don't worry, sir, I think, smiling to myself. *It won't be the last.*

I pay for 12 months' insurance, top up a fresh gas card, and drive the shiny blue Lincoln Mark VIII out of the lot and head out of town for its inaugural outing. I open and close the electric windows with childlike glee as I drive, grinning. Would Dad would be proud of me? I like to think so.

I drive for hours, enjoying the purr of the Linc's powerful engine. And, finally, I arrive. I go to the trunk and get out the materials I need, nervous and eager that this day has finally come.

I walk up to the front door of the log house, eyes following the smoke rising from its chimney and then bring my attention back down as I knock twice, loudly. The door opens and there she is, a smile breaking across her face.

"Jeff?" Mom says, pulling me into a hug, her arms tight around me. "I thought you weren't coming until new year."

"I wanted it to be a surprise," I say with a grin, and step back so she can see the car.

The West Virginian morning sun reflects off the bonnet, highlighting the pretty, deep blue duco and reflecting in Mom's eyes. The large, red bow I affixed to the roof is bright and sleek and shiny against the glare of the mountain snow and I look back at her, almost holding my breath, to see her reaction. She stands with her hand over her mouth, tears cascading over her cheeks.

"Jeff," she manages, eyes glistening.

"Merry Christmas, Mom," I say, dropping the keys into her hand. "Thank you for everything."

Everything has been worth it for her expression alone.

*

"Ich spreche kein Deutsch" is the first phrase I learn when I find out that Juice Plus+ is expanding to Europe. Specifically, Germany.

I don't speak German. How am I meant to start a team in a country where I don't speak the language? Europe is an enormous market, and being able to grow my team across the pond would be the opportunity of a lifetime. But how can I share the product and business opportunities we offer in a country I've not only never been to but also have no clue about the language?

If only I'd turned out to be a language whiz on top of my business skills.

But, as they say, the bigger the problem, the bigger the paycheck—and I'm more than ready for the challenge.

Can't manage on your own? Recruit somebody who knows what you lack.

I place ads in the newspaper for English–German bilingual speakers and meet with everybody who responds. Some interviewees are more promising than others, but in the end, I luck out on the first few people I meet: Tom, Mark, and Jacque. The sons of German immigrant families, they are polite, young, and enthusiastic. And more than willing to cut me some slack for my shoddy German.

I meet each of them in the lobby of the Hyatt hotel in Sarasota. Sipping on my coffee, I explain my plan to the tall young man seated across from me. "If you go with me and open up Europe," I tell him, "we'll start in Germany and then we'll expand into Austria, Switzerland, Italy, all over…" Watching his face, I add, "I can help you become one of the top marketing directors in the company."

Jacque looks suitably impressed, and the other meetings prove to be just as successful.

After a few weeks of training, I take the three of them to a Juice Plus+ conference. The light in their eyes reflects my own excitement.

After the conference, I fly to Frankfurt.

The arrivals hall is bustling with people, and I look around, wondering what to do next. This is my first time outside of North America, and while my team will be meeting me here, for now I'm on my own.

I'm pleasantly surprised at how many people speak English, although I can't get to the safety of my room fast enough. By the time my team are in town to meet me, I'm buzzing, ready to start our European expansion.

Under my direction, the guys hire a hotel conference room every day for a week and place ads in multiple local newspapers for the presentations. When I walk into the room, the patterned carpet and beige curtains demonstrate chic professionalism. The lectern at the front of the room is ready for my translator, the products are set up on the table, and the partner application forms sit alongside them, ready. The room is ready, the team is ready, I'm ready.

I have come to live by a mantra called *tell, show, try, do*. When I sign up a team member, I say, "Let's do this together. I'll tell you, then I'll show you, you try it, and once you're ready, I'll cut you loose."

As the room fills with hundreds of people, their hushed voices a gentle susurrus in the large space, I clench my fists by my side, pumping them a few times to maximize my energy. Almost every seat in the room is full. It's an impressive turnout.

"Welcome to the Juice Plus+ Company." My voice booms through the room. "The company with a heart."

"Willkommen bei der Firma Juice Plus+," Mark says, smiling at the sea of faces. "Das Unternehmen mit Herz."

The presentation flies by, and by the time I finish, the room is buzzing with energy. Feeling good, I go on to talk about the history of the company, the products and what they can do, while Mark translates with easy confidence.

At the end of the session, people crowd around the tables at the front, eager to fill out application forms and ask questions; their motivation to become involved is almost palpable. It sets an incredible precedent for the coming months.

As the weeks go by, the numbers are never quite the same. Sometimes there are three, four, or five people in the room; other times, they bring their friends and there are 15 or 20. If I've learned anything from my mentors, however, it's to remember the law of averages. If we show up day after day, presenting with enthusiasm and heart, results will follow.

A couple of weeks in, I notice something funny. I start telling the company story and the product story, and after I finish a line, one of the guys translates but talks for much longer than the sentence I've just finished. And then I realize they've translated me so many times that they know the whole spiel by heart.

Every night I go back to my room and pop a CD into my Walkman. I listen to a lot of experts; I always feed my mind. I truly believe that you have to keep yourself in a peak resourceful state, to show up every day and put in the work. Success breeds success. I am primed for success, and my time in Germany is already showing results.

We spend 90 days in Frankfurt, 90 days in Munich, 90 days in Berlin; my team is thriving and working with them on creating their success is a dream come true. I am fortunate to have chosen a very coachable team and they respond incredibly well to my leadership.

"Simple disciplines equal multiple rewards because you don't have to do a thousand things," I tell them. "Just do a handful of things a thousand times over, and then over again. Consistency is required, but if you keep going, you will reap the rewards."

And reap they do. I build five frontline National Marketing Directors during my first year in Germany and then we move on to Switzerland, Austria, Italy...

Five years I spend creating a team in Europe, ultimately building 40 frontline marketing directors around the world. My biggest lesson is that it's never about you. It's always about the person in front of you, meeting their needs, adding value to their lives, and creating raving fan relationships.

After five years in the US and Canada, then five years in Europe, I keep cranking out daily action for another ten years. Long-term relationships equal long-term success, and the years I spend in Europe—making almost one hundred trips to the continent—set me up for many years to come.

*

The auditorium, 10,000 people strong, erupts into applause as I take the stage. The music is pumping, and everybody is on their feet, clapping and yelling encouragement. What an incredible crowd, I think as I walk to the lectern, checking one last time that my over-ear microphone is securely taped to the side of my head so I can gesture freely during my speech. I'm introduced as the #1 top earner in the company, and I'm ready to inspire this audience of beautiful people.

"I think the reason they bring me up here is to show you guys that if I can do it, anyone can do it," I say, and a few whoops of agreement and support arise in the audience. "My outcome today is to create an experience—to move people emotionally. To keep it real, to keep it transparent, to keep it authentic with some emotional sincerity."

I adjust the collar of my black shirt. *It's so hot under these lights.* Beads of sweat form on my back and across the top of my brow. I spend 30 minutes speaking to a generous audience who I hope are captivated and encouraged to take massive action after my presentation.

In the next break, a few work friends come and talk to me and in about a ten-minute period, congratulations on my speech are followed by about five different ways of asking about my health. I know what they're talking about. I love traveling for work, meeting people, talking, engaging, learning about their needs, and entertaining. Months fly by, full of lunches, dinners, and drinks with more team members than I can count. It's definitely the best part of my business, but it's come at a price. I've gained about five pounds a year and have reached 270 pounds.

Only last year I lost my brother Paul to a heart attack—just like Dad. He was only 49 when he died, and a small voice in my head constantly warns me that I could be next.

I make an appointment to see a cardiologist and the news is not great.

"You're a walking time bomb, Jeff," the doctor says. "Especially with your family history. Honestly, it's not a matter of if—it's when."

This sobering news follows me home, and I retreat to my office and reflect. As I sit down at my desk, I look at the framed picture of my parents on their wedding day, my dad tall and dapper in his bow tie, and I start to cry. I take the picture off the wall and hug it to my chest. It feels like it's been a lifetime since I last saw him and heard him say, "Hi, son."

After returning the photo to the wall, my gaze moves to the picture on my desk of me, Paul, and Jonathan, Paul in fluorescent paisley shorts and me and John in bright Hawaiian shirts. Immediately, the tears intensify. I'm alone at 2 am, sobbing in my office, the uncertain light of the moon outside my window adding to my raw anguish.

I can't let my mom bury another son.

This is a defining moment in my life. *Enough is enough.* I look around the office at my beautiful display of Juice Plus+ products: the capsules and the Complete protein shakes. *They'll work better if I actually take them,* I muse, and almost manage a laugh.

When daylight comes, I go for a walk on the beach. Weeks later, my walk becomes a run and soon I'm flying high on a health kick that turns into a daily part of my lifestyle. I take responsibility for my own health and treat my body like a temple, not an amusement park.

Soon I show up as an example, rather than a warning. It's not for vanity; I just don't want my mom put through such intense grief ever again.

At the next conference, people react very differently to me. I have a new product story because I'm walking the talk. More than once I hear versions of, "Who is this guy?" and I'm thrilled to find that I'm inspiring other people on their own health journeys.

When I leave the conference, my phone starts ringing with requests.

"Jeff, can you come present...?"

"Jeff, can you please talk to my team?"

"Jeff, we want to know what you've been doing."

The *ping, ping, ping* of my phone every few minutes alerts me to the multitude of calls, texts, and emails asking me to speak to a new era of Juice Plus+ entrepreneurs.

Over the next six years, I keep the weight off, life is great, and the flood of requests has never stopped coming. Simon Bowler, from Corporate in Europe, calls. "Would you be willing to come over and do a big tour for the month of September?" he asks. "Everybody misses you and we haven't seen you in forever."

Poland, Israel, Spain, Italy, England, France, Germany... I smile as the town car slides soundlessly down Highway 75 to take me home. Go back to Europe? I'd love to.

When I arrive home to my beach house in Siesta Keys, Florida, I make my way to my office, sit down at my desk, and look out at the ocean.

My youngsters over in Europe do business very differently now than when I was in my twenties. They have social media and videos and smartphone apps, when we used to celebrate being able to send faxes! They're called influencers now—and they've certainly influenced me! I'm honored to do what I do, and to make a real difference in people's lives every single day.

A few years ago, I was self-medicating and drinking; now, I don't drink. I've come so far. I'm happy, I'm healthy, I'm at peace. I've grown so much spiritually, emotionally, and physically. I put God first, and my life flows with harmony.

I'm a totally different person now and I'm at a different stage of my career. I'm more of a mentor, a role model, and an ambassador. I still work with my team and I still recruit customers and partners, but I pass them onto my leadership team. I still show up and provide value; I don't just do nothing—I'm still very plugged in.

I'm 60 years old. Maybe I should slow down, but I don't feel like I'll ever retire. I love what I do too much. Now I take time to scuba dive, kayak, and paddleboard and play pickleball and tennis. As I watch the world go by, I thank God every day for the life I have been able to build. I'm so grateful.

My *why* has evolved, and maybe now, after 36 years in the business, it's about *leaving a legacy*. About paying it forward. I'll never forget the defining moment of filling out my application and getting signed up, and now I want to inspire the next generation of partners and leaders.

I hope I did you proud, Dad.

CHAPTER 2

Set the world on fire

Shelly Mackey

"Gosh, Mom," my daughter says, right after my birthday toasts, "in five years, that's how old your dad was when he died of cancer."

Happy 52nd birthday to me.

I feel a stabbing pain in my heart and the wind is knocked out of me as the realization hits me. He died so young—25 years ago— and I can still see the way he looked at me with such love. "Hey, Sassy Britches," he'd say in his quiet mid-western voice, trying to hide his amusement at something I'd said or done. Where do the years go?

My oldest daughter Morgan reaches out to touch my arm, her brow furrowed as she frowns at her younger sister. "Gosh, Marisa, you're gonna make Mom cry."

Marisa is right, though. My children didn't even get to meet my father; he passed away at only 57, before they were even born. I'm healthy, though, right? And fit. *I look pretty darn good for my age*, I think, casting a sideways glance at myself in the buffet mirror.

"No, no, no, it's okay," I say. "I needed to hear that." My words come from a place of wanting to pacify my middle daughter, rather than from a belief that I, too, might genuinely be in the potential path of a premature death.

The next morning, I just make it to my favorite pew in time for church to start. I love the feeling I get from connecting with God among fellow Christians, and I smile at the young lady getting up to share the reading. "Don't you know that your body is the temple of the Holy Spirit, who lives in you and who was given to you by God?" she says, reading from Corinthians.

Well, of course I do, I say to God. *I know You live within me.*

Do you? He replies. *Do you treat your body as such?*

I look around, curious to see if anybody else is receiving this same message from the reading. Everybody gazes up at the pulpit, but no faces betray the listener as experiencing the same internal dialogue as me.

The priest nods at the reader, swishes his robe, and leans forward on his knee as he hoists himself up the altar stairs to share the gospel. Today he reads from Matthew, and a few lines in I know there is a message coming through for me today, loud and clear.

"You blind Pharisee! First wash the inside of the cup and the dish, and then the outside will become clean, too."

I'm sure he looks straight at me, sitting in the front row, as he says this.

I mean, I try to eat healthy, and I think I look pretty good for 52 years old, especially when I've had four kids, and...

Then I stop my runaway train of defense. What does the inside of me look like? Do I have cancer growing, like my dad did?

God, I hear you.

On Monday morning, I enrol in a course about the science between diet and disease. Based on science, I learn the truth about dairy, fruits and vegetables and how important they are, exercise, the physiology of the body, the psychology of the body, and how important water is to the body. Each segment of the course focuses on a different area of nutrition or disease, and when I am immersed in the whole foods segment, a few of the terms seem familiar... and then I realize that I've consumed whole food based concentrates before. I was taking Juice Plus+ a few years ago.

I was attending daily mass at church, and a nurse named Allison would stalk me every day after the service. "Shelly, you should get on Juice Plus+," she'd say, running along beside me as I tried to dodge her on my way back to the car. "Your kids should be on Juice Plus+."

"Is that like Sunny Delight?" I asked her once, unaware that the two products bore absolutely no resemblance to each other.

"Oh no, it's nothing like it," she snapped. "That's not even orange juice."

Every day I'd leave mass feeling refreshed and pious, and every day I'd climb into my car feeling harassed, slamming the door and fumbling through my keys, eager to get away from her.

Eventually, I caved. I just wanted her off my back, so I fished around in my purse and produced a credit card. Allison reverently picked it out of my hands and entered my details into her little book. A short time later my order arrived, and Allison never approached me again. In fact, I didn't even see her much after that and my morning peace was restored.

Unfortunately, the children weren't terribly enthused about consuming more products in the morning. At that time, my kids were on multiple allergy and asthma medications, and the idea of adding to that was a burden they didn't wish to endure.

"Fine," I said, shoving the Juice Plus+ containers to the back of the pantry, before calling and canceling my future orders.

A couple of years later, I meet a lovely lady named Susan at Bible study, and after a pleasant conversation, she invites me to lunch. Sitting at a local café, I glance around at the lovely décor before focusing my attention back on Susan, who smiles warmly across the table.

"So… do you work outside the home?" she asks, taking a sip of her sparkling water.

"No, I'm a stay-at-home mom," I reply. "But I do a lot of volunteering at church and school." It feels good to have somebody interested in me, which sometimes doesn't feel the case when you're in the 'mom' category.

Susan looks at me with a flat expression, as though unimpressed, and I quickly remember my manners. "Let's talk about you," I say. "What do you do?"

"I'm a Juice Plus+ distributor," she says, her mouth turning upwards into a broad smile.

Here we go again.

"Oh my gosh, I've got that junk piled up in my pantry," I say, leaning back in my chair and considering my exits.

"Well, first of all, it's not junk," she says. "And secondly, you should pull it out tonight and get your kids to start taking it."

"They don't want to take it," I reply, cognizant of the fact she doesn't know my kids at all, or what a task this would be.

"Just read them all the ingredients that are in it and ask them if they'd prefer you cook that for dinner," she says. "Broccoli, parsley, tomato, carrot, garlic, beet, spinach, cabbage…" She rattles off a list of ingredients that I know my children would prefer to avoid.

So, this is what I do. I come home and assert my mom-power. "I'm the mom and you're going to take these, and that's the end of it," I say, acting as authoritative as I can manage despite feeling a lack of confidence inside. Of course I want my children to be healthy, but with four young people to manage, it can be challenging to muster the energy of an authority figure at all times.

Susan is different from Allison, and I know that she is not going to leave it at just having the kids taking the capsules—I know she's going to come after me to start selling it. And try she does—

for nine years. Almost a decade passes, with her regular phone check-ins. Every time she calls to invite me to an event, I say no.

"Susan, I know why you're inviting me," I say. "You think I'm gonna get there and then I'm gonna sell Juice Plus+. But I'll tell you right now, that's not gonna happen."

I'm no longer anti-Juice Plus+; This is more about me feeling uncomfortable with 'selling'. We are fortunate that my husband, a CEO, earns a great income, and we don't want for anything. I also had a bad experience with another company in the past and don't want to go down that road again.

Maybe there is a pattern in my behavior, but eventually Susan wears me down.

"Hey, Shelly," she says on that last call, "you know the last time I talked to you, you told me you were trying to figure out why your dad died of cancer? Well, there's a nurse coming to Kansas City; she's a holistic nurse, and I think you will really identify with her."

A few weeks later, I'm at the KU Edwards campus, sitting in the audience as nurse Staci Joy talks, glued to every word she says. The room is huge and the energy is high; her fascinating words have enraptured around 300 people, and the collective enthusiasm is contagious. Staci has been an ER nurse for 15 years and oozes California vibes with her pantsuit, backpack, and blonde pixie haircut. Her energy is chilled, laid back, and coupled with a very science brain—very opposite to me! Overall, she's enticing, engaging; you can't wait to hear what she'll say next. Her talk is called 'One Little Thing,' and it isn't the sales pitch I'd feared. I can tell she deeply cares and that is what speaks to me. She discusses not eating dairy or gluten. Despite coming from a third-generation dairy family, I am aware of the issues cow's milk can create and have been dairy free for six months, but I didn't know that gluten is the protein in wheat. We're in Kansas, after all— the Wheat State. Stacey draws in the audience with compelling research-based evidence about the way you're currently eating and makes it clear that she loves you right where you're at. She also draws you into change without making you feel like you're a bad person.

"When you make a change," she explains, "your body is like a GPS that just takes a short time to recalculate your route." Her words encourage us to make one small change that will impact our lives in a large way.

It's so intriguing that I decide to attend the second day of her presentation. First thing Saturday morning, my daughter Marisa and her friend Shalin sit beside me in the front row of the lecture hall. Long tables have been set up with about ten people across, and a long aisle runs down the middle. A lot fewer people are in attendance today but the energy is still high. A short time into the presentation, I realize that today is not as much about the products as it is about the company and the business opportunity—but as we're squarely in the middle of the front row, there is no escape. As the day progresses, my fears dissipate, and I'm pulled into the possibilities. A company that's been in existence for many years; whole food based capsules, not vitamins; legitimate Gold Standard research with double-blind, placebo-controlled tests... This is the real deal. Towards the end of the session, they do a drawing and give away five free tickets to the next Juice Plus+ Live Conference in Orlando, Florida.

"Yes! That's me!" Marisa calls from beside me. She jumps up in her seat, high-fives me, and bounds up to the stage to collect her prize.

"Oh! That's me!" cries Shalin a few moments later, running to join Marisa at the front of the room.

It looks like we're going to the conference.

*

The 5000-strong animated crowd outside the convention center impatiently pushes against the doors. I feel closed-in in the sweltering heat, dragged along by another forward surge every time the music crescendos. Surely it's almost time for them to open the doors? We've been here almost two hours.

"As soon as the doors open," Susan told me on the phone last night, "I'll run and save seats."

"What for?" I asked, naively; this was obviously going to be my first Juice Plus+ conference.

"Well, Juice Plus+ people are the kindest, nicest, sweetest people you'll ever meet... except for one time they are not nice people," she replied. "And that's when the conference doors are locked and they're getting ready to open them up."

And she's right. Looking around me, with the limited view I have given the sea of thousands of heads, all talking and jumping and perky, I can see people lined up like they're going to eat their last meal—it's borderline psychotic. I cannot believe the intensity of this crowd, and I've been to see Tom Jones.

"You're gonna want to get as close to the front as possible," Susan says, standing beside me.

She doesn't need to tell me twice. I may not be a Juice Plus+ convert quite yet, but I'm front row all the way. We don't know which set of doors they are going to open first—nobody knows. It's like a lottery. I'm looking to both sides, ready to rush forward when I see an opening. I'm ready.

Suddenly, the doors directly in front of us swing open, and gasps crescendo behind us like a cresting wave. A sea of bodies pushes us from behind, and I'm off, charging towards the front of the convention center. I used to play sports, and I know how to take the angle. Hundreds of people sprint forward; I stay at the front of the pack. A woman in front of me loses a shoe and tumbles down into a heap on the floor... and I hurdle her. A surge of guilt overwhelms me and I call over my shoulder, "Are you okaaaay?" as I keep running. I'm sure somebody will help her.

I reach the front rows and know that I'm safe. Except that a large group of men and women are throwing Australian flags across the full second row of seats. "Oh, heck no!" I shout, pulling every item I own from my purse and strewing them across the five seats we'll need. We're safe.

I look around with a satisfied smile to see where my group has ended up, and see Susan jumping up and down, waving her hands, apparently looking for us to show us the seats she's managed to nab... about 30 rows behind. I catch her eye and her jaw drops for a moment before she breaks into a grin and mouths *Whaaaaat?* at my near-front-row position. Running down to hug me, she says, "How did you get here?!"

"I hurdled someone," I say. We both laugh hysterically and wait for the girls to join us.

The room hums so loudly with anticipation that it practically vibrates. Thousands of warm, eager bodies quickly fill the room, many singing and tapping to the music that throbs through the open space. The room is enormous, cavernous, and the ceiling is high, so the sounds and emotions are tense, loud music reverberating inside the space.

After getting settled and introducing ourselves to the people around us, our attention is diverted by loud music and lights coming from the stage. Bam bam bam! The music intensifies and three figures stroll onto the stage, smiling and waving. The crowd jumps to their feet, screeching and clapping in time to the music. How can you help but love this company?

The professionalism of the conference is astounding. Marisa is beside me and regularly grabs hold of my arm to whisper in my ear. "Oh my gosh, Dad would be dying at how professional this is," she says numerous times. And she's right. I am genuinely shocked by the sophistication of the presentations and the stature of the speakers. Dr. Sears, the world's most famous pediatrician, is joined by impressive speakers like Julie Herbst – the face of Juice Plus+, and Juice Plus+ Company founder Jay Martin. I already know Juice Plus+ products are phenomenal from my own use; I heard some of the research at the presentation in Kansas, and now this.

The second day of the conference is just as fantastic, the stories shared by the National Marketing Directors (NMDs) are inspirational, and the closing speech by Jeff Roberti is both endearing and rousing. The whole experience is unbelievable, and every hair on my body stands up with the inner knowing that I have to become a bigger part of this company.

We stay for the weekend with my sister Kathi, who owns a beach house in Englewood Beach, Florida, only a couple of hours from the conference venue. On the way home, I can't stop talking about our experience. "You guys, how can we keep this to ourselves?" I gush. I've been keeping quiet because I was embarrassed about what people might think if I dare to 'sell' something. Now, I no longer care what people think. This product is incredible and the company is rock solid. Why is every doctor in America not sharing this? We owe it to people to share what we've learned.

When I return home, I immediately visit my girlfriend Lesley, who owns an athletic club. She's been taking the products for a long time, like me, and has also seen benefits but didn't think about selling them because she already has a successful business. She ushers me into her office, and I close the door quietly behind me, then rush to sit down.

"Oh, my goodness, Lesley," I exclaim, "we have to start telling everybody about Juice Plus+. You and I have just been sitting on this, and we have to share it!" I tell her all about the conference and what I've learned.

"Okay, okay," she says, and pulls out her calendar.

The only flaw in my plan is that I don't know how to share the news, so I contact Susan, who sends me a DVD and a box of information, and we set to work. Lesley sets up a time and sends out invitations for our first event, and on the night, fear takes over. I drive to the venue down a dark, two-lane road, begging God, "Please do not let one person ask me a question because I will not know the answer."

Armed with the little 13-inch TV/DVD player from my children's bedroom, I set up on top of the refrigerator in the smoothie area of the athletic club. Ten people sit in front of me and are politely attentive when I introduce myself and my history with Juice Plus+. I tell them about how Lesley got started with the products.

"Lesley, you're the healthiest person I know," I say. "Do you get seven to thirteen servings of fruits and vegetables daily?"

"Well, heck now, who could do that seven days a week?" she responds, and a number of people smile or nod in recognition, and a few lean forward a little when I hit play on the DVD, *Bridging the Gap*. The 11-minute video features eight doctors talking about micronutrients and Juice Plus+ and is an excellent overview of the product benefits.

After the video, I tell them about my children's and my experience with Juice Plus+. Then I tell them about how my husband called Juice Plus+ snake oil for the first five years, refusing to take it. Then, once he started taking it, the added nutritional support helped provide the foundation of health that he needed and he's been a fan ever since. "Do you have enough Juice Plus+?" is the first question he asks whenever we pack for a trip.

I have laid out order forms along the smoothie bar, and everyone clamors around to fill them in... and nobody asks any questions.

*

It's April 2014, and I'm in Phoenix for another conference. The energy and intensity are the same as in Orlando, and when 26 year old Katie Ravey from the UK takes the stage, I am mesmerized. She has reached NMD level in only 18 months, which is not common.

"How did she do that so fast?" I ask Susan, who is once again beside me.

"Oh, they have a different marketing plan," she says.

"Well, that shouldn't matter. I'm gonna do it fast too," I proclaim, my former third-grade school teacher mind kicking into action for how I'm going to achieve this. I want to make it so simple that anybody could duplicate this, but I also still feel uncomfortable making money from people. My solution is to make everybody a partner rather than a customer, and that way, they earn rebates on their own purchases.

I come home from the conference and map out my plan on the 'blue and white sheets' with a slew of colored highlighters. Then it dawns on me. It just takes five people… If I help five people pay for their own product, then they will help their family and friends pay for *their* own product… The wheel of success is born.

I start holding weekly events in my home—Thirsty Thursdays. Every Thursday evening, I have an open invitation for people to come over after work for water, wine, and smoothies. I provide carrot sticks and hummus for the people who come straight from work. I show them the capsules. "These should come out of your health or your medical budget because these are going to help your cells, your tissues, and your organs," I say. I show them the Complete whole food-based shake mix that will replace snacks and meals. "These will come out of your grocery budget," I tell them. At 53 years old, supported by friends, I take the show on the road and Thirsty Thursdays blow through Kansas and Oklahoma like a category five tornado.

Ten months later, I am a National Marketing Director.

*

They call me Mama Mackey. I was raised by a single mother and saw how hard she worked to take care of us. She sang in a band and we never went hungry or relied on the government, but I always knew it wasn't an easy road. My mother would never have been able to afford to buy the extra product for us kids, and she'd have to choose one child to sponsor for free—something I love about Juice Plus+. I have a heart for single moms, and I think that's why God put so many single moms on my team.

My heart is to help them pay for their product, if that's all they want to do. "Bring me seven to ten people," I say. "I'll help you get them signed up and support them in adding extra nutrition to their diet. Your closest family members and friends can be healthier, and you will get your product paid for. You won't have to struggle." The fact that the company gives us this amazing product backed by research and at a really affordable price just makes it easier for people to share.

Our goal is to get everybody's product paid for and we've duplicated ten people to NMD or above since I got there myself at the end of 2014. This isn't normal, plus we have more in the team who are close. We don't quit. We are persistent. We are consistent. And we love hard on people.

Today, it's my job to help people go share this gift. The gift for me is that it's given me flexibility. My husband is a very successful man, and his money is my money, but there's something about growing up on a tight budget that makes it hard to receive from others, despite how freely they give. So, the money I earn allows me to give. I love to give gifts, and it's very freeing to be able to do that. My mom hasn't had a new car since she was 18 years old, and I'm able to buy her one for her 83rd birthday, five years before she passes. It might sound materialistic, but it's a gift for me at the same time and it sets my heart on fire.

Fire is my theme... I want people to get fired up at conferences and events, which is exactly what happened to me. I want to create desire in others and inspire them to go out into the world and make a difference. So, it is perfect when I am asked to close the Austin Juice Plus+ conference with a 50-minute presentation.

"This girl is on fire..." pumps out of the speakers; lights flash, and flames shoot out of big jumbotrons on either side of the stage. I feel confident in my white pants and black top, its cape flowing out behind me as I stroll across to grab the microphone.

Towards the end of my presentation, I share something close to my heart with the audience.

"My mom died two months ago." There is a collective sigh of sympathy from the 10,000-strong crowd. "She was my person, and she was a single mom who raised five kids alone... Although we sang together, I am on a very different stage than she was, but her legacy lives on through me as mine will and yours will through this mission."

The crowd are hyped, hands are in the air, and the air is full with joy and passion; I can feel the support and energy emanating from the beautiful sea of bodies.

"I believe God gave me this 'Business Ministry' because he knew I would need a really big family to support me and a purpose *way* bigger than me!"

The music starts to swell and I see the DJ start to walk on stage to play my exit song. People are ready to sing and dance with me; emotions are high, and the feeling is electric.

I speak my final words. "Everything was a song in our home growing up and the last thing I want to say to you in all encompassed in this song... our new theme song."

"Sing it out loud and then go out and **set the world on fire!**"

CHAPTER 3

Promises made, promises kept

Harriet Sulcer

"I don't like the idea of you driving into Atlanta alone tonight," my husband Lou said. "Take the Karate Kid with you."

Our 14 year old son, Kevin, having won a national Taekwondo competition, would be my bodyguard.

We entered the buzzing conference hall, and knots twisted my stomach; my limited work experience declared I couldn't do my own home business. I listened as the conference speaker showed us the business model, involving numbers and percentages. The Karate Kid was powerless to hold back the fear crushing my chest, and all I could do was worry: if I don't understand the math, I can't do this.

Concentrating on the big picture, I reminded myself that all of this, it was about team building. Immediately, the fear faded. I'd help others accomplish their dreams and reach mine in the process.

I was all in!

Leaving the hall, I declared, "Kevin, this is it! Curt Beavers was right; this is the opportunity we've been praying for. Let's dive in and go for the top!"

Kevin asked, "Mom, does this mean we're going to get rich?"

"Rich?" I laughed. "Right now, let's just pay some bills."

In addition to selling water filters, my first goal when I started was to find five key people who would join our team and begin to duplicate the process. My inspiration to join, Jackie Beavers, was also working closely with her son, Curt. In his early twenties and newly married, Curt mentored Kevin in learning to install water filters. He wisely encouraged me to concentrate on reaching our highest management level through team building. One year later, I was presented on stage as a National Marketing Director. A vision achieved has to first be believed!

It's easier to control a train of thought than a train that wrecks. My life began to come off the rails faster than I could brake. My daughter Christy got married and moved to North Carolina. Andrea was headed to the University of Alabama as a freshman. Kevin was beginning his junior year in high school.

My husband, Lou, had such physical strength and ability that the men in our community called him 'Super Lou'. However, multiple surgeries and health conditions plunged him into depression. We were on a fast train and the bridge was out.

"I'm going under and I feel as if I'm dragging everybody down with me," Lou said, his voice trembling. "This family would be better off without me."

Tragically, in the same week our youngest daughter left for college, Lou packed his things and left. That night, while cooking, I prayed quietly, "Lord, please help me to be strong for Kevin."

For 25 years, I made dinner special at our home. We always sat down to a hot meal and, without distractions, reconnected and shared the highlights of our day. But I knew that this first night without Andrea and Lou would be indescribably difficult. By candlelight, I served Kevin's favorite meal. As our hands clasped for dinner prayer, we couldn't not see that our family circle was broken.

"Well, Mom," Kevin said quietly, "I guess it's just you and me now."

"Yes," I replied, fighting back tears. "But we're gonna make it, Kevin." As I spoke the words, I hoped we really could.

Although our personal world was devastated, my confidence in Jay Martin and the stable company he had founded kept my family anchored. From the beginning, I fully embraced Jay's mission statement: to help as many families as possible to realize their dreams. Of course, at this stage, all my energy and determination were poured into recovering from bankruptcy; realizing dreams would come later.

However, a difficult transition was just over the horizon. Big box stores began selling in-home water filters, which put Jay Martin in a squeeze. His pivot was stunning: move from water filters to fruits and vegetables in a capsule.

"Are you kidding me?" was the question everyone asked under their breath. Yet, with fierce loyalty to our company, Kevin and I grabbed those orange boxes and set out enthusiastically to share the value of Juice Plus+ with our friends and family.

Scientific research would later prove that our product was truly a nutritional breakthrough. However, it didn't come fast enough for my key leaders. My strongest line, in Tennessee, was made up of veterinarians who were marketing our air filters to their animal lovers. My team in Jackson, Mississippi, was led by a successful builder who was installing our water filters in all his condominiums.

Nutritional capsules weren't on their radar. I felt so hopeless as the team I had worked so hard to build fell apart. It was like being at the beach and seeing the waves wash your sandcastle away. My choices were limited: throw in the towel and quit, or throw my heart back in and rebuild. There was no debate because there was no plan B. I loved team building, so if finding five key people and helping them accomplish their goals made me successful once, I'd do it again—helping families to thrive!

Throughout my 34+ years at Juice Plus+, I've relied on God to guide me to the right people and empower me to share my vision. Early on, He led me to an impressively successful business owner, Cheryl Beaudreault. She desired a healthy diet but was too busy to be consistent. I gave her a compelling video about Juice Plus+

capsules. After several follow-up calls, I learned Cheryl hadn't viewed the video. She informed me that her TV was broken. Bold and determined, I got creative and committed to one of the most audacious presentations I would ever make.

After checking to be sure she was in her office, I quickly loaded up my heavy TV/VCR. I'm sure I raised some eyebrows as I rolled through the office lobby in Atlanta's upscale Buckhead business district with a TV/VCR on a dolly.

"I have something for Cheryl Beaudreault," I cheerfully announced to her receptionist.

Moments later, Cheryl, looking like a fashion model, came out of her office with a concerned look on her face. As I held my breath, she broke into a warm smile.

"Anyone who has the nerve to do what you've just done deserves to be heard. Come on in and let's watch your video together!"

I'll admit it was crazy, but it was worth the risk. The next few awkward moments turned into a delightful partnership that would become a deep friendship. The impact on my business was unimaginable. While keeping her current business thriving, Cheryl became passionate about sharing the research behind our Juice Plus+ products and also saw the long-term financial opportunity in team building.

One day, Marty, her team member in St. Louis, gave one of our audio tapes to Wendy Campbell, a former nursing instructor, wife, and busy mother of three teenagers. The first visit at Wendy's home told me she would be successful. Her love for people, and her wealth of knowledge about the impact of good nutrition on long-term health, was impressive.

"Harriet, you need to understand that I am not interested in making money," she told me. "My husband has an excellent corporate job, so I'll only be sharing Juice Plus+ products." Looking back, her words seem comical, because soon she called and in a passionate voice said, "We need to talk about this marketing plan!"

As Wendy began sharing our JP+ products, her belief and enthusiasm were contagious. She poured herself into helping others become successful, and her business exploded.

"This is not just about adding to the team," she exclaimed. "It's about multiplication. You are duplicating your time and energy through other people as you transfer your vision. It's like passing the baton to the next runner in the relay and cheering them on."

Now, over twenty years later, Wendy has inspired, trained, and developed thousands of Juice Plus+ distributors. Today she's one of the strongest earners in our Juice Plus+ company. What a powerful impact the Campbell Team has had on my family. And to think it all started with a gutsy decision, a TV/VCR, and a dolly.

Years earlier, after becoming a National Marketing Director with the environmental products, I called my lifelong best friend, Rusty Armstrong. Rusty and her husband Joe owned a horse farm in La Mesa, New Mexico. Because I lived in Atlanta, we rarely saw each other.

"I miss you!" I said. "Can you put me back in the saddle if I come out for a bit?"

On the flight out, my mind was flooded with memories of growing up with Rusty in the Mississippi Delta. We cheered together at football games and stayed up half the night sharing secrets, but we were happiest when we were on horseback, exploring new trails on Midnight and Dixie.

"We have so much catching up to do," Rusty said as we drove away from the airport. "We may have to stay up all night."

I smiled. "Well, it won't be the first time!"

There's something so comforting about being with a friend who knows everything there is to know about you and loves you anyway. Now, after all these years of friendship, I couldn't wait to bless them with an invitation to join my team. I shared our product and plan with them, and after taking a careful look at the long-term potential, they locked arms with me and began building a second income.

Over the next few years, I made an annual week-long trip to Las Cruces. While Joe was busy as head of the Equestrian Dept. at New Mexico State, Rusty was working to build a successful franchise. One thing about horse ranchers—they're resilient and fiercely determined. So, when our company transitioned from environmental products to Juice Plus+, they were determined to rebuild.

By that time, Rusty had become a National Marketing Director and earned great respect with our corporate staff. Together, Rusty and Joe began hosting a summer boot camp in the beautiful mountain resort town of Ruidoso. Juice Plus+ distributors from Texas, Arizona, and all over New Mexico gathered there to be trained and inspired and to make lasting friendships.

Looking back at sharing our business opportunity with them reminded me of skipping stones on the creek in front of my home in Mississippi. The ripples keep going out in an ever-widening circles. Rusty started a powerful ripple effect when she shared our Juice Plus+ product and business opportunity with Criss Reep, a mom of four boys whose husband, Jeff, was the head basketball coach at NMSU.

Later, when Criss and Jeff moved to Springfield, Ohio, and added another son, Criss' solid business allowed her to homeschool the boys. Firmly settled in Ohio, Criss accomplished her goal of becoming a National Marketing Director. She then shared Juice Plus+ with her personal physician, Dr. Jan Roberto. Another major ripple! While continuing her practice, Jan became a National Marketing Director. She is a highly respected speaker for Juice Plus+ and one of the most positive and powerful voices for our community.

Life and love gave me two young granddaughters in Jackson, Mississippi. I had attempted to make a team there, and now I had a major incentive. I mused, "I need to find a well-respected medical professional who will embrace Juice Plus+ and give us credibility." Together with my daughter Christy, we made a list, booked a meeting room, and made some flyers for a luncheon.

I invited a physician from Anniston, Alabama, to come present the research and share his confidence in our product, but I couldn't shake my nerves.

"Mom, you got this! You do it all the time," Christy said, attempting to relieve my anxieties.

"Yes, I do, and I know too well what it feels like when no one shows up."

We didn't have the response I had hoped for, but I remembered that the head-count is not important as long as the right person is in the room. After the meeting ended, Dr. Doug Odom, easily recognized as the most well-known and loved OBGYN in Jackson, approached me.

"Harriet," he said, "I have been searching for a quality substitute for prenatal vitamins. Today, I'm convinced you have brought me that product. I need more information." Later, I shared more details, and he immediately began making capsules available to his patients.

Almost a year later, Dr. Odom and I met for coffee at the hospital café. He was very impressed with an audio tape made by a highly respected infectious disease specialist from Atlanta, Dr. Ric DuBois. I could tell this solidified Doug's belief in our product, so I wasn't surprised when he told me he had several hundred patients taking Juice Plus+.

What did surprise me was the sudden change in his direction.

"I don't really want to concentrate on the JP product today," he said, glancing at his watch. "I have one hour. I want you to walk me through your marketing plan."

Doug was attentive as we progressed through the sequential steps of achievement, aiming at our highest position. His eyes widened when I showed him the average income of a National Marketing Director, along with the generous benefit package and expense allowance available at that level.

As we finished, I tried to read the look on his face. I only had to wonder for a brief moment before he said, "I've been observing the lifestyle you have. If you will help me reach that top level, secure the benefits of flexibility and solid income, I'll retire from my OB practice and do GYN three days a week. The other days, I'll devote myself to building a solid team."

Doug Odom is a man of his word. With fierce determination and an impressive work ethic, he put together a strong, committed team that enabled him to quickly achieve his goals. The day he was promoted to NMD, he gave up his OB practice and poured his heart into helping families thrive.

Over two decades later, his impressive leadership team continues to have an impact on our Juice Plus+ community: Renee O'Neil, Mary Koenig, Maria Word, Nicole Lamar, Angel Faulk, and many others who are rapidly rising through the ranks. It's been a joy and a privilege working with Doug and his wife Walterine. Our company was blessed the day Dr. Odom said "Yes!"

Back on the home front, Kevin graduated from Rocky Mt. School of Art and Design in Denver, Colorado. He returned to Atlanta, worked in graphic design, and then started his own business, Prodigal Design. Soon he reconnected with his high school sweetheart, Brittany. In no time he was married to his best friend and love of his life. Oh, what a beautiful wedding it was.

Late one afternoon, the phone rang. "Mom, Brittany and I would like to drop by tonight after dinner. We have an idea to run by you."

Later that evening, as we began our meeting, I realized Kevin was about to share something immensely important.

"Mom, being home this past year, I've observed the amazing quality of life you have," Kevin told me. "Brittany and I are realizing that time flexibility is as important to us as the freedom to say yes more often. I'm sold on Juice Plus+. I wouldn't go a day without it. I'm also equally attracted to the business opportunity, seeing how it's worked for you. How would you feel about taking on a partner?"

Fighting back the tears, I exclaimed, "This is what I've always dreamed of, but I didn't want to ask you to give up your career."

It's been 34 years since Kevin was my young bodyguard at our first business meeting. He tirelessly worked alongside me that first year, and now he was ready to join forces again. The timing was perfect, as I was overwhelmed by the rapid growth of my business. Having Kevin on board gave me a burst of new energy. Together we aimed for him to be a National Marketing Director. Those years were so memorable and fun. Kevin has his dad's sense of humor, which helped us laugh through the difficulties as we traveled to support our team. What a joyful reunion!

Another astounding answer to prayer was on the horizon, when my marriage was miraculously reconciled after ten years of separation. Family and friends concerned for me advised against it. However, an experience eight years earlier assured me this was a supernatural breakthrough.

After a weekend of soul-searching and earnestly seeking God's guidance, I began to clearly see how Lou and I had gone off track. Sobbing my way through these moments of revelation, I took full responsibility for my failure and totally forgave Lou for his. That profound experience empowered me not to divorce and trust God for a miracle.

God used our grandchildren as a sweet resource to work on Lou and I. Christy gave us a precious baby girl who immediately stole our hearts. A new bond grew deeper and stronger with the addition of each grandchild. By the time the third grandchild was a year old, Lou and I were reunited and the entire family was overwhelmed with gratitude.

The grandbabies kept coming, and eventually there were nine. The last two were a wonderful surprise. Lou and I had gone into Atlanta that afternoon and as I was fighting my way through the heavy traffic his cell phone rang. "It's Kevin," he said with a grin. "I'll put it on speaker so we can both hear." We knew Kevin had taken Brittany in for a sonogram and they might have some news for us.

"Dad, it's boys!" Kevin blurted out.

"Boys, as in more than one?" Lou stammered.

"Yep! We're having twins!" The excitement in his voice said this was beyond his dreams.

He adored his precious baby girl and also longed to raise a son. Now, he would have the challenge of double trouble, and he was eager to take it on.

God brought about restoration in our lives in such a way that we would have never dreamed of. But to share that, I need to step back in time and recall a very precious memory, one that began 20 years earlier.

Shortly after Lou and I married in 1964, Lou exclaimed, "I can't wait to take you camping in the North Georgia mountains."

"I would love that," I replied with a warm smile.

There was something very endearing about his boyish excitement as he looked forward to sharing that experience with me. Fortunately, I loved the outdoors and had done a fair amount of hiking and camping growing up.

That September, he kept his promise and we headed up into the North Georgia mountains. The beauty was breathtaking. The fall weather transformed the mountains into a magnificent display of brilliant red, yellow, and gold glory.

As we arrived at Vogel State Park, my anticipation soared. Lou decided to pitch our tent beside Wolf Creek, so we could hear the water cascading over the rocks as we sat around our campfire. He was excited about trout fishing, too, and I was thrilled to join him.

That night, after we stuffed ourselves with smores, we were quietly watching the last flickering flames of the fire when Lou's determined tone broke the silence. "Harriet, someday we are going to have a place up here in these mountains."

Snuggling closer, I whispered softly, "Promise me we'll do that."

He kissed me gently on the cheek and said, "I promise."

As the years rolled along, we continued our adventures in the Blue Ridge mountains. Tent camping with the children from early spring through fall and renting cozy cabins in the winter were family bonding experiences like no other. The kids grew to love those mountains as much as we did. They also loved the promise Lou made, so during every trip they would echo it: "Someday we'll have a place up here." However, when our tranquil family train horrifyingly derailed, so did our dream of a mountain home. The pain from our family fallout silenced any mention of it for years.

Let's fast forward to a magical moment in time. Lou and I had been reunited for almost ten years when I suggested that we ride up to the mountains for the day. Although he was facing some life-threatening health challenges, I thought a walk down memory lane might lift his spirits.

"I can't remember when I've seen you this relaxed and happy," I remarked as we finished our lunch in the quaint mountain town of Helen, Georgia.

Our last stop was at Vogel State Park, where we relived our very first camping trip. What a wonderful day it was. As the sun was setting, we headed home, quietly reflecting.

I abruptly broke the silence. "Lou, we didn't keep our promise!"

With a startled look, he said, "What in the world are you talking about?"

"We promised that someday we would have a cabin in these beautiful mountains. Our children believed us, and we never followed through."

He looked away, sadly shook his head, and in a broken whisper said, "We've waited too long."

"Lou Sulcer," I said emphatically, "It's never too late to fulfill your dreams." I reached over and took his hand. "Honey, can you imagine what a wonderful gift it would be for our children and grandchildren?"

He smiled, and we were dreaming again.

Wasting no time, bright and early the next morning we rang our realtor. In those early years, we had pictured our family enjoying long weekends in a tiny cabin by a trout stream. Now our family had grown considerably, and thanks to Juice Plus+, so had our income. We sat out to make a dream come true, building a lake house for our whole family to gather during holidays and summer vacations. God planted us at Lake Nottely.

We began fulfilling our promise, and Lou, although suffering in health, came alive. From the doctor's perspective, nothing had changed, but our family saw a new level of energy and excitement that gave us renewed hope. Lou's experience as a builder, and Kevin's gift as a designer, proved to be a powerful partnership and deepening friendship. Our family was delighted the lake house was complete and ready for festivities just as school let out for the summer.

Surrounded by family around the campfire, Lou and I shared for the first time with our grandchildren the promise we had made 47 years earlier. Lou chuckled as he told them, "Your nana and I were dreaming about a cabin on the river, and here we are with a lodge on the lake." As everyone laughed, Lou continued in a more serious tone, "You know, I think we've been greatly blessed to find this beautiful point—almost two acres right on the water." Everyone agreed.

"Let's name this place," I exclaimed. "Let's have a contest and everyone submit a name!"

Brittan, our oldest granddaughter, spoke up. "Nana, there's no contest. You and Grandaddy kept your promise. We should call it Promise Point!"

Time is such a bandit. A decade seems like yesterday. Lou and I enjoyed three wonderful years together at Promise Point before cancer ushered him into God's presence. I recall the last time we left Promise Point together, Lou reached over and put his hand on my shoulder.

"Well, we've hung in there for almost 50 years."

"Against all odds," I replied smiling.

After a moment, he added quietly, "And these last three years have been the best."

It seems there should have been a cloud of sadness hanging over us at that moment, knowing what lay ahead, but instead deep peace calmed us. Our journey had not been easy, but we were ending it well.

Having lived 82 years, I've learned what really matters in life, especially as a great-grandmother. People matter, not fame or accomplishments or money. People you helped to reach their dreams and family who loved one another through the nightmares.

Be encouraged, tenaciously keep your family strong, and never, ever give up on your dreams.

CHAPTER 4

Mean for more

Nila Mason

⁓⧼•⧽⁓

This isn't me. I can't go on! I softly sobbed onto my robe.

Then, as if he were standing beside me, I heard my father say, "Nila, you've got grit." He'd told me that before and I'd believed him. I needed to believe him now.

Warm tears trickled down mascara-smudged cheeks as I slouched in my pink terrycloth bathrobe. It seemed 4:00 pm came so quickly, yet would never end, days and nights meshing into a fog of despair.

We had married ten months earlier. Following my job resignation, we were to have worked together in the same industry. However, he was fired. We both were without jobs. Shock, anger, and sadness temporarily were waylaid when playing dominoes, cards, and puzzles. I was so scared.

And then it happened. I started recalling lessons I'd learned as a girl on our 180-acre Iowa farm: You don't stop feeding the cattle just because the mean bull is glaring at you. You don't stop baling hay just because it's 104 degrees. You don't stop farming because insects have destroyed your crop. You plant another one.

That's all I needed, reminders. I looked at the *Kansas City Star* to see who was hiring, scheduled interviews, and took a shower, warm beads bouncing from my smiling cheeks again.

I interviewed with National Safety Associates (NSA), a company marketing water filters. I knew nothing about them but agreed, the water really did taste better.

The next Saturday I attended a regional training, showing me a bigger picture of what was possible. I sat quietly in the back of the hotel's huge conference room. Despite being encouraged by success stories and informative training, I was still apprehensive.

What if I fail?

My mother had always encouraged me, "Nila, just do your best."

Maybe I can do this. After all, I was an English teacher, ten years in Iowa—if I could reach and teach high schoolers, I could probably teach adults about clean water.

Following teaching, I received a master's degree in social work. I had always enjoyed inspiring people to become more of whom they wanted to be. *Perhaps my people skills will be needed for this job, too.*

After graduate school in 1981, I moved to Kansas City looking for a job. Unfortunately, but fortunately in retrospect, I could not find one in my field. With the economy's decline, social work positions were not to be found. I resorted to the *Kansas City Star*, looking for other possibilities.

The US Chamber of Commerce wanted someone to train, manage, and motivate a small sales force. I interviewed; I got the job.

"We want you to sell memberships to business owners throughout Iowa, Kansas, Nebraska, and Missouri," the interviewer told me. "If you are going to train a team how to do that, you need to know how to do it yourself."

Sell? I'd never sold anything before except cinnamon rolls at our 4-H bake sale and magazine subscriptions for my class trip to Washington, DC. Feeling desperate, but willing to learn, I accepted the job. I created a plan where I sold $500 a day, $10,000 monthly. I had desire, a goal, and discipline. When I was told 'no,' I pictured the next business owner saying 'yes.' During my six years with the company, I was among the top producers and often ranked #2 in the country.

Reflecting on those experiences, I decided on Saturday I could be successful again. This time with sweat trickling down my mascara smudged cheeks, on May 31, 1988, I signed my distributor application with National Safety Associates. I knew, too, if it was to be, it was up to me.

Unlike today, when I work from home or anywhere, I drove to a tiny office in a dingy warehouse. At the time, when network marketing was unappreciated, having offices seemed to legitimize the business. Each morning I would sport a smart-looking suit and prance out the door in my panty hose and three-inch heels. I enjoyed helping families get cleaner water. I was excited about recruiting a team and teaching them to be successful. I was elated I could earn as much as I wanted. *Happy days are here again.* Then reality came to call.

People come; people go. Some stay; some are loyal. That was a scenario I had to learn.

Shortly after I'd become a distributor, my sponsor quit. *Now who is going to teach me, go on appointments with me, guide me further?* I rolled up to the next guy. Looking to him for guidance, I realized, much to my chagrin, that he was new, too. After a few weeks, he quit. I rolled up to another guy who was quite a character. He quit. I then rolled up to an out-of-state gentleman who eventually quit, also. By then, with a chuckle and chucking aside my 'poor me' mentality, I mused, *I guess none of these people had learned the values of growing up on a farm.*

At one conference, I was mortified to learn I could have given my National Marketing Director speech there. *If only someone would have guided me, believed in me. It would have made all the difference.*

I had made NMD in two years, four months, and was recognized at the next conference. Instead of being angry, I was grateful for the benefit package. I focused on what I would say and wear on that huge stage under glaring, hot lights in front of thousands. With my perfectly coiffed auburn hair, I pictured sporting my cream yellow suit with tiny black and cream pinstripes, oyster-colored blouse and panty hose to match my three-inch heels. A rush of excitement filled my body.

At conferences, I treasured hearing Jeff Roberti and Bob and Sue Burdick talk to their teams. I loved hearing them train on the main stage, passionately imparting wisdom, direction, and encouragement for growing large teams. Sharron Rankin and Cheryl Cortese were my role models. They were beautiful, smart, and successful. I wanted to be like them. They all had joined the company a few years before me. I so respected their determination, integrity, and loyalty. They all are still with the company today, excellent role models for those who choose to stay, valuing loyalty. Lesson learned: Your upline isn't going to make you successful. You are!

All work and no play won't create a loyal team. In December 1989, my husband and I cohosted a Christmas party with our neighbors, everyone inviting friends and coworkers to my home. I had a beautiful 3000-square foot, five-level home, perfect for a party. That night, cinnamon-scented candles and fragrant fir wafted through the air. The gleeful band played from the sunroom, a gregarious bartender entertained in the hot tub room, and festive food adorned the dining room. I loved treating my team and coworkers to a fun evening. Everything was perfect—except for a haunting phone call I'd received earlier that day.

My brother Reid had called and said he was having surgery the next day in Minneapolis. "I know, Nila, you are having a big party tonight, but if you could come up and be with me tomorrow, I'd really appreciate your being here," he said.

With no hesitation, I replied, "I'll be there."

It had snowed several inches during the night and swirling flakes angrily pelted drifts the next morning. On the drive to the airport, we had a blowout. Fear ricocheted through my body as I forced back tears.

Fortunately, a car pulled over and a well-dressed businessman asked, "Do you need some help? I'm going to the airport if anyone needs a ride."

With quivering lips, I eked out, "Yes, I do!" I grabbed my bulging suitcase and bolted into his car.

I arrived at the hospital to learn Reid was already in surgery. The important thing was that I would be there when he awakened. As the nurse gently wheeled him into his dimly lit room, Reid weakly opened his eyes and whispered, "You're here."

"I will always be here for you, Reid," I assured him. With that, he gave me a little smile as his lids slowly closed over his blue eyes. And I always was, day and night. I stayed at his home 20 minutes away, driving his car to the hospital every morning. Those were special times for us. We told each other secrets. We laughed and reminisced. I told him stories.

We made plans until his passing, February 18, 1990. I miss Reid every day. Below is the poem I wrote for Reid's funeral program.

Protective Palms

Carefully cradled within my palms,
Chiseled features frown with pain.
Gently I soothe your furrowed brow,
And chase away the dreams.

Oh, my kind and very special one,
Your gentle eyes meet mine.
Our depths of blue hold so much love,
Just thankful for the time...
   We laughed,
   We played,
   We cried,
   We prayed,
Holding tight to what we'd shared.

For soon we know the day will come,

Our earthly parting nigh.
The wind beneath your wings grows weak,
As I sadly say good-bye.

But know, my strong, yet gentle one,
All will be well again.
For you and mom will lie side by side,
Carefully cradled within His palms.

After readying Reid's house for a sale, I returned home in April. It was then I learned most of my team had quit, all except Sean and Jennifer Myers. That meant rebuilding. That meant appreciating who was loyal.

Upon my return, I learned National Safety Associates had introduced air filters. *Hmm. Another learning curve.* I didn't mind. I was grateful for a company that hadn't fired me because I had chosen to care for Reid. More realizations came to light. I understood even more why NSA was known as the company with a heart.

Gut punches were not done with me yet. February 6, 1991, my father passed away following heart surgery. With my mother having passed in 1983 and recently my brother, I truly felt my father died of a broken heart.

Loneliness haunted me even more. My husband and I were not as close. I soon discovered why.

One day when cleaning bedroom drawers, I found multiple membership cards to various 'clubs,' and other secrets as well. It became clear why he hadn't answered my calls when I was gone.

Once again, I thought, *This can't go on!* I felt my father softly say, "Nila, you've got grit."

With that, I knew what to do. My divorce finalized in 1992. After much thought, and many tears and prayers, I realized I must:

Reach out to family and friends, for they will support me.
Reach up to my higher power, for He loves me.
Reach in, for I am stronger than I think.

I decided to dive into my business full force. Local distributors held opportunity meetings every Tuesday and Thursday nights so we could introduce our products and business to others. Meetings were divided into four parts. One male distributor proudly talked about the company. I nervously talked about the product. A male distributor confidently showed the marketing plan. We closed with success stories. There was a saying: "The man with the pen makes the rules." I never got to hold the pen. I felt like the soft cream in the middle of an Oreo cookie.

Well-meaning male NMDs in our Kansas City coop shared: "Nila, you talk too slowly and show too much emotion. Pick it up." Our products attracted more men. Indeed, they had a different style of presenting. Then, it truly was a male-dominated business.

Respecting their advice, I made changes so I could more effectively attract more men onto my team.

I decided to think like a man, present like a man, but still act like a lady.

It worked. My team grew, giving confidence to other women. My monthly recruits enjoyed our Saturday training. I kept reminding myself, *Tough times don't last. Tough people do.*

The early 1990s was a tumultuous time for NSA. Stores competitively sold water and air filters and many distributors left for other companies. My Colorado team was ravaged, with well over 30 distributors leaving. I regularly received stacks of materials enticing me to join another company. I got numerous three-way calls from people who sheepishly introduced me to their leader so I could defect.

My response was always the same. "I am honored you thought of me, but NSA has been loyal to me and I am remaining loyal to them. Besides, I trust Jay Martin, its president. Thank you. Good-bye."

I was ready for some good news. I wasn't the only one. In 1993, NSA introduced Juice Plus+ into the marketplace. I must admit, distributors, men especially, were perplexed why a company that once successfully sold appliances would switch to fruit and vegetable powders in a capsule.

I don't know how to talk about these capsules. I don't know if they do any good. People are used to taking vitamins.

Then I remembered. Our intention was to "improve the quality of people's lives around the world." Of course. Jay Martin's foresight and wisdom prevailed again. He had understood timing and need. It was a home run!

I felt like I was in the World Series when John Blair, VP, asked me to join his team along with Dr. Humbart 'Smokey' Santillo, creator of Juice Plus+, for the Silver Anniversary Tour. John strongly felt women would play an important role in the future of Juice Plus+. Therefore, a woman, a doctor, and a corporate leader comprised each of the three teams. NSA was turning 25 years old in 1995. To celebrate, create more customers, educate distributors, and attract more, the teams toured 50 cities throughout the United States.

When invited I pondered, *Why me?* I was not the top female earner in the company. Maybe it was because I was single, wouldn't have to leave a family, and would be an example for others without a spouse. Then I remembered. John Blair had heard me speak in Minneapolis and Wichita. Perhaps he'd seen potential. Regardless, I was beyond elated and very honored.

Two weekends a month, for a year and a half, we spoke in assigned cities. Friday nights Dr. Santillo gave an insightful health talk. Saturday, John, in his articulate and inspiring way, trained an hour on NSA the company. Dr. Santillo trained on the intricacies and benefits of Juice Plus+. I trained for three hours on how to go from being a new dealer to National Marketing Director.

By the time I timidly walked upon the stage, tightly gripping the podium, my mouth was dry and my blouse was damp. As I gazed around the hotel's crowded conference room, hundreds of expectant eyes and hopeful ears waited for me to give them the secrets.

How can I do this? I want to help everyone be successful. I don't want to let down our team.

About that time, all I had to do was look towards the back of the room where John often sat. Seeing my fear frozen face, he smiled, nodded, and gave me all the reassurance I needed. Once I felt his comforting belief in me, I took a deep breath, loosened my grip on the wooden podium, and began my team-building training: "Geese Don't Fly Solo."

It was gratifying to see the audience's puzzled looks progressively dissolve into gleeful flashes of insight and determination. Once curious attendees, now confident, ordered.

Those looking for hope and a vehicle for their future joined NSA. It was obvious to all. They were with a forward-thinking company, always ahead of its time, offering something everyone needed and hardly anyone had. They were overjoyed seeing a path to follow.

As a result, people humbly understood Jay Martin's mission statement: *To build a stable and lasting company that will help as many people as possible realize their dreams.* Attendees felt a sense of peace, knowing they were meant for more. They indeed were in the right place at the right time.

Our team felt so good about inspiring so many when we flew home on Saturdays. John was especially happy as that was 'date night' with his beautiful wife Christine. I learned that trusted friendships are precious and saw that loving, authentic relationships could last forever.

I am so very grateful for this touring experience. I learned so much from John and Smokey. I made so many great and lasting friends with distributors in each city. It felt so good to help them grow larger teams as well as my own. Below is a poem reflecting the ecstasy I felt during this time, grateful for God's guidance. I was busy. I was learning. I was growing.

Fresh Beginnings

Dancing in the shadows,
Spinning out of step,
Always in a hurry
So promises are kept.

Late for a facial; my crow's feet are squawking...
Find a personal trainer so abs and glutes can be seen...
File that extension; heard Uncle Sam is very mean...
Rush to the airport; what city is today?
Find the ticket for my dry-cleaned suit; hope my Power Ball
will pay.

Is it PMS or PVC? If I pay the price I then receive...
Change the Pennzoil in my right front tire and rotate all my
oil...
Is it algae ala sprouts and more inside my Frigidaire?

Dancing on the incline,
Seeking solace, being centered.
Sneak one quick breath just long enough
To gasp: "Where is my mentor?"

All I had to do was ask and then...
Listen,
  Listen,
His soothing words brought such relief,
A calming warmth with gentle peace.
Find your purpose.
  Perfect your mission.
  Smell the roses and
  Forget me not.
  I'll love you always, my precious one.
  I've never ever stopped.

Dancing in the sunshine
With my partner's guiding hand.
How much I love my life and you
Feeling His promises transcend.
  NRM—1994

I spoke three times on the main stage at international conferences with thousands attending. I often wondered if the audience could hear the *thud thud thud* from my microphone as it tried to keep rhythm with my pounding heart. If they did, I guess they didn't mind.

At one conference, I met a very handsome gentleman from Puerto Rico. We had a great time dancing at the Saturday night party. Weeks later, during one of our phone conversations, he said, "Nila, please come to Puerto Rico. You can develop your business here, too." I could almost see his warm brown eyes as his inviting accent melted my objections.

Pausing for what seemed like many minutes, I finally replied, "Yes, I'll come to Puerto Rico."

It was exhilarating flying into San Juan. The minute I stepped off the plane into the steamy airport, I was swept away by gleeful smiles and melodic Spanish conversations as passengers met loved ones. *This will be fun.*

With regular presentations at my hotel, my team grew quickly. Soon we traveled across their lush, beautiful island where I met their friends, giving more talks. When not working, my team took me dancing to lively music, for a sassy salsa or merengue. Sometimes my friend and I walked barefoot along the beach, sand squishing between our toes just long enough until another gentle wave washed it away. White lights from cruise ships decorated the night as echoes from Coqui frogs captured our imaginations.

I loved attending and speaking at bootcamps, casual settings for training. My team and I traveled to a destination, rooming together. The camaraderie, memories, and bonding were priceless. Impactful training combined with fun activities attracted many who realized they were meant for more. Bootcamps fostered growth, cemented relationships, and were instrumental for one's success. They still are today.

Mark Hair and Yvonne Cunningham hosted the 'Banff Beavertail Bootcamp,' a real highlight. Following training, we snow-skied around the picturesque peaks of the Canadian Rockies. I valued working with Canada's leadership, staff, and teams, treasuring my new friends from the north.

Reno's 'Winterfest Bootcamp', a true adventure, was hosted by Chris and Nikki Cotton. One of my best friends, Janet McGinn and I always had so much fun together. We all skied *Heavenly*. On the way back to our hotels, we stopped at the oldest bar in Nevada for a little cheer and a mischievous tradition.

Sean and Jennifer Myers hosted Colorado's 'Summer in the Rockies Bootcamp'. White water rafting jolted sedentary souls. As eight rafters rhythmically paddled over gushing cold waters, towering pines welcomed us with clean mountain air. My adrenaline surged as we navigated rapids, nearly capsizing as we careened around clusters of protruding rocks. *Ah, it feels good to be alive.*

Georgia's 'Padgett Bootcamp', hosted by Bobby and Lisa Padgett, was particularly special. Filled with laughter and jokes, it created much fun. Especially memorable were Jay Martin, Elton DuBose, and Leslie Padgett harmonizing behind the mic with some of their favorites.

It was another rewarding experience when Guy De Boo invited Wendy Campbell and me to speak at the first International Bootcamp in Belgium. It was exciting meeting European staff and distributors. The melding of hopes, dreams, and a path resulted. Wendy and I enjoyed a festive dinner in Brussels prior to our flights home the next day. Once again, great memories were created. Mutually respected bonds were cemented.

With each speaking engagement, I gained more confidence. Perhaps that's why John Blair invited me to join him and Dr. John Wise on a European speaking tour. John's wife Christine and Dr. Wise's wife Lois joined us. With trepidation I asked John Blair, "I'm going to feel like a fifth wheel. Would it be possible if I invited a distributor on my team?" He agreed. Becky Ennis joyfully joined.

We spoke in Copenhagen, Paris, Milan, Amsterdam, Frankfurt, and London in a little over a week's time. Between events, we all went sightseeing to capture everything we could: Copenhagen's Van Gogh art museum; Paris' D'Orsay art museum. London's double decker buses; Buckingham Palace; the River Thames. Amsterdam's canals. Souvenir shopping for family at Milan's Galleria. Such treasured memories. NSA understood that to avoid burnout, everyone must find time for fun. My resolve: Work hard. Play hard.

I loved continually growing my teams, speaking in their homes and cities. I met their spouse and played with their children. It was then I better appreciated their whys, challenges, and vision. I got to know their hearts and they got to feel mine. I shared: "If I can do it, so can you. I believe in you."

I adapted to changes. National Safety Associates became the Juice Plus+ Company, expanding into 25 countries. Technology improved. Bag phones, beepers, cassette tapes, DVDs, overhead projectors, fax machines, and offices disappeared.

Today, network marketing is a respected profession offering freedom and flexibility. Men have joined our business, realizing that by blending their skills with their wives, their family business can be even more successful, fun, and lucrative. They realized, too, that telling stories and showing emotion aren't detriments, but assets when being real.

Distributors are called partners. Closed meetings, no more. Teams work together harmoniously, sharing knowledge, giving support. 'One Team One Mission' created 'The Juice Plus+ Family'.

Today, I get to hold the pen. Gone is my pink, tear-stained, terrycloth bathrobe. I now proudly wear tears of joy and gratitude, knowing I am secure, appreciated, and loved.

I am a Presidential Marketing Director+ and 100 club member. I value having been with this great company for 34 years. My personal growth and income have allowed me to freely give to family, friends, charities, and church, to travel, and to enjoy a lifestyle and freedom that this Iowa farm girl never imagined. I am 'Aunt Nila' to my partners' children. I still get a little scared when I speak sometimes, but when I find a smile and a nod in the audience, that makes all the difference.

My path to where I am today as a 75-years-young lady prompted realizations, included rewards, and required resilience. I am truly blessed!

CHAPTER 5

Bob & Sue Burdick

I stood and stared as the phone rang a third time, each ring becoming more insistent. I knew who it was on the other end, and I felt guilty for dodging him for the past three weeks. Worse than that, I stood him up for a luncheon the previous week because "I was just too busy." I comforted myself with the knowledge that I was saving him from another rejection on a sales pitch, and I was saving myself the awkward *NO* that I was resolved to deliver. I almost walked away, but the guilt won out. and I grudgingly reached for the phone to spare us both a fourth ring.

"Hello," I said, managing my best attempt at a smile and some fake enthusiasm.

"Sue!" came the excited response from my friend, Dave. My dread was proven correct; I cut him off before he could extend his next invitation to another luncheon or meeting.

"Dave, I bought your product. Isn't that enough?"

I wanted to be firm but gentle; however, Dave caught me off guard when he replied, "No! It's really not enough."

The curveball left me momentarily speechless, and while my brain scrambled to assemble a witty response, Dave upped the ante by saying, "I have a friend here who wants to say a few words."

Oh my God. He brought reinforcements, I thought as his friend, Jeff, introduced himself and said, "Dave tells me you have a lot going on, and we just happen to be looking for busy people."

As a 37 year old mother of five teenage boys, I was skilled at juggling many simultaneous tasks so, as Jeff began talking, my mind was focused on one goal—ending this phone call as quickly as possible with our friendship intact.

Jeff's words pulled me away from my escape plan when he said, "I don't think you understand that your negative attitude could possibly jeopardize the financial future of your children."

Don't be so dramatic, I thought as I caught myself laughing. But the laughter hung in my throat as I realized that there might be some truth to his words.

"You don't have to buy, sell, or join," Jeff said. "We just want you to take a look at this business. You know you owe it to yourself and your family to come and look this over."

I knew well the parable of the man stuck on the roof of his house in the ravages of a flood, pleading to God to save him, even as he turned down offers to evacuate and rescue attempts from a boat and a helicopter. His prayers to God were being answered, but he was blind to them amidst the chaos of the moment and his belief that "God will save me." Could this opportunity be my rescue boat in the flood?

"Okay, I'll come look." The words blurted out of my mouth before I could filter them, so I quickly added, "But, I want you both to raise your right hand and promise that after I look and say 'No', that you'll stop calling me and we can still be friends."

"Great!" was Jeff's only reply as he rattled off the address and time for the meeting the next afternoon.

On his way out the door to his construction job in the South Florida heat the following morning, my husband, Bob, said over his shoulder, "Don't take the checkbook to that meeting today. There's no money in that account and I don't want these guys talking you into anything." Like most of our friends, we lived paycheck to paycheck, always fearful of the future, and struggling just to make ends meet. There always seemed to be more "month at the end of the money," rather than the other way around.

The morning minutes were eaten up with chores, mundane tasks, and rummaging through my closet for what constituted my best attempt at business attire—jeans, heels, and a light jacket over my tank top. The hour-long drive to the meeting was just enough time for me to reflect on, and regret, my decision many times over.

An impressive chiropractor's office in Boca Raton served as the meeting place and, in a room filled with three-piece suits and plenty of testosterone, my decision-regretting process reached new heights. I was out of my element, and I was the only woman in the room. In an effort to mask my anxiety, I boldly strode to the front row and claimed a seat with the nonverbal statement that follows stiff posture, arms folded, and a serious look on my face.

I stubbornly sat there and watched several suits milling around the front door along with a flashy young kid, barely older than my oldest son, wearing a black velour jacket. Eventually, the sparse crowd slowly took their seats and a distinguished guy sporting a heavy Hungarian accent opened the meeting. As he spoke, I knew I wasn't doing a good job of disguising the negativity on my face.

What am I doing here? I thought. *I shouldn't have come here. I have too much to do today.* My thoughts struggled to focus on the presentation of this company and their new 'revolutionary' product, but I kept thinking, *These guys are looking for businessmen, not some housewife. What do they want with me?* Nobody in this room looked like me, and the gnawing feeling that I was in over my head and out of place continued to eat at me.

The indecision was growing and, with it, a level of anger. Anger at myself for being forced into this. Anger with them for being so insistent. *Why did I let them put me in this awkward position?*

When the Hungarian, who called himself Rudy, began turning things over to the next speaker, I was a little shocked to see the flashy kid take the stage and be introduced as Jeff. This was the friend of Dave's who convinced me to come today.

Here was a target for my frustration. My eyes narrowed and I imagined everyone behind me staring at the back of my head, questioning my presence in the room.

What is she doing here?

She doesn't belong here.

She's just a housewife with no education.

The questions weren't real, but I heard them all the same. Stripping away my confidence and eroding any hope of my forming an objective view of this 'opportunity'.

Adjusting his jacket with an air of confidence and swagger, Jeff began by thanking the room for being there, but he spoke with a relaxed intensity that made everyone in the room feel as if we should be thanking him for being there. He spoke with ease and gravitas beyond his years and said, "Millionaires are going to be made in this room!"

I was sure that a little steam could still be seen coming out of my ears from a combination of self-induced humiliation and anger, but I noticed that my arms were now uncrossed and I was leaning ever so slightly forward in my seat.

Millionaires?

I have lived every day of my life broke. I grew up poor in rural Mississippi in a house with no running water and no electricity. My parents grew and hunted nearly everything we ate, while my father was a share-cropper on a cotton farm. Plowing fields with mules, my father was the second youngest of 17 siblings. The word "millionaire" was never even spoken in my childhood. It was as foreign to me as the Hungarian greeting that Rudy opened the meeting with.

After losing my mother at 12 years old, I later dropped out of high school and was married with five sons before I turned 26. Poverty was the only life I had ever known.

The words of a country song drifted up from the recesses of my mind: *I was raised poor, but I wanted more.* I had always felt that but never allowed myself the risk of believing.

As Jeff laid out the marketing plan, my brain was swept up in the energy and excitement of the moment. "You don't have to quit working full-time on your job in order for you to work part-time on your fortune."

My mind, usually consumed with an endless litany of tasks and chores, was cautiously curious about what I was hearing, and I caught myself paying attention. Paying close attention.

Retailing a product and becoming a millionaire was a stretch for my mind. But I had once heard a saying, "It's better to earn 1% of 100 people than 100% of yourself." As Jeff drew out a team-building component to this business, something clicked inside me. The retail income was only part of this. I could build a small team and earn commissions on the sales of my team.

This is the missing link. The thought struck me, and the room around me seemed to spin. This didn't require years of experience. It didn't require a college degree.

As high school dropouts, Bob and I only knew manual labor. I've worked so many jobs that I've lost count—from construction jobs with Bob to cleaning houses and teaching aerobics, and even grooming dogs.

I subconsciously reached up to scratch an imaginary flea in my hair and said to myself, *This is something I can do.*

The warnings from Bob were suddenly nowhere to be found in my thoughts, and the cloud of daily tasks, shopping lists, dinner menus for five picky-eating boys, and a mountain of house chores awaiting me at home all seemed to fade away as I watched and listened to the presentation that presented more than some home-based business. It was offering hope. It was offering the potential to change my life. It was offering a whole new world for my entire family. And this offer was right in front of me.

A wave of adrenaline rushed through my veins and panic briefly grabbed me as a thought struck me like a brick. *I almost didn't answer that phone!*

*

Buyer's remorse. I had heard the term before, but never really attempted to understand its true meaning. As I bustled around my house, mentally checking off my to-do list, I knew that I was purposely averting my gaze from the end of the dining room table, where I had assembled my own makeshift office. My phone was perfectly placed with my list of names to call and a brochure with a script to follow. It was there. Ready to go.

It was me who wasn't ready. That phone loomed like a creature from a horror movie every time I walked through the living room, looking anywhere but in its direction. Grabbing a basket of clean sheets from the laundry room, I hurried back to the bedroom, eyes down, scurrying like a mouse when the light flickers on. Safe in my bedroom, I set about being 'productive' by stripping the old sheets and remaking the bed. As I grasped the sheet and shook it hard, the sheet turned itself into a parachute of paisley and slowed in the air, softly floating back down toward the bed. For a moment, the sheet blocked out the room in front of me. As it drifted downward, it revealed the mirror on the dresser directly across the room from me. And there, I saw the thing I feared the most. My own reflection stared back at me. I knew that look. I could read it anywhere. Procrastination in its worst form.

"Don't look at me that way," I said to the reflection. "I know where it is. I saw it there." The reflection looked back at me coldly as if asking me, *How long are you going to put this off? To make excuses?*

I had no answer. Procrastination was the thief of dreams and my reflection spoke to me plainly. *Are you a fool? You can stand in here making beds... or you can pick up that phone and make a fortune.*

With a deep breath, I left the bed, the sheet, and the room, and turned toward the phone.

Beside the phone, the table was stacked with a formidable pile of products that represented my 'new business venture.' Bob had been as enthusiastic as I was when I dragged him to a meeting the night before. As a carpenter, he knew numbers in ways that most men don't, and he saw the potential for income almost immediately. But the next morning, with the high and exhilaration burnt off, the pile of product on the table represented just one more bad decision. We had to borrow from our savings just to get started, and now, Bob had real misgivings about what I had 'made' him commit to.

"I can't believe I let you talk me into this," Bob snarled as the door shut behind him. The morning had been rough, and doubt crept into us both. Bob has supported every business venture I have tried, and this was no different, but his doubt was real and the product on the table represented more than just rent money. "That is a bunch of *stuff!*" Bob shouted. "I never should've bought this *stuff*. We don't need all this *stuff* and you can't sell *stuff!* That STUFF is going to sit there and rot!" Except he wasn't saying 'stuff'.

I understood his remorse, but the frustration transformed for me into a promise as I stood at the table, looking at the pile, then at the phone.

I'll show him, I thought. *I'll sell this... stuff.*

*

The next four months became a whirlwind. I sold *lots* of stuff. That morning in my dining room, I stared at the phone for what seemed like an eternity. I knew I needed a positive first call.

Who do I know that won't say no to me?

The answer popped into my head—the father of my best friend, Pat. Pat and I had been friends since we were 10 years old but never guessed that she would go on to become my sister-in-law. We had long ago devised the system of "You ask my dad, and I'll ask yours" and found it to be wildly successful, so Mr. Starling became my very first attempt at a sale. He gladly agreed to let me perform a demonstration and, as I hung up the phone, that "yes" became the spark that fueled my morning momentum. I didn't put down the phone until I had made 40 calls on my list of 100 names. The calls I made that morning and the demonstrations we went on to do that night, and in the coming days, laid a foundation that was too big to be ignored.

Within four weeks, I knew I couldn't keep up with the number of appointments, follow-ups, and team that I was building. I needed Bob. More than just during the day, and not just for a few stolen hours after his construction work, I needed full-time help to take this to the next level.

"You need to quit your job and help me."

"You're crazy."

The conversation began much as I had anticipated. I knew that, in order for me to take this part-time business to the next level, I needed his help on a regular basis. However, after a quarter of a century working construction, quitting his job to be a 'salesman' would require a massive leap of faith on his part.

I had met Bob in a South Florida bar in 1968. Leaning against the wall, his long beard and tattoos were enough to catch my eye when I walked in. He stood out from his motorcycle club friends with his quiet demeanor and easy smile. This was the 1960s, so... 90 days later we were married, and we had five sons over the next six years. Growing a family of this size, this quickly, meant that Bob worked a lot. Since construction was what he knew, it was impossible for him to consider any other line of work. No matter how much he supported me.

To say that my husband had a difficult upbringing is an understatement. With a single mother who possessed only a driving work ethic, my husband grew up a gypsy, bouncing from trailer park to trailer park, with the belief that if your back wasn't hurting and your hands weren't dirty, then your day had not been spent 'working'. His entire wardrobe consisted of cut off Levi's, worn-out t-shirts, and well-worn work boots.

During the previous few years, with all five of my boys in school, I attempted to enter the workforce. I had no education so I found some 'personal development' courses and took a few seminars. I convinced Bob to join me at a couple of these seminars, where we repeatedly heard the mantra "For things to change, you have to change," but the long-haired construction worker beside me was not convinced that this applied to him. Looking back, I'm certain that he felt as out of his element at those seminars as I did entering my first business presentation in that chiropractor's office.

In the first weeks, he grudgingly fell into a routine of me making the calls, scheduling appointments, training my rapidly growing team, and running my business, all with his occasional help with the 'grunt' work of carrying things or setting up. But getting him to explain our compensation plan to a handful of people was out of the question. His work ethic was unmatched, but he was painfully shy and totally unwilling to talk to new people.

Then I got my first paycheck.

When I opened the mail that day, my mind froze. Looking at the numbers and the attached pages of my team structure, I was overwhelmed and overjoyed. Bob and I pored over the printout and saw that my early work was paying off.

Bob had a grasp of these numbers, and the structure of the business I was growing was crystal clear. But seeing it laid out on printed pages astonished him. The *numbers never lie* had been his personal motto, and the proof that my business was working was now right in front of him. This was the largest single check that either of us had ever held in our hands. It was more than he made in months of working construction, even after 25 years of experience and a broken body to show for it.

We were giddy with excitement looking at our printout as he explained to me what this meant for *our* next month. I recognized that the passion and understanding he had for explaining this far exceeded my own attempts at teaching this information to my team.

That night, in our living room, just like every night for the past few weeks, my fledgling team assembled with their guests, to learn how to build their own team and create long-lasting structure. When we reached the point of laying out the compensation plan and explaining how to earn the most money at each of our company's positions, I called on Bob to come up and tell us all about it.

There was a moment of silence as I stretched out my arm, marker in hand. "Bob, why don't you explain to them what you saw in our printout today."

He was briefly caught off guard, but his excitement over those numbers won out and he took the marker from my hand. He pulled out the printout and launched into his first impromptu presentation of our compensation plan.

His shyness and anxiety faded away at that moment, and his confidence with this aspect of the business brought out an entirely new aspect of his character. Our friends were on the edge of their seats, and his words began to sow the seeds of hope in a room full of people.

With a marker and a flip chart, Bob added an element to our business that launched us to a whole new level. This became our routine. Exponential growth was a new term to us, and we were suddenly living examples of it. Our rapid growth was exhilarating, and Bob could see that our business needed him home to work with me. But giving up the security of a job and weekly paycheck was still too much for him to imagine.

My second paycheck did it. With just a little contribution from him, we tripled our earnings from the previous month. A few days later, Bob came home in the middle of the day. When the door opened, I knew something must be terribly wrong, because Bob never worked half days.

"I just quit my job."

I almost fainted. I could feel the panic well up inside me, and I choked back a sob. My heart was pounding.

"Well, if we don't sell… our kids won't eat."

"And our boys like to eat."

We both laughed nervously at our predicament, but the unspoken commitment became another bond between us. This was real for us now.

Bob took the leap of faith with me and together we went to work. I began adding to my list of names through my endless contacts with Cub Scout troops, church youth groups, baseball and football teams, music lesson moms, PTA volunteer committees, and all the other organizations that mothers typically get drawn into.

While Bob's circle of friends was quite small, mine, like most mothers, was massive and growing bigger all the time. I made calls to those on my list while my new team members created lists of their own and I helped them make calls to their lists.

The days flew by in a flurry of activity and excitement. After starting our business in June, our world seemed to turn upside down. I tried to grasp the moments as they whisked by us. Each day was a new issue and a new opportunity to learn. To grow.

We had yet to travel outside of south Florida, but every day I walked into my living room to see a growing number of calls on my answering machine. 13 messages surged to 21 messages, which soared to over 50. I struggled to keep up, but the struggle was a snowball of energy and momentum. By October, I felt as if I hadn't slept a full night since June.

"I have nothing to wear to something this fancy!"

My complaints to Bob fell on deaf ears. All he had to do was rent a tux and show up. I stood for a moment, consumed with worry about what I was going to wear when it dawned on me that Bob had never worn a tuxedo in his life. If I was going to get Bob Burdick into a tuxedo, I had to have the best dress I could find.

This was our first leadership conference with our new business and the excitement was electric. We had argued about our phone bill doubling last month with all the long-distance calling we had been doing, but airline tickets to New Orleans were another pill for us to swallow. We had been promoting the conference to our team throughout the entire five months of our business. Our sponsors had gone overboard stressing the importance of being there and bringing our team, so that had been one of our primary goals since the day we signed up. We were committed to rolling into New Orleans in style.

With 22 team members at our side, we had five partners who had achieved the highest sales position possible, and we were all in awe of this experience. I felt like Cinderella at the ball. As we walked the hallway of our fancy hotel, headed toward our first awards dinner, I found myself face to face with the mirror that once scared me. My reflection looked like a different person. Gone was the look of procrastination and uncertainty. Nowhere in this woman's eyes was there any fear or doubt.

I look like a movie star.

Bob looked like Paul Newman had nothing on him, and I was overwhelmed with pride for us both.

The room was packed with black-tie formal wear and ball gowns as nearly 2000 people gathered to celebrate. I was shaking hands and strutting in my heels with a smile you couldn't slap off my face.

As we took our seats and dinner was served, I was pleasantly surprised to find our table in the front of the room, right beside the main stage. Steak and lobster rolled out, and no expense was spared in making us feel like this night was one to remember.

I had never seen anything like this except in movies. When the president of our company took the stage, enthusiasm from the crowd erupted like a volcano. I was laughing, smiling, and crying all at the same time. His quick wit and humor kept the crowd laughing, but the room became serious with anticipation when he made an announcement.

"It's time to recognize the top ten producers in our company."

I couldn't wait to see this. I kicked my heels off under the table and refilled my glass of champagne, leaning forward to watch the action on the main stage. Applause shook the room with each name that was called.

"Who do you think is next?" Bob asked me.

We didn't know many people in the room, but we had heard the names of many of the big earners during our previous few months.

"I don't know!"

I couldn't even imagine what it felt like to be one of those people, floating on air as they made their way to the stage after being called. It just felt like a red carpet at the Oscars.

"Next up are a couple of newbies from Fort Lauderdale, Bob and Sue Burdick."

Bob jumped out of his seat.

"Did they call our name?" I shouted at him.

"Yes! Come on!" said Bob.

"You've gotta help me find my shoes!"

I scrambled under the table to find my heels as I clung to Bob's tuxedo coat to keep him from racing to the stage without me.

I was hopping toward the stage, pulling on my second sequined shoe—they perfectly matched my dress—still in shock as the applause roared around us.

I have no lipstick on!

Bob paused at the bottom of the steps and I grasped his arm.

We looked at each other, the moment freezing in my mind, then strode together onto the main stage.

CHAPTER 6

I am enough

Wendy Campbell

❧

God has such a sense of humor to have moved me, one of the most imperfect, insecure people in the world, into a position of passion for teaching on the relationship between nutrition and disease and allowing me the honor and privilege of becoming the top female income earner in our company. It truly is crazy because I began this journey, the same as many others in my lifetime, with those incessant toxic voices singing, *Who do you think you are? You're not enough, you're not enough, you're not enough!*

28 years ago, I was a 43 year old stay-at-home mom. My children were six, ten, and eleven, and even though I was an RN, I had absolutely no interest in nutrition. I was focused on putting good food on the table but didn't put much thought into the specifics. When my neighbor shared "fruits and vegetables nutrition in a capsule" with me, my first response was, "Give me a break! What are they going to think of next? I already eat plenty of fruits and vegetables."

At that time, Juice Plus+ was just a concept. There was absolutely no research and just one measly brochure. And this neighbor not only expected that I would buy Juice Plus+ from her, but even had the audacity to suggest that I join her team to sell it.

What? An MLM? NO! I am a nurse, not a salesperson.

Besides, my only experience with network marketing began with an invitation to go to dinner... and ended up at some 'meeting' where people were trying to sell me soap. And I never even got dinner. "No, thank you," I said politely, at least on the outside, while inside I was screaming, *No way!*

However, it was the education, not the 'sales pitch', that lit up my nursing brain and shocked me into research mode. *Why do we need more fruits and vegetables?* I pondered as I headed to the library. I was barraged by articles describing the sheer power of phytochemicals, antioxidants, the importance of variety as well as quantity, and how the produce was far less nutritious than years past. I felt pure shame over the fact that I, as an RN, was so oblivious to these facts. *You call yourself an educated nurse? How have you missed this?*

As I kept researching, I was shocked to the core that children were getting diseases that in my early days of nursing had been reserved for the elderly. I thought back to when I was supervisor of a clinic in Hawaii from the mid-1970s to early 1980s and realized that I had not taken care of even one child with diabetes. And yet now, the stats were clearly showing that diabetes had become an epidemic in America. I soberly reflected on the fact that I had taken care of only one child with cancer back then, and it had broken my heart to take care of 3 year old Jeremy... and yet now, hospitals were sprouting up all over the place geared towards nothing but pediatric cancer. On top of that, adults seemed to be getting diseases at younger and younger ages as well.

I struggled with why. Could this transition away from fruits and vegetables and into processed and fast food over the past 40 years really be the critical factor in the demise of America's health?

There was a stirring in my heart. I got hooked on wanting to learn more.

Could I, should I, as a NURSE, be proactive in reversing this trend?

Could this truly be God's plan for my life?

"NO!" I screamed.

I don't want to do it. Please don't turn me into a salesperson!

God lit me up with a lightning bolt. I was MAD, MAD, MAD over what I was learning. I felt invigorated, alive, with a fire in my belly for this newfound passion. Here I was, considered by society to be over the hill, still seemingly healthy, looking and feeling good, I suppose, but maybe a little bored with the routine of life, when instantly I felt like I was back in the 1960s. We were standing up for African American rights, women's rights, equal pay, protesting the war, and experiencing the exhilaration of not just complaining about the world but actively making a difference.

I truly believed in President John F. Kennedy when he rallied us with his explosive call to action with, "Your Voice Matters!"

I immediately ordered Juice Plus+ for my family, my mom, and even our dog. I told everyone in and off my path about what I had found for our family and why it was so amazing.

"What have you been up to?" my family and friends would ask.

"I am having the time of my life!" I would unashamedly burst out. So, of course, they would want to know what and why I felt that way. If they asked more questions, I'd offer up more. But sometimes people didn't ask for more. Or sometimes they would raise their eyebrows and make some scathing remarks. And sometimes I would react by thinking, *Hmm, I thought you were a smart person... I guess I was wrong.* But deep inside I knew that my sarcasm was just a cover-up for the fact that every raised eyebrow, every "no", and every rejection or criticism of any kind felt like someone had put a stake in my heart. *I'm not strong enough to handle this rejection.*

Don't ask me how I got there, but only two months after partnering with our company, I'm sitting in the audience with one of my first teammates at my first conference in Florida.

I'm only here to learn more about fruits and vegetables. I'm a nurse, not a salesperson. If they think that I'm going to set goals and set myself up for even more disappointments at this stage of life, they are barking up the wrong tree.

Hmm, sure feels good to be dressed up for business though... I'm not just a mommy here.

At the conference, a one-page sheet of paper was passed around titled, "Why Am I Eating Juice Plus?" by Wendy Campbell, RN.

"WHAT?" I sputtered. "That's me. I wrote that!"

How did it get here? These people don't even know that I'm here. I AM Wendy Campbell! Hmmm, maybe I do have value here?

My confidence just got its first spark. But then other fears appeared.

I went to a business training session and saw the income possibilities moving up the ladder of success, but not only did I not believe that I could accomplish that top position, but I didn't want to even try.

I don't want to make a lot of money. I'm not going to dream, and you can't make me!

I didn't feel worthy or deserving of the blessings I already had—a loving husband with a six-figure income corporate job, wonderful children, a beautiful home... I didn't WANT to WANT more. But why NOT?! I really didn't know, but I knew something was holding me back.

The answer came when I happened to read an article about the "adult child of alcoholic parents syndrome". It talked about feelings of self-criticism, fear of abandonment, unworthiness... I thought everybody had those! MY parents were alcoholics. Could this subliminally be affecting my ability to dream?

Maybe, but the "fear of success or being rich" might have been a little deeper. In short, my dad was an entrepreneur, became wealthy, philandered, and divorced multiple times. Consequently,

I always had it in my head that money was the root of all evil. I've since learned through the past 25 years of bible study, however, that money is not the root of all evil. It is the love of money that creates issues. When the only reason you do anything is for money... That is the problem. On the contrary, money gives us choices and opportunities to give and give and give.

Unfortunately, my dad, despite his wealth, didn't seem to see the value in paying child support (or valuing women in general), and he for sure didn't value investing in education for me, his only daughter. I'm done with blame, anger, and resentfulness for my parents. They did the best they could with what was given to them. Strongholds over money are not uncommon. Alcoholism is a disease. The end.

I wish God would have given me that wisdom sooner.

I didn't know any of that when I left home as a sweet, naive 18 year old off on a one-way, standby student ticket to Hawaii... all alone... with only two goals:

To never have children... stemming from fear over reading that 75% of abused children unknowingly abuse their own children.

To never be rich... stemming from my father, who was rich in money but extremely poor in loving relationships.

Regardless of my fears, and despite the "I'm not going to do this as a business, I'm not going to dream, and I don't want to be rich" mindset, I kind of became a 'star' in our Juice Plus+ Company very quickly. I climbed to the top level of our company in just 16 months, which was unusual at that time. At each conference, more and more people would stop me in the hallways and exclaim, "Are you Wendy Campbell? I can't believe I am meeting you!" Surprisingly, they seemed to be putting me on a pedestal, like a hero. Initially, I tried and tried so hard to be that perfect leader that they were expecting, but it was inauthentic and exhausting. *Wow, they really think I'm something special. If they only knew...*

I know now that God gave me the people, the words, and the wisdom to be able to achieve this success. The only thing that I can 'claim', so to speak, is being obedient and responsible in the follow-through. However, for a while, I could have been accused of being on an ego trip. I was trying way too hard. I think it was less egotism and more overcompensation because I just did not want to disappoint and let down these amazing servant hearted people. It's at that point when my biggest fear began to show its ugly face: *Yikes! Everyone is going to find out I'm not that smart and not that great.*

Enter my wonderful and smart husband, Jim, who believed in me before I believed in myself. My brain was filled with negative self-talk: *How could he think I could master this? I thought he knew me.* I would berate myself for every little thing, like not being able to figure out PowerPoint and accidentally erasing half my contacts from Excel.

Once I worked for six hours on training, without saving, and my computer crashed. All of it was evidence that I wasn't a capable person.

As I cried tears of frustration, zillions of times, Jim just patiently taught me computer skills and fed me books like the *7 Habits of Highly Effective People* by Stephen R. Covey, because he got sick of seeing my sticky notes all over the house, and *I Dare You,* by William H. Danforth, whose concepts catapulted me into a place of CONSISTENT daily action steps, deeper healing, and exhilaration.

I was so tired of the stronghold about money and what I considered to be nonsense about being a salesperson. However, as my belief in Juice Plus+ grew, based on the growing body of research, my voice became louder. I became bold and confident, sharing the product I had fallen in love with. *I'm a nurse. I have an ethical and moral responsibility to share Juice Plus+,* I would tell myself.

A lightning bolt from the heavens changed my concept of 'selling' into that of 'gifting'. I began to see that I was empowering people through a series of educational and relationship building exposures by giving the gift of education, which became the gift of health, which moved naturally into the gift of an invitation to the team, as I relished waking up to passion and purpose every day. *I can do this. Empower… not sell! I'm going to care as much about creating a better life for people as I do their health.*

"Honor God: Serve People" became my motto.

My dream then and now is to have Juice Plus+ on the kitchen table of everyone in America, but I knew instantly that I couldn't do it on my own and, magically, a team was born.

"You're a blessing whether you do a little or a lot" is my mantra, as I invite people into our team, because I want to make sure they understand that their voice, small or large, is important. "You will certainly touch at least those friends and family members about whom you care the most and maybe a few other people who may have otherwise been missed by someone else," I suggest.

As my beliefs grew for the possibilities for my own life and my families' lives, others were empowered as well. My business kept growing exponentially, to the point that our family was able to make some fantastic choices. Within a few years, my husband joined me on this mission, so we had not only increased supplemental income but time flexibility together as well. Our family dreams BIG. When Jim and I moved from the Midwest back to the California beaches, our kids transferred high schools and colleges to follow us. When 16 years later we decided to move to Montana, two out of three of our kids and their families followed us again.

Hallelujah! My kids love me!

God can dream bigger for you and for me than we could ever dream on our own.

"I don't know what God's plan for your life is, but neither do you," I often challenged others. "Come on along," I urged. Whether you make a little or a lot, either way, I truly believe we are getting paid to do philanthropy. I surmise that 99.9% of our team members would bring up Juice Plus+ in conversation whether they made a dime or a dollar and are just as surprised as I was when the promotions and business growth happened anyway.

"We are a mission-driven team!" I screamed from the rafters.

Despite my confidence in the product, my belief in the business, and my support of my team, I was still constantly fighting down the toxic voices in my head—*You're a fake! You're not enough! You're not enough! YOU'RE NOT ENOUGH!*

The drama of my life, despite being watered down through the years, still gets in my way at times. Even though I've gone through the Bible study *Breaking Free* by Beth Moore, three times, it turns out I'm not alone in this torment.

Cut back to the young, cute, naive girl alone in Hawaii.

With the sun shining and the palm trees swaying in tune to the tropical trade winds blowing, my first day in Waikiki found me skipping down the main street of Kalakaua in a short little muumuu. Rebirth! Freedom! It was like I was flying and the whole world was available to me. Yep, I needed a job, but that didn't scare me. I'd worked regularly since I was 12, mostly for all the extras my mom couldn't afford—deodorant, perfume, and prom dresses—but now it was all about survival. The basics like food and shelter were all on me. The rest of life was my responsibility.

God allowed many 'bullet holes of life' to grow me along the way. I'll minimize the emotions of, for instance, rape... and simply move into the best part—I didn't let the bad guy win. That fool could have stolen from me the ability to trust men for the rest of my life. He could have stolen from me the joy of intimacy for over 41 years with my fabulous, handsome, and sexy husband. Nope, by the grace of God, he didn't win. I didn't give him that power.

I've been trying for all my life to not let the bad guys win. I came to an understanding with God, and as he helped me move into compassion, forgiveness, and nonjudgement for others, I was released from that prison of anger and resentment.

The remaining roadblock, however, was how to embrace that same compassion, forgiveness, and love for myself. I dabbled with a few coping mechanisms—mostly overeating and smoking—as a great way to stuff my feelings and hide in loneliness. I am an overachiever and the class clown, and it certainly doesn't take Psych 101 to recognize the insecurities that these represent.

I've learned that gratitude is the key to an abundant, joy-filled life. My morning ritual now is to shout to the heavens… "I choose gratitude and joy today!"

So, what happened to the young girl skipping down the streets of Waikiki? Too many bullet holes and too little faith.

But in His perfect timing, God showed up and showed off.

I remember clearly the day he sat me down speaking softly, as a father to a child. "Wendy," He began, "you are right. You aren't the smartest and you aren't the greatest… without Me, anyway. I allowed every one of those bullet holes—the betrayals, the physical and verbal assaults, the hurts, and the disappointments—all as pieces of my plan to help you towards compassion for others, to move you away from unwarranted 'judgment' so that you could serve others well. I've been pouring light and love into you from above so that your broken heart and body would be a vehicle to shine that light, my light, out into the world."

"But what did you do?" He admonished. "You covered up the bullet holes with band-aids and trapped it all for yourself. Haven't you been studying my words? You are holding back in fear and insecurities that are no longer acceptable. I want you, in all your imperfections, to rip off those band-aids and let my light shine right through those holes out into the world."

Okay, God, I hear you now.

Pray, listen, act, and obey and then give Him the glory. That is the true secret to success. I'm sure God's ego doesn't need the edification, but when we acknowledge Him, the word 'luck' becomes synonymous with 'God's Grace', faith is replenished, and we begin to live on earth as if we are in heaven, free from scarcity and fear.

All I know is that when I do move through those pearly gates, I don't want to be apologizing to God for not using the gifts, talents, and abilities he bestowed on me.

I am a warrior angel on a mission.

Allow me to count my blessings, one by one.

First blessing, my husband Jim, the love of my life, the wind beneath my wings. Having experienced and appreciated the value of having my own personal cheerleader, I'm frequently suggesting to my team to "Get yourself a Jim." However, I quickly clarify with, "Not my Jim; get your own Jim!"

Second, my children and grandchildren, who have been a continual stream of joy for almost 40 years. Katie, my daughter and best friend, has become my lifeline to continued emotional and technical skill building, and we work and play side by side almost daily.

Next, God gave me important and satisfying work, if you want to call waking to passion and purpose every day and being surrounded with the most caring and loving people ever work. Since our company generously pays us to do 'philanthropic work', I'm reminded by the words of Confucius, "Choose a job you love, and you will never have to work a day in your life."

My company has sent me throughout the USA, Europe, the UK, across Australia, and Canada. My husband has been by my side during most of these adventures. I was also able to plan month-long vacations centered around the European conferences for myself plus each one of my children, before they were married with their own children... just myself and each one at a time... cherished memories forever!

How do you qualify and quantify the value of creating these bountiful memories for a lifetime? Let me share with you a quote from Joyce Maynard, an American writer, that might help you think a little more broadly about your role as a parent:

It's not only children who grow.

Parents do too.

As much as we watch to see what our children do with their lives, they are watching us to see what we do with ours.

I can't tell my children to reach for the sun.

All I can do is reach for it myself.

When my children are being asked about me, their mother, I hope they will say, "She climbs mountains that most people wouldn't dare."

*

"We are the messengers, not the message. Get over yourself."

I've been known to say this in exasperation while coaching those who seem to be wallowing in a muddy pond of self-doubt. I believe it's imperative that each person on our team knows that you don't have to be perfect to be flat-out amazing. On our team you are not only acceptable as you are, but highly respected and valued as you step out of your comfort zone, sometimes in boldness but maybe initially with timidity, to proactively do something important in this world.

If anybody at my graveside says, "Oh, she was such a good motivator," I will literally get out of that grave and haunt them for the rest of my non-life! I don't want to be remembered for motivating. I want to be remembered for inspiring. To me, a motivator pushes their beliefs onto others for their own gain. NO! I want to inspire people to feel worthy of desiring, accomplishing, and experiencing the internal satisfaction of doing good for the world, their families, and their own selves. I want to inspire them to use their God-given talents and abilities during this limited time on earth so they can die knowing they've left a legacy of servant-hearted people who will continue doing good through future generations. I want them facing their higher power without excuses and shame, but with a gratefulness that God gave them this journey and they were obedient to His path.

Our company founder, Jay Martin, emphatically stated in his mission statement from years ago that he wanted "to build a stable and lasting company that would help as many people as possible realize their dreams"—not the company's dreams, but *their* dreams. In our company, you have full permission to have both altruistic, mission-driven goals as well as income-driven goals, because we will coach you, believe in you before you believe in yourself, and help you to attain them.

I don't know what God's plan is for your life, but probably neither do you...

I've been allowed to live a life of excellence within this company as one of the most imperfect and insecure people in the world. But I'm done with, *I'm not enough, I'm not enough, I'm not enough...*

I AM ENOUGH, bullet holes and all.

CHAPTER 7

Becoming me

Janice Neigum

The shrill ringing of the phone woke me from a night of restless sleep. *This can't be good*, I thought as I tried to shake my exhausted body awake. I instructed myself to hurry before it stopped, feeling along the wall in the dark. The ringing stopped, but I knew I could check the caller ID. My heart felt heavy; I knew this call would change my life.

Our family had received a call like this early one morning so many years ago—the gut-wrenching call that my brother had been tragically killed in a car accident.

Please, God, don't let it be another call like that.

Confirming the phone number, I tried to swallow the lump in my throat. It was my former husband; I knew in that instant our son, Justin, had been in an accident. My mind raced, jumping from one disconnected thought to another and I was unable to focus;

Please, God, let him be alive.

My mind slipped back to our last conversation, his promise to call me and to pull over if he was tired. Why, after working a 12-hour shift in the blazing hot sun, had he insisted on the four-hour drive that night? I'd had a nagging feeling, a sixth sense, that he shouldn't go. I had hugged him as tight as I could, looked deep into his eyes, and said, "I love you, Justin."

"I love you, Mom. Don't worry, I'll be fine." As he rushed out the door, I was left with an unsettled knot in my stomach.

Why didn't I insist that he stay? Why didn't I beg him to leave early in the morning? Why, why, why...

I tortured myself with unending thoughts. Maybe, had I insisted, this call would not have happened. I recognized the guilt; it had haunted me so many times. I prayed I was in a bad dream. I didn't want to entertain what I might hear; perhaps my mom guilt would be too much for me to live with.

As I answered the call, I braced myself for what I would hear. Trembling inside, I said, "Hello, it's me." I held my breath and listened.

"I have bad news..." said the voice on the other end. "Justin's been in a serious roll over—it's bad, and he's unconscious. The RCMP sergeant said he is likely paralyzed."

"Please, don't tell me that," I said. "He's not a doctor; let's not believe the worst before we know for sure." My fear made me defensive; I didn't want to entertain those possibilities. I wanted my son alive and well.

Collect your thoughts, I commanded myself. Inside I was trembling, and an old, uneasy, and all-too familiar feeling was back. As I dialed the emergency doctor's number, I thankfully remembered to take long, deep breaths, to help calm my mind so I could pay attention to what the doctor would say.

Janice, you must shift your consciousness out of the funk you've been stuck in these last four years. I will become a confident, powerful woman.

My daughter and closest friends often encouraged me to look inside and become the confident woman I was destined to be.

"Justin needs my support," I said to myself. He needed to have the most positive reinforcement of his 40 years of living, so I declared to myself that I would be that for him.

I hung onto every word the doctor said.

"Justin has limited movement in his lower extremities," she explained, "more sensation than movement, lacerations on his head, and his L4 looks cracked with possible lower fractures in his spine."

My heart sank. Yet, despite the prognosis I had just listened to, I clung to the fact she didn't say he was paralyzed. And like my life up till now, I still had hope.

Seeing his 6'4" listless body was a shock; he had a swollen head, black eyes, and cuts and dried blood everywhere, plus a tube breathing life into him.

Just breathe, I reminded myself. Justin needed me to believe he would be well again. It was a miracle he was alive, and I needed to watch for the smallest miracles every day and support his belief that he would walk again.

We'd been advised that only two immediate family members could visit, and with Justin's father at his bedside, my husband Jim said, "I'm going to go home," and left to take care of business. My next challenge was to overcome my paralyzing fear of driving by myself in a city of over 1.5 million people.

Fear turned to anger. Why did I have to lose the security of my husband by my side? He was my rock!

I had to move past this, I decided, and I put on my big girl pants to prove to myself that I was strong enough to weather both storms.

I thought about the course I'd signed up for a month before this accident that had caused tension between Jim and I. I had taken dozens of courses over the last 20 years, but there were still all those dark days that settled in like a wild snowstorm. I'd had glimpses and moved forward with hope, and then someone would say something hurtful and I'd hit rock bottom. My patterns get revealed; I swear I'll climb the mountain, and then I slip on those craggy rocks and down I go. I felt like I'd made progress with all of those courses and I had peeled back many layers from my first insights... but there was still so much work to do. Why was I so afraid of the darkness when the light has always overcome the shadows?

I promised myself this three-month course with meditation would reveal more of what I was ready to move through. More personal development, just one more deep dive, but this time would be different. I had the faith and courage and I believed that this time, I would finally slay my dragons. The mantra I chose was simple, powerful, and calmed my fears; it was part of my healing to help me unravel and understand why I was so prone to depression.

I am whole, I trust, I am love, I am.

I was so proud of myself for driving safely back and forth for two weeks. I gained more confidence each day, and it was the best feeling I'd had in years. "I am capable!" I said out loud, smiling to myself in the mirror, knowing how far I had come in such a short time.

With my new-earned confidence of having conquered my fear of driving in a big city, I went from extreme anxiety to calm and collected. My river of tears were of joy, knowing that at 69 years young, I did it.

*

The journey of a thousand miles begins with the first step, I thought to myself. How many times had I taken that first step? How many times was it met with failure? I can still feel how scared I was as a young woman of 17, walking down the aisle in white, five months pregnant, embarrassed, yet hopeful to live 'happily ever after.'

I had an old, familiar feeling of shame that I seemed to carry with me, silently, into every moment. I did not know how to talk about it, which is exactly what shame needs to grow—silence. My shame eventually erupted into paralyzing depression. My marriage was so difficult; we were so young, and there was so much responsibility. We didn't know how to communicate, and constant unfulfilled expectations led to endless fighting. I was worn out.

Somehow, even after ten years of chronic struggle, attempted suicides, and so many fights, I still had an inner flicker of hope that I could get life right... Why? Because I had two young daughters.

Where did the shame start to find its silence? Reflecting on my childhood, I kept hearing, "Keep the peace, Janice"; "Stay positive, just keep smiling"; "Do what you're told; what would a good girl do?"; "Be, say, do what you are supposed to do"; "Don't ruffle the feathers."

In my reflections, I was a happy child; I was a positive person, the kind of person my friends and family expected me to be. I didn't know I'd learned to put on an act. I became a people pleaser. I believed that if I was quiet or funny or behaved a certain way, maybe then my parents would get along, maybe then everyone would like me. It took years to perfect my outer smile, all while I was crying on the inside. I was adept at stuffing my feelings way down, especially when it seemed to keep the peace at home.

There was no transition from childhood to adulthood, not really. Naturally, I felt ill prepared as a wife and as a mom, and out of desperation, I fell to my knees and found my way to church. I walked the path to be 'born again'. I felt accepted, and because of that, I felt happier than I had been in a very long time. I was forgiven for getting pregnant so young. I was forgiven for all the lies I'd told. I was forgiven for all the guilty thoughts that I had. There were fewer better feelings than being told I was forgiven. Church became a safe and comfortable place to ask all my questions, to learn how to parent and how to be in marriage. I felt my confidence ebb and flow; I felt more good and less bad. I cherished those foundational years at the church, feeling accepted and learning how to be more patient and kind. I was hoping I could be the loving mom I always wished I had.

My marriage to my children's father crumbled, and even though I had some highs, it made my lows even lower. The dark thoughts were swallowing me up; I heard the voices say, *I am not good enough, I am not a good mom, I am an inadequate wife, I am not a good daughter, I'm not a good sister, and I need to be a better friend...* and in desperation and to quiet these incessant voices, I took an overdose. I wholeheartedly convinced myself that my family and the world would be better off without me.

To God's grace, after the storm came the calm, and I knew it was not my time; I had more to do, and more to give. I had a new lease on life and enrolled in a course at a local college that helped me feel like I was moving forward in my life. The course was called Business Readiness Training, and I was getting ready.

My history repeated itself, with highs and lows that became as rugged as the Rocky Mountains. I tried my hand at network marketing—selling jewelry, household products, supplements, and make-up. I loved each company and their products, but I bought into all the old stories in my head, and even though I was excited at the possibilities of having my own business, earning my own money, and becoming successful, I quickly learned that I was always my biggest customer, and as such, my businesses crumbled right alongside my self-esteem. The feeling of failure was as bitter as having my stomach pumped. The familiar feelings of shame and embarrassment led to discouragement, and my loop of negative thoughts once again took over. I tried dropping to my knees again; this time, I stayed down for quite a while.

After our separation, we decided to make a go of our marriage again. I was so much happier being a family, and giving birth to twin boys was the icing on the cake. I felt settled and happier than I had been in a while, and my family felt content to be together.

However, the honeymoon phase didn't last. My unhappiness and depression returned with a vengeance, and we were soon in the throes of a nasty divorce. My self-deprecating thoughts were on the rampage. Thoughts that I had let my kids down, I was taking them away from their safe place, I was a terrible mother, went around and around in my head.

I felt like I was cheating on my girls by leaving our beautiful home again. Somehow, I convinced myself that renting a townhouse would make my life easier. I never could have imagined how difficult it would be for my children.

My heart hurts as I think about all the poor choices I have made throughout my life and the ripple effect it has had on those I love.

Divorce, hard times, inner trust, and a lot of personal growth led me to meet my soulmate. The challenges were not over as we blended two families. It is rewarding looking back at all the good intentions, the fascinating and hilarious holidays, pride-filled graduations, career moves, grandbabies, and new friends, all which have led to my personal growth and the realization that this is what my life is about: change, trying something new, meeting someone new, and making choices, right or wrong, good or bad. I am learning that change is slow, patience can be my friend, love covers a host of wrongs—and I am doing the best I can.

Most importantly, each time I perceived myself as having failed, I also started over; again and again and again, I trusted one more time. This time I asked myself if I could try another network marketing business.

Was it too good to be true?

What if I failed again?

What if I succeeded?

*

I reluctantly picked up the phone and dialed, waiting to hear my daughter's voice on the other end. She answered cheerfully. "Hi, Mom!"

I immediately launched into my tirade. "I don't want to do this business anymore; I just suck. I want you to have my customers and partners because you deserve it all. You are the one attracting so many wonderful team members and doing all the hard work. I feel guilty and so undeserving, you created Team Bee and you deserve to have my team and customers..."

It felt good to get that burden off my chest and tell her how I really felt.

I managed to reconcile that I couldn't make another MLM successful because I just didn't have it in me.

Jim and I had been going through turmoil. We were going back and forth about how this decision, to give up again, would affect our lives. This business was sucking the life out of me; my negative thoughts were almost out of control again. Another business failure.

I am not a leader, no one trusts me, this is too hard...

I felt guilty about all the hard work my daughter Nicole was doing while I was just reaping the benefits from her. It didn't seem fair.

"Mom," she said, "you were the one who built your business 16 years ago. You were the one going to trade shows, farmers markets, hosting parties, bringing in doctors, sharing with passion all your health benefits." My girl, supporting me as always. "Why are you forgetting all the hard work you did?"

Why could I not receive her encouragement and grace? I had loved the early years when I was first introduced to the concept of plant nutrition versus vitamins. I remember my overwhelming excitement at my first Wellness Expo in Edmonton, which I attended with my boss. I was vibrating with emotion and could barely take it all in. The enormous building buzzed with electricity as rows and rows of exhibitors lined up to share the latest technology in health and wellness.

A woman standing in front of her booth reached out to shake my hand. She was as excited to share her information as I was to hear about it. I thought, *Can someone really be this happy, this passionate, about capsules packed full of phytonutrients from fruit and veggies?* The concept was so foreign to me, yet I was so interested and wanted to learn more. I knew that plants could heal, as I had done a 30-day detox only nine short months before that had changed my entire health status.

She literally made me promise that if she gave me this life-changing information on cassette tape, including research from four medical doctors, that I would honestly listen to it.

"Yes," I promised. "Yes, I will listen to the information... Why wouldn't I?"

I was starting to get uncomfortable at how insistent she was because, even though I had said yes, it was like she didn't believe I would. Her beautiful smile and sincerity were definitely charming, and I did love her enthusiasm. Little did I know this conversation would change the trajectory of my life.

After many more conversations and questions, I said a resounding "YES!" to the product, and in spite of my past NWM attempts, I even said "YESSS" to the business. After all, even if I was my best customer, I wanted the discount! I knew Jim was not going to be happy with me asking him to spend more money and take more supplements, or that I was going to work the business. I started with, "I promise we will actually save money and feel better; we will finish off these other supplements and this is all we will need." I confidently defended my point of view, unwavering in my knowledge deep down that this was something to go to bat for. I ended with, "I know you are skeptical; just take them for four months and we will see."

I was my own evidence—waking up at 6 am sharp after a restful eight hours and no alarm!

I began my business as I tested the power of concentrated plant-based nutrition that is whole food based and as close to nature as possible. With a healthier lifestyle, I felt that I had more energy, which was the icing on my cake.

A passion was born. I loved sharing Juice Plus+ products to make healthy living easier by helping my friends and family bridge the gap between what they should eat and what they did eat, every day. I was so excited.

My big mission became helping Nicole to understand how she could help her daughter, Ella, improve her nutrition battle for a healthier little body. The convincing was not as easy as I thought. Where was all this resistance and stubbornness coming from? I always considered Nicole to be open minded. How could she think Ella would not benefit from eating all the extra fruit and veggies in a delicious gummy? With no after no, I realized I needed to come up with my best mom strategy. I would wait until her graduation from nutrition school, fly out to visit her, and bring her a CD from her favorite doctor, Bill Sears. My plan was set.

"Now that Ella is in bed, I thought we could take 15 minutes and watch your favorite doctor explain all the benefits of Juice Plus+." I realized I had her cornered, plugged in the VHS tape, and pressed play. I saw her resign herself to watching and then soften as it played. I saw her eyebrow raise and her head nod along in agreement... She leaned in!

Did she finally believe me? I was certain that she was ready to try anything and everything to resolve Ella's health concerns. I was concerned she might be thinking that if the naturopath couldn't figure it out after a year, how could something as simple as fruits and vegetables be the answer? I was prepared to show her.

"Just sign right here, Nicole... Yes, it's only $50 to join... No, you don't have to work the business if you don't want to... Yes, you can just try it for four months." My full-blown excitement at her joining me in the business could not be contained; I hugged her so tight that I was sure her ribs hurt. She was quick to see the benefits and the improvement to Ella's health, and everything started to make sense. The more research I read, the more bulletproof I became with the naysayers.

It felt like a punch to the gut when someone I considered to be a friend threw me under the bus. The excitement I felt had been building after planning for months to host a talk at the college with a well-respected pediatrician in our business. Putting on an event like this was a new experience, and I learned as I went how much work went into making all the pieces fit.

I reached out to the principal of the school my friend worked at and shared details of the upcoming event. I asked her if she had heard of this doctor, and she said yes. It was all coming together with the number of people that would be there, and I already felt the excitement building. Parents would learn about how to get their children to eat more fruits and veggies and Juice Plus+. How could anyone not want to learn from a well-respected pediatrician who specialized in child obesity? I considered the value to parents:

the doctor was giving up his time for something he believed in, it was free, nothing was sold, and they would have more choices... surely this would be a win-win. I really did have a servant's heart, and I was proud of what it took for me to put it all together.

While I was busy on my computer, I received a message from the principal. Her words stung me like a bee. She accused me of being unethical, that I hadn't told her this was one of those MLM companies. As my heart sank, I thought of what I could say to her and drafted up an email. I explained as best I could that this well-respected doctor would not make money from his presentation, that we were only there to educate and no product would be sold. We just wanted parents to have easy solutions to bridge their child's nutritional gaps. I even asked her if we could speak on the phone, but it fell on deaf ears; she was already convinced I was trying to scam them.

It was times like these that I wanted to throw in the towel, because I cared too darn much about others' opinions of me. Although it took years, when I accepted that my part was simply to share, and that their opinion of me was none of my business, the stories in my head started to collapse. Many experiences shook me to my core, made me question my purpose and consider leaving, but the people in the business, the doctors and the research, and my own success stories picked me back up and pushed me forward.

I know my son's accident gave me newfound courage. I needed to feel capable, powerful, and loving, and to thrive through this season in my life. My son has embraced his new reality, as have I, and we both share in the faith that he will walk again. I see how tirelessly he works every day. I know how tirelessly I have worked each day, and I am so proud of where we both are. I know I am not finished with my personal growth journey, but I am finished caring about what others think about me and my passion.

I am beyond grateful for the life I have created with my teams—Team Bee and Balance Builders—our upline Shining Star International. I love hard on each new person and all these amazing humans I have met across Canada, the US, and globally.

The fun we continue to have attending conferences, working with our team here in Calgary, hosting events online and in person has given all of us so much joy. I know it is this community that keeps me inspired because as a collective we have impacted thousands of families throughout the world.

We bought our dream home in Mexico recently. Having Nicole purchase her dream home in the same city so we can finally have time to enjoy the sun, ocean, and adventure makes up for all the years we lived apart. With so many inspiring people joining our teams, I share unapologetically both the power of plants and the power of a wonderful network marketing family.

I continue to put one foot in front of the next. Every time I thought I failed or quit, I actually just started anew. I believe in this product; I believe in me, my teams, the science, NWM, the Juice Plus+ Company, and our president, Jay Martin, whose mission statement is "to inspire healthy living around the world."

Because my daughter believed in me, I learned to believe in myself. I remind myself daily that I do deserve the paychecks I earn, I deserve our home and life in Bucerias, I deserve a healthy, fun, and loving life—and I believe the best is yet to come!

CHAPTER 8

Make a life, not just a living

Curt & Lori Beavers

Saturday morning, there was a pounding on the front door. My mom hurried through the living room to answer the insistent knock. My father wasn't around, not that that was anything new; he hadn't been around much for years. The only time I remembered him being present was when he coached my all-star baseball game, when I was nine years old.

I was 13 now.

The men at the door were speaking to my mom, but I couldn't understand exactly what they were saying. Later, I found out what was happening. Our house, car, and even Mom's wedding ring were being repossessed.

"Mom, why did they do this to us?" I asked.

"Your father's business collapsed," she said. "We're bankrupt."

It was 1976, and the country was on the heels of an economic crisis. I'd known my dad's furniture business had been falling apart, but I hadn't known things were this bad.

*

In the years that followed, my mother struggled to take care of me and my brother. She shielded us rather well, as she persevered and maintained hope. Despite the fact she had no job and no prospects, she empowered herself with a quote she'd read in *Man's Search for Meaning*, a book by concentration camp inmate Viktor Frankl: "Those who have a 'why' to live, can bear with almost any 'how'."

My mother's 'why' was obvious: she wanted to give me and my brother a good life. My brother and I were the reason she got out of bed every morning, determined to do her best, despite all the obstacles. While the details of this time were foggy for my 13 year old brain, she sowed the seeds of my future hopes and dreams, which would be realized in years to come. Her tenacity and dedication to her family left their mark on my soul.

Fast forward a decade, and I found myself married to my beautiful wife, Lori. We knew we wanted to have a family and raise our kids, who would fascinate and delight us as we watched their lives unfold.

Lori wanted to be at home to raise them and make our dream for them a reality—but we weren't sure how we could make it happen.

"I want to have children, but I can't imagine putting them into daycare for 40 hours a week," Lori said one morning. "Curt, I don't want anyone else to raise our kids—I want to be there for them, especially when they're young. It's fine if other people want to do daycare, but what I want is to be a stay-at-home mom."

I agreed wholeheartedly. "If that is what we want, then we are going to trust that God will help us find a way to make it happen."

For months, we ruminated over this problem, looked for solutions, and prayed for God to provide. We didn't want to be stuck in the vicious cycle of being slaves to the clock, trading hours for dollars, and seeing any future children we might have only on the weekends and evenings.

Our *Kairos* Moment

One Sunday, our pastor got up to deliver his sermon, and little did he know that the message was for the two of us. Pastor Stanley's sermon was about getting out of debt and living the financial life of your dreams. We were amazed at God's timing!

"You need to think about how you can repay your debts, since a borrower will forever be a slave to the lender," Pastor Stanley intoned, his deep voice resonating through the church. "Who are you in bondage to? What is holding you back? What do you want out of your life—and what do you need to do to get there?"

Something in the pastor's words struck us, deep and true. This moment confirmed in us that our dreams of Lori being able to stay at home with our kids could happen with our determination and our faith in His timing.

Later that day, I said to Lori, "We have to do something about this. Dreaming's not changing anything. We have to make the change happen ourselves. We have to move on with our dream—and take the next step. For things to change, we've got to change."

This moment reminded me of a quote I once heard, "Faith carries a shovel." Sometimes God does things for us, beyond our wildest imagination, but what I have also learned is that He often invites us into actively making something of our lives. You can faith there will be a ditch, but it still has to be dug. Although we didn't know exactly where to go, we decided that day to quit dreaming about our life. We decided that it was time to make the life we wanted with God's help.

The ancient Greeks had two words for time. First was the word *chronos*, which refers to chronological or sequential time—just those typical seconds, minutes, hours, days, or weeks of your life. *Chronos* time represents your comfort zone when you're doing everything you should be doing, taking no risks. But this moment was a different type of time for Lori and I. This was our *kairos* moment. *Kairos* was used by ancient Greeks to describe moments in time that dramatically impacted people, nations, and systems. It is a moment when something happens that breaks the normal timeline, leaving you forever changed. When we experience *kairos*, we are left with an opportunity to seize the moment, reflect, and take action.

For Lori and I, this was one of the most defining moments of our lives together—it was our wake-up alarm, our revelation, our epiphany.

As Lori and I discussed the next steps, we agreed that if this was what we really wanted, we had to take initiative. If we didn't want to just go with the flow of whatever the world threw at us, then we had to do *something*.

"We're not really budget kind of people, but I think we should make a budget," I told her. "Let's figure out what we need to do to be able to have you stay at home."

How Much Is Our Dream Worth?

Lori was working as a legal secretary on the executive floor of a major bank downtown and didn't make much money. She was probably the lowest-paid person on the floor. Even as a recent college graduate who didn't earn much, she still had to play the part, dressing for success.

After taking a deep dive into our finances, we decided we needed a thousand dollars per month for Lori to be able to quit her job. We had no idea how we would find that money, but we were determined to make it happen.

We began to share with our friends at church what we were thinking. These were the people we 'did life' with. They were the people who we could turn to when we needed wisdom and guidance. Lori and I took the moment to be transparent.

"We need help," we explained. "Lori's looking for a way to make a thousand dollars a month. We want her to be able to quit her job so that she can stay home with our future family. If you hear of anything, please let us know."

Over the next few weeks, we kept putting out feelers and asking for help. We started researching at-home businesses and prayed fervently for an answer.

God answered our prayers.

One afternoon, the phone rang. I answered it and heard a woman's voice.

"You don't know me, but I'm Fran," she said. "I'm a pastor's wife. Somebody at your church told me y'all are thinking about your future family and Lori wants to stay at home. I used to work for the airlines, but now I do something else from home. I think what I do might work for y'all too. Could my husband and I cook dinner for you and tell you about it?"

When I hung up, I recounted the conversation to Lori and said, "Do you think this could be God providing what we're looking for?"

Lori was excited. "Whatever it is, let's at least check it out. Even though we don't even know her, she wants to cook dinner for us! I mean, who does that?"

The following week, we drove over to their house, which was in a very quaint, rural part of town. It was a couple of weeks before Christmas and the houses we passed twinkled with decorations. We pulled up to Fran's surrounded by a peace beyond our understanding.

Fran and her husband turned out to be the sweetest couple. As she spoke to us at the table, I realized she was the mercy-giver personality type, the kind of person you'd want at your bedside if you were sick.

"We're so glad y'all could come over," Fran said, as we dug into dinner. "I just thought you two sounded like you have the same problem I had. I was trying as hard as I could to find a way to replace my income as a flight attendant. When I found this company, I hit the jackpot."

She went on to explain more about her business. The thing was, she did not strike us as a Type A, go-get-'em salesperson. As

Fran shared her story of what she did for a living, she could not even fully explain the technicalities of her business all that well. But we could tell she loved the product, loved the business, and was extremely passionate about life.

Driving home that night, we reflected on the conversation,

"Lori, you know what she said that really shocked me?"

Lori couldn't stop smiling. "What's that?"

"She said she made $80,000 last year!" I exclaimed. "She wasn't bragging, but, still, that's what she said. And, hey, $80K is nothing to sneeze at."

"If she could do it... then we certainly could," Lori agreed. "I mean, we have every bit of potential as she does."

"If not more," I chimed in.

So that was it. We were all in.

Finding Our Purpose With Juice Plus+

In our first month, Lori and I were already making supplemental income with Juice Plus+.

When we started our business, we were very nervous. We were naive and innocent, hoping beyond hope that we could make our dream come true by going into business for ourselves with the help of the Juice Plus+ company. We needed this business to create the life we wanted to make. We needed—and wanted—it so badly, we could almost taste it.

In our initial training, which took place in a meeting room at a local hotel in Atlanta, they told us to make a list of 300 names of potential customers.

Together, Lori and I sat down and made that list. The first 150 names were easy.

"Let's use our wedding guest list," Lori suggested. "And how about our church directory and our high school and college yearbooks?"

"Yeah, and what about our neighborhood directory?" I added.

That's when we stalled. The second 150 names were much harder to come up with. Suddenly, the worry crushed down on us once again. Failure hovered over our heads like an impending storm. We just couldn't think of anyone else.

"If we don't get to the 300 names, it's just not going to work," Lori said, her voice trembling. "This is what they told us to do."

Reluctantly, we dialed the company. I held the receiver tightly, trying to hold on to control. "We have our list, but we don't have 300. Um, we're having a lot of trouble... coming up with 300 names."

Imagine how flabbergasted we were when the man on the other end of the line said cheerfully, "No problem! Just get out the yellow pages!"

In the back of my mind, I thought to myself, *There is no freaking way I am going to start calling names from the yellow pages.*

Still, I smiled at Lori, cleared my throat, and asked for more information.

The man explained. "This is the way we do it. Listen, the yellow pages can be a great tool. It's basically a directory of people— from anthropologists to barbers to chiropractors to doctors to exterminators to fence builders to garage door salesmen. As you walk your way through these categories, trust me, you'll think of other names to add to your list."

And sure enough, when I got to hardware stores, I remembered the man who had sold me a green Lawnboy lawn mower when I ran a lawn cutting business in high school. I added that man to my list (and eventually he ended up buying our product). I remembered the guy who had installed the garage door at our house. His name went on our list, too. Before we knew it, we had 300 names.

Armed with our precious list, we landed 38 customers in our first month. We were so excited! And, out of those 38, 13 of them were also interested in joining us in the business. Some of our other friends wanted to hear our story—how we'd started our business so that Lori could stay home with our children. Five of these friends joined us as partners in that first month, and we never looked back.

Fran and her husband hadn't tried to lure us in with the promise of a get-rich-quick scheme. She didn't tell us we could make a zillion dollars in the first month. However, what she did say turned out to be true: if we were willing to work hard, take some risks, and keep remembering our purpose in life—the "why we're doing what we're doing" kind of thing— then we would ultimately find success.

Deep in our hearts, we knew our 'why.' It was so that we could start our family with Lori able to stay home. Our 'why' was the purpose that God laid out for us, as individuals and as a couple. Armed with a steadfast commitment to our purpose, the 'how' was taking care of itself. Fran was put in our path as the messenger. Juice Plus+ was placed in our path as the vehicle. All we had to do was fit these pieces together to figure out what we needed to do next.

Building Our Business

As we got started in the business, we learned very quickly that building a strong customer base is crucial. This was not difficult, since Juice Plus+ is such an amazing product: number one in its category and one of the most researched nutritional products in the world.

After building that solid base, we had to build our team. In this business, you're not working alone. Recruiting, training, and developing a team is vital so that you can leverage your skills through other people—and stop trading dollars for hours.

The people who joined Lori and me in our business became lifelong friends. We cherished these people and felt grateful for them each and every day. One insight we learned early on was you have to expect the unexpected. You never know who you're going to talk to and whether this will be the person that makes your business explode. Not every team member becomes a superstar, but most people have a connection to a person with exponential potential. Some people you come into contact with will be the doers, and some will be the connectors, the ones who are great at finding the right people to partner with them. It's all a matter of finding the combination that works.

Multiple Generations

When Lori and I started with Juice Plus+, we didn't imagine having multiple generations of our family working with us. It has become a family enterprise.

My mother eventually joined us. She had worked in direct sales when my brother and I were teenagers, to put me and my brother through college. I learned so much from my mom. She taught me to pour myself into others. That pouring, she said, would overflow and let me reap the rewards ten times over.

My mother was a very wise woman.

Juice Plus+ became a business my mom could really sink her teeth into for the last half of her life. She enjoyed working with her family and doing something she loved and was good at.

Fast forward a generation, and we now have our daughter, Hope, working with us. After graduating from college with a mass communications degree, she began looking for jobs because that was what all her friends were doing. To be honest, she didn't really want a job. What lit her up was people. She considered her parents, who had always modeled working for themselves from home. Hope had seen us there for her and her brothers at every school or sports event they ever had throughout their childhoods. She saw the community, the friends our business built, and the freedom we had in not being slaves to the clock.

She learned very quickly in her life that she wished to have that freedom, too, and what we had modeled was exactly what she had wanted.

Hope began to build her own Juice Plus+ business. It was indeed a different era for her to start with Juice Plus+, as she has tools like social media and online marketing, things we did not have when we first started. However, she was able to leverage these modern tactics to skyrocket into success.

Putting our heads together, joining up strengths, and filling in for each other's weaknesses, our family has tag-teamed the Juice Plus+ enterprise and supercharged what we were able to do. That's how it worked for our family.

Make a Life, Not Just a Living

A few years ago, I asked Lori, "What if I took my story and put it into a book? Do you think it could help people find a life like we have?"

Make a Life, Not Just a Living became the story of our journey in this business. It's not about how much money we made or how successful we came to be. Instead, the crux of our story is our journey to finding what our purpose was and then pursuing that purpose with our whole hearts.

When I was a kid, my mom would take me to church, where God put some amazingly inspirational men in my life. These men became father figures to me. One of them was a businessman, a vice president with Franklin Covey, a time management company. This man told me two things. One, "Get up early every day and start the day with a quiet time. Don't let the world fill you up, but let God be the fuel of your life." The second thing was, "You need to know your God-given purpose, and then you need to pursue that purpose."

I must admit, these lessons went right over my 13 year old head. However, this man planted seeds in me that have yielded so much wisdom over the years. Most people probably would think it's crazy, but I get up at 4 am every morning to spend two hours of quiet time, feeding my mind and body and getting it right. I spend this time pouring the things into myself that I know I want in there before the world just dumps its own values into me.

The concept of 'making a life' is something Lori and I have always been passionate about. It means we know our purpose. We built our business to be the fuel and foundation to raise a family, do what we love, serve others, and live well.

I genuinely believe that everybody deserves to make a life, not just a living. Living this way is learning how to live on purpose.

And when we're living fully in our purpose, we can create the life we want to live. So many around us have a life they desire, but what they do to earn a living is the biggest obstacle. It needs to be the foundation for that 'life.'

For us, Juice Plus+ has been the vehicle that allowed us to earn in a way that did not interfere with the purpose we had set for ourselves. Thankfully, Lori and I could understand this early on in our lives. From the very beginning of our marriage, we could see our God-given purpose for being on earth as parents, as a couple, and as a family.

This search for meaning and purpose is what's driven us to build our business and to make the choices we made. We longed for the flexibility and the freedom of time and money to spend with our family. And we got that by ignoring the typical path and refusing to do what everyone else around us was doing.

This business has done more than we ever dreamed and made a huge difference in our family, impacting three generations. Our business is in all 50 states and over 20 countries—it has been an incredible journey. Working for ourselves through the Juice Plus+ company has allowed us to make a life, not just a living.

CHAPTER 9

The best is yet to come

Melissa Hyde

She caught me totally off guard. She had been calling me almost weekly for an entire year, and I had managed to avoid her until now. I answered my phone before I saw her number. I knew better. I knew she would be calling. She was so persistent. What made matters worse was that she was always so nice, so it was hard to say no to her, let alone get off the phone. I was just not interested.

But you see, Nicole refused to give up on me.

Twelve months earlier, I had basically quit with Juice Plus+. The opportunity she presented was just not for me. Instead, I made the decision to focus on my personal training business.

Quitting was an easy decision after the first home party I hosted. Sitting in the empty kitchen/living area, it was all too easy to stare at all of the empty seats. Smoothies, snacks, and bottles of capsules were lined up along the bench, along with piles of hopeful-looking application forms.

I waited.

And waited.

Then four friends skulked in the door and forced small talk.

Eventually, I realized, *nobody else is coming.* I thought for sure that they would be interested in the product; I mean, what a simple way to get more nutrition into their diet. Everyone knows fruits and veggies are good for them, so I thought they would be excited about the easy solution offered by Juice Plus+ capsules. At the very least, I thought they would show up to support me as I had done for them when they hosted their own parties.

My guests sat there politely as Sherri, my sponsor, shared the product and business information. To say that everyone looked awkward was an understatement. It felt like one of those parties where everyone felt obligated to buy something.

At the end, when asked if there were any questions, three people just shook their heads. One friend broke the awkward silence, but all she said was, "It sounds good—I'll think about it."

I felt deflated. I thought for sure I would have everyone ordering at least something. After everyone left, Sherri reassured me, saying, "This is normal. Not everyone who says they will attend shows up, and not everyone who shows up will buy. You'll probably get a few orders in the next couple of days once people have time to process the information."

Two orders trickled in over the following week. Not much, but better than nothing.

The next week, I hosted my second party. Again, I invited pretty much everyone I could think of. I got a few maybes. It was not the response I was hoping for. I let Sherri know and she said, "That's okay; people often show up last minute."

Well, this time they didn't. Not one person.

I was so embarrassed. I had dragged Sherri to my house for a second time to do a business presentation and no one showed up. I had totally wasted her time and mine. I was really beginning to doubt myself. I thought, *If my close friends aren't even interested, how can I possibly get started, let alone grow a business?*

"These home parties are just awful," I said, disappointed. "I will never host another ever again."

Sherri just smiled as she replied, "Me neither."

"And what about these 9 pm training calls we're supposed to tune into?" I said. "I'm not doing those, either. They're way too late; I'm usually not even home. It's ridiculous for them to expect us to get on a call so late in the evening." My voice dripped with distaste.

"Yeah, I totally agree," Sherri replied. "I haven't really been tuning in, either. I don't really think this business is for me."

"Yeah," I said. "I'm going to just focus on taking more courses for my personal training business."

It was in that moment I decided I was done. I quit.

Now, holding onto my phone, a wave of discomfort washed over me as I heard her voice, cheerful as ever, say, "How are you? How is your personal training business going?"

I had nothing new to report. Nothing had changed. Guilt and shame began to sink in. Yes, I had taken several new courses, and I was studying weekly with a mentor of mine; and yes, I was learning a lot, but the actual business itself had not grown at all. My revenue was the same.

"We have a local business training event this weekend," Nicole said. "Why don't you come? I'll pick you up. I'll buy your ticket and we'll go for lunch. This will give you a chance to really learn about the products and how we work this business, and see the bigger picture."

How can I say no? I'm not busy. I have no other pressing matters, and worst of all, nothing has changed. I don't have any excuses to give her.

Reluctantly, I agreed.

"Really?" she said, her tone lifting. "Okay, great. I'll pick you up at eight o'clock."

"Sounds good," I replied, half-heartedly.

I was so frustrated with myself for agreeing to go. I kept trying to think of a good excuse to give Nicole, but I couldn't come up with anything that would justify me cancelling last minute. It would be too inconsiderate. So, I resigned myself to going and thought, *Well, I guess I really don't have anything to lose.*

The venue was exceptionally nice. I'd be lying if I said I wasn't surprised. I think I was expecting the meeting to be held in a musty old church basement or a windowless room in a community center. I had envisioned fluorescent lights that hum annoyingly, filthy, worn-out gray tiles, beige walls, and wooden chairs sitting around rough-edged wooden folding tables.

This room was very bright and cheerful. The walls were a soft grey, and the décor was white, modern, and beautiful. Silky white sheers framed the sun rays that streamed through the floor-to-ceiling windows that spanned three of the four walls. Looking outside took my breath away. The golf course it was located on was pristine. It looked like a painting. The greens looked like velvet and were surrounded by the most colorful flower gardens I had ever seen.

There were a lot of people chatting in groups throughout the room. Far more people than I had expected. I couldn't quite put my finger on it, but they, like Nicole, all seemed so happy and healthy. Everyone had this glow about them. You could feel the positive energy in the room.

And then the meeting started, the information washing over me like waves.

A global company? Operating in over 20 countries? And it's been around for more than 40 years? What?

I was blown away.

I had no idea how big this company was. I hadn't really given much thought to the company at all, but I had no idea it operated in so many countries. That they had been in business for so long and had revenue in excess of $1 billion dollars. I just wondered why, in all my years as a personal trainer, I had never heard of this company or its product before.

I had only signed up as a rep so I could get a discount on my own order. I already had a personal training business and a crazy schedule because of my kids and their sports. I had zero free time, so I was not looking to add another business. I did entertain the thought that it would be nice if I could make a little supplemental income. Then I just laughed and thought to myself, *Yeah, right. As if.* Clearly, I just had no idea.

But I was beginning to think very differently. I listened as Dr. Hardy, an expert in his field, started sharing all the research that had been done on this product, compared to most companies, which tend not to have any clinical research done. If they did, it would only be one or two studies at most.

Wow, I had no idea what great quality Juice Plus+ is!

He also said, "Olympic teams are using it along with tens of thousands of other athletes."

Oh, my goodness. I'm an athlete and a personal trainer. I need to start eating Juice Plus+ again. Why did I stop?

When I decided to quit 12 months earlier, I didn't reorder once I ran out. A poor decision on my part.

My kids need this so badly. They're training such long hours every week. No wonder they're so tired. They desperately need more nutrition. Why did I stop?

It was also clear to me now that I had an obligation to share this with all my clients. By only focusing on the exercise component with my clients, I was doing them such a disservice. Without the good nutrition of Juice Plus+ to assist their bodies with repair and recovery, exercise was speeding up the aging process. The exact opposite of what I thought I was doing and what my clients wanted. I felt so bad.

I have to explain this to all my clients and spread the word to as many athletes and coaches as possible.

This product would be a game changer.

I was finally seeing the big picture and beginning to realize so many possibilities. I looked over at Nicole and shook my head. "Oh, my God."

She just smiled and said, "Aren't you glad you came?"

"Absolutely," I replied.

I don't know if it's because he was a man, or because he was an accountant, but when I heard a gentleman named John Shaw speak about his career with the company, my perception of this business model completely changed.

For whatever reason, I had envisioned a group of women sitting around a kitchen table, just chatting and casually sharing this business with others—much like a book club, or a hobby, not the serious viable lucrative business model that John shared.

Then John said, "Last year I actually retired from being an accountant to do this business full-time."

My jaw dropped to the floor. I looked at Nicole again, stunned and in awe.

She knew what I was thinking and said, "Yes, there are so many people in our company that are earning full-time incomes yet only working part–time hours."

I listened to one story after another. Everyone had such different backgrounds, but there was definitely a common theme… how much this business had changed their life, and how it was the best decision they had ever made.

My shock began to turn into excitement, my stomach filling with butterflies. I was starting to get restless. I wanted to start telling people all about this amazing product and business. I now understood the opportunity I had in my hands and what was possible. And why everyone was so happy and healthy.

My mind was spinning. I didn't stop talking the entire way home. "I have to share this with everyone," I said to Nicole.

She just smiled.

I hadn't felt this excited since… I couldn't remember when. I was starting to dream again.

What if I could create a better life for my family…? I wondered, sifting through all the possibilities in front of me.

*

Today was the day, five years after that dreadful party. I couldn't believe it was actually happening. I had dreamed about having an event like this for athletes and coaches since that first business meeting Nicole dragged me to.

I personally had invited over 200 people. And what better place to have it than at an actual sports school. Students that were gifted athletes had to apply to attend and were only accepted based on their athletic endeavors. These were my people.

My friend Jaime was the head of the Phys Ed department. She was equally keen to have a sports physician educate the students about the power of whole food nutrition. Months of planning had taken place. We had to jump through hoops to persuade the principal to even allow an outside speaker to come into the auditorium, as this meant canceling all previously scheduled events for the entire day.

The hardest part, we thought, would be to get the students interested. To our surprise, the majority of the students were super excited and had been inviting friends from other schools. They even invited their coaches and parents. Before we knew it, schools from all over were calling and asking if their students could attend.

"Hey, Jaime, I'd like to review the presentation with you one last time," I said.

"Sounds great," she replied.

I went to make sure everything was ready in the gym.

It was filled wall to wall with hundreds of chairs. We had finished the sound check and everything was good to go.

As I stood on the stage at the podium, looking out over all the chairs, I felt a brief twinge of fear, of doubt. *Are we really going to fill all these seats?*

The buses started arriving one after another. The parking lot was a sea of yellow. My excitement continued to build.

There wasn't an empty chair or even an empty spot on the floor. People stood shoulder to shoulder along every wall. The double doors at the back had to be propped open to allow others to stand in that hallway just outside the main room. The room felt so alive, and all I could think was, *Wow, it's really happening.* I wanted to squeal with excitement.

The room became silent as Jaime gave a beautiful introduction. "Dr. Phillips is an emergency physician, a sports physician, and an accomplished athlete. He has competed in many triathlons and has even competed in several Ironman races."

All eyes were on Dr. Phillips. The entire audience was captivated. Everyone listened to every word as Dr Phillips explained the physiology of exercising.

"Whole food nutrition is as important as your training," he said. "If you are not eating a diet rich in fruits and veg, you will not be able to perform at your best. And actually, you are speeding up your aging process."

Did I just hear gasps?

He asked, "How many people ate two servings of fruits and veg yesterday?"

Most hands went up.

"How about five servings?" Again, most hands went up.

But when he got to ten or more servings, there wasn't a single hand still raised.

Oh, my gosh, it really is true.

Just as I had been told and was now seeing it with my own eyes, no one eats enough fruits and veg. Not even these elite athletes whose career depends on them performing at their absolute best.

Yay, me. So glad I organized this event. I stood a little taller and the smile on my face got even bigger.

I was so happy that these students were learning about nutrition.

Not just to improve their athletic performance, I thought, looking around the room at the engaged expressions on the sea of faces, *but also to experience better health for the rest of their lives. What a lifelong impact this event will have on them.*

I was covered in goosebumps and my cheeks hurt from smiling, but I couldn't stop.

I've found my purpose.

"Would you like an easy solution to be able to eat more fruits and veg every day?" Dr. Philips asked everyone. "Would you like to know my secret?"

Every single head nodded yes in unison. It was really a rhetorical question as by now everyone in that room understood the power of whole food nutrition and wanted that competitive edge.

"Let me share with you Juice Plus+. It's just fruits and veg in a capsule. It's the most researched product of its kind…"

What's that? I wondered as I heard a change in the crowd.

Suddenly, out of the corner of my eye, I saw movement. People were shifting to allow someone to squeeze by them. Someone started walking up the aisle.

I turned to see the school principal thundering his way to the stage. I froze. Row by row people started to turn their attention away from Dr. Phillips to watch the principal.

What was going on?? Curiosity had me frozen.

I held my breath, my palms starting to sweat. My entire body was tense. Dr. Phillips had stopped talking and was also watching the principal approaching the stage.

All you could hear were the principal's heavy footsteps. He stomped up the stairs and barged in front of Dr. Phillips to reach for the microphone.

I clasped my hands together and pressed them against my lip in anticipation for what was next. Fear washed over my entire body, and I could feel my face getting hot and red.

The principal leaned forward and in a deep, angry voice, he bellowed into the microphone, "Attention, students, this school does not condone these products. This presentation is over.

Everyone back to their classes and guests go to your buses immediately."

For a moment it was silent. It felt like time stood still, as no one moved a muscle. We were all in shock. What had just happened? My mind raced as I tried to make sense of things. I didn't know whether to cry or scream. On the one hand, I was so humiliated to have all my guests experience this. If I could have disappeared into thin air, I would have. But at the same time, I was livid.

All I could think was, *How dare he? How dare the principal prevent these kids from learning such important information?!*

I was so angry because I knew full well they were not teaching nutrition in school. I felt so bad that these students were lacking in such vital information. They were so interested in learning how to improve their athletic performance!

At the very least, he could have handled himself with a lot more professionalism. He could have let Dr. Phillips finish his talk and allow the kids to take in all of this information. And, at the end, simply thank Dr. Phillips for his time and say something along the lines of, just to be clear, the school does not promote these products. We are just providing education. Something like that would have sufficed.

"Melissa, you just jeopardized Jaime's teaching career!" a fellow rep hissed at me.

Panic overcame me. I had to find Jaime to see if this was going to impact her.

I caught up to her in the hallway. I couldn't tell if she was angry or scared. But she looked like a deer in headlights and her face was glowing, it was so red.

"I am so sorry," I said. "I don't know what to say. I had no idea this would happen."

"Me neither," she said.

"I'll call you later after I speak to the principal," she said as she turned and left.

I went back to the auditorium and found Dr. Phillips packing up. He looked up and smiled.

"Well," he said, "that's a first! What a shame. I think everyone was really enjoying my talk. And even after the principal said it was over, so many kids came to the stage to ask me questions, but the principal wouldn't have it. He just yelled at everyone to leave. Who knew fruits and veggies were such a controversial topic?"

He almost appeared giddy with excitement, despite what had just happened.

I learned that day to never give up…

*

The sun sparkled on the lake, a warm breeze tickling the hairs on my head. I could hear nothing but the beautiful sound of nature—this was the dream. As contentment washed over me, I looked at Nicole, who looked just as peaceful.

"Can you believe it's been 15 years and I'm still here?" I said, smiling. "Life is amazing. I truly never dreamed that what started out as simply a good idea for my family's health could grow into an international business."

"I know. It's so awesome." With a laugh she added, "Good thing, because we are unemployable."

"Isn't that the truth," I replied. "Time flexibility is my top value. I couldn't imagine someone telling me what time I have to start work, what time I finish, how many holidays I can take, or how long my lunch break is."

"Oh, my gosh, I can't even imagine working for someone else. So many people were laid off or had pay cuts during Covid, but our businesses grew dramatically. I'm so grateful that we can offer people solutions like this."

"Right!" I replied, beaming with pride and purpose.

I was quiet for a moment as we watched the sun glisten on the water and saw a mama duck and her five babies swim by.

"Now more than ever," Nicole said, "I realize how rewarding it is for me to be working with a company that provides solutions to problems in the world today. I couldn't be prouder."

As we sat back and gazed out to the water again, I thought about my extended family and the various health issues many of them had. My grandpa had diabetes; my grandma had heart issues; Nanny had Alzheimer's; and my mom's only brother, my Uncle Alan, lost his battle with stomach cancer at only 39 years of age, leaving behind my aunt and my three young cousins.

The timing of Nicole coming into my life had been fortuitous. She had introduced me to Juice Plus+ and all those health professionals, and I had learned to make healthier lifestyle choices for my family.

Reminding her of that, I said, "You changed our lives forever that day."

"Oh, friend, you are so welcome," Nicole replied, smiling through tears. "Isn't this the most incredible work we get to do?"

And it is. My family is far from perfect, but my kids do eat their Juice Plus+ daily, without me even having to ask. They would probably never admit this to me, but sometimes I hear them talking to their friends about health and nutrition, so I know they've learned a lot.

I couldn't imagine what our future might look like had I not learned healthier habits and started eating Juice Plus+.

With all I've learned over the last 15 years, I've become an even better personal trainer, so my clients get better results faster. And I'm also helping them improve their overall health for the rest of their lives. It's a mystery why nutrition is still not part of a personal training certification.

I reflected back on when I just wanted to earn $500 per month to cover the cost of my products and car payment. Then my goal was $1000 per month. I wanted to be able to stop personal training and be at our cottage with the kids—now it's our full-time home.

I feel like our team—although it is the largest in Canada—is just getting started. I feel Juice Plus+ has been the best kept secret, and it's time we get loud and proud. Everyone needs to know about what we do because I truly believe we provide solutions to so many health problems in the world today.

"What about your coaching business?" Nicole asked again, with the same curiosity all those years ago.

"I love it, and it's growing nicely." I grinned. "Who would have guessed 15 years ago I would have an online course and be doing one-on-one coaching."

"Wow, that's so awesome," Nicole said. "You have so much knowledge to share. What do you think makes your coaching different from all the others?"

"Three things, I believe," I said. "Firstly, I specialize in keeping them accountable to the goals they set for themselves. It's so easy to get excited, but that doesn't last. People need to have someone to keep them accountable. Secondly, I help them discover their niche. Once they know their niche, it makes doing this business easier, a lot more fun, and they achieve more success. And lastly, I help my clients find their why. That's what keeps them going on the tough days, because they know what they are working towards. They have a vision for their life. And it changes their approach from selling to consulting. Nothing lights me up more than seeing others realize their goals and dreams, knowing I helped in some way."

"I love that. I can see how you can really help coach people with their business. Anything else?"

"Well, my big crazy goal is to be a trainer on the Go Pro stage," I said.

My phone buzzed, indicating a new text.

Hey Melissa, we hear you do a great training called The Riches Are in the Niches. We'd love for you to do this training at our Business Reset Event. It's taking place in Eric Worre's personal studio in his home...

"The best is yet to come," I said to Nicole, sitting back as pride and excitement washed over me.

Keep dreaming—the best really is yet to come!!!

CHAPTER 10

There are no excuses, only priorities

Dany & Debbie Martin

***

January, 1990

I was the Golden Boy for much of my grocery career. Youngest grocery store manager with the company at age 21. Chosen to operate the first showcase supermarket at age 29. Setting sales records and setting the bar for the entire region.

But things have changed. I'm NOT the Golden Boy anymore. There's a new supervisor in town and he Does. Not. Like. Me. Not surprisingly, the feeling is mutual, and I know it shows. He didn't come up through the ranks like I did, but he thinks he knows everything. I must explore other opportunities.

The living room of our new home is crowded: me, Debbie, my wife of six months—both my sisters and their husbands, and a few other people I don't know. Word has gotten out to a friend of my oldest sister that I'm looking for another job. I'm ready to get out of the grocery business.

Could this be the chance we're looking for?

But it's got to stay on the sly. 'Cause when you've successfully become the Golden Boy, no one can know that you are miserable. No one can know that you're looking for something else, because then you could be forced to look for something else before you've prepared to leave.

Debbie sits in a chair by herself, arms crossed, concentrating, worried about what I'm going to do. She found me sitting on the floor in my office almost in tears of defeat after attempting to write my resumè. She helped me all she could. What can you do with only a high school education and you've worked for only one company since you were 16 years old? Probably shouldn't mention my previous failed marriage. Eighty-hour work weeks don't leave much time for family. My very average grades in high school won't help, either, but growing up in my world, average was good enough. I've always had an exceptional work ethic, but how do I adequately translate that into the third line of my resumè?

So now I'm listening to this big, tough-looking guy from a small town in south Louisiana, who has a heavy Cajun accent, who's sharing a 'business opportunity'. My sister's friend connected the two of us after a chance meeting with him, and we've been talking over the phone. He wanted me to get a few people together and have him and his wife come to visit. My first day off in two weeks, a Sunday afternoon, and I'm sitting here wishing I could be anywhere else—while also praying that this will lead to something. I really need a new job.

"How's the job search going?" my brother-in-law asks. "Any prospects?"

"I'm interviewing, seeing as many people as I can," I respond. "I don't want to go to a competitor because if I'm going to stay in the grocery business, I'm already with the best company out there. But the industry is changing and I must get out."

"What are you trying to do?" he asks.

"I'm looking at the insurance business or maybe sales," I explain, absently picking at a loose thread on my shirt. "Everything I'm looking at, though, is for a lot less money, and many of my options are commission only. I don't know how that will work. We have bills to pay, a mortgage, child support... not a lot of wiggle room in our budget to take a big cut in income." I sigh. "I'm used to knowing how much I'm going to make down to the penny every month. It's a lot to cope with."

The scary Cajun guy is talking about making money selling some kind of water filter, about recruiting others to sell with me to reach more people.

I don't know that many people. I know people from my job, and they aren't going to buy a water filter from me! I'm the store manager, for crying out loud.

I look over and see Debbie's brow wrinkling further. She is watching closely and listening hard, but I can't read her.

She's the professional salesperson with a college degree—not me. Is this one of those pyramid schemes? Oh, my God, how am I going to get these people out of my house? What am I doing? The big guy told me he's been in the BOXING business most of his life. He's going to be hard to throw out!

A few hours later, Debbie and I sit at our kitchen table, having had time to think about what we've heard.

"A lot of what they said makes sense," I point out. "We recently started carrying gallon bottles of filtered water in our stores, so there must be something going on that people don't want to drink tap water anymore. The timing might be right to sell some of these things." After a moment I add, "Let's try the demo filter they left us. If we like it, we can sell a few and make some extra cash."

Debbie starts crunching the numbers. "It looks like if we put up about $200, we can buy five filters on credit, pay them off over the next few months, and see what happens."

I continue to think aloud. "If I can make a little extra money with this, I can keep looking for another job and can afford to take a cut in pay somewhere else with the extra income. Then I can work hard and work my way up in the new company, prove myself, and build up my income to what I'm making now. At that point, I wouldn't have to sell water filters anymore. And maybe I could work more normal hours."

Debbie continues to recall things we had heard earlier that day. "That boxing guy said that if you work hard, you could possibly make $1000 to $1500 a month, in a reasonable amount of time. If that's true, that would be a big help. It could give us some choices."

"Which credit card do you want to use?" I ask. "I do like the taste of the water."

Hope blooms, skepticism flourishes; we may be turning the corner.

Early 1997...

"A passport... you're telling me I need a passport already?" I ask, my confusion, frustration, and excitement bleeding into my voice. "In just a few weeks? Where do I get a passport?" I stumble over my words and finally get out, "You realize I've only been on a few flights in my entire life, and now you're telling me I need to be ready to go all the way to the other side of the globe in just six weeks? I've just finally learned how to spell Australia and now I'm about to fly there? This is moving a lot faster than we talked about."

"Get ready, Dany," our company's VP of International Operations tells me. "You said you would support this if it ever happened, and it is happening NOW. We need you to go and manage some of the unexpected crises that have come up with the new master distributors we've partnered with. You're about to get a crash course in international travel and business."

The company that Debbie and I joined in 1990 to sell water filtration products, National Safety Associates (NSA), had an opportunity to move into the whole food-based nutrition industry in 1993 with a product called Juice Plus+. It was their third product line after marketing heat and smoke detection from 1969 to 1979, followed by water and air filtration from 1979 to 1993.

Debbie and I are getting ready for me to get on a huge, double-decker jet and fly more than 10,000 miles from our rented condo to a country we have dreamed of doing business in. We've spent thousands of dollars trying to secure leadership on the ground in a place we've never been to with people we've never met, all in hopes of our business and personal sacrifices paying off. Although we knew we would eventually have to travel to Australia, circumstances had changed such that we needed to go much sooner than anticipated. Everything is moving faster than we originally planned.

The expenses seem endless. We have been on overseas calls costing over $1/minute, not to mention the cost of all the faxes going back and forth. Eventually, we will have to invest in one of those new home computers that people are starting to talk about. We've shipped thousands of dollars' worth of Juice Plus+ products from our personal inventory. We've invested in mind-blowing amounts of marketing materials. We have placed our financial future in the hands of people we don't even know. And we have heard horror stories of how our future business partners settle disputes with their fists in the 'car park', which we finally discovered was the Australian term for parking garage.

Oh, dear Lord! What are we doing?

Debbie reminds me of a few things. "Dany, you know you don't have any proper luggage to travel on a 'real' trip, right?" My mind starts to race. "And, babe, I think they're in a different season over there than we are right now. I don't think you have enough proper clothes to wear for days of back-to-back business meetings in a different climate." She sighs. "We're going to have to find you some suitable outfits to wear."

My heart beats faster. The walls in my small dining room/office start to feel like they are closing in on me. I'm breaking into a sweat.

Debbie continues to study her notes and research. "How are we going to communicate while you're gone? Our phone plan doesn't have anything but regular long distance, and I'm hearing that the rates to call home from other countries are outrageous.

Is there something we need to do differently to get international rates on our landline? We'll have to work out a schedule so I can be sure to be here when you're able to call home."

I think I'm going to be sick. I'm a man with a blue-collar upbringing, no worldly experience, very little travel, and no big business background. Yet, I'm about to embark on a massive, month-long journey away from my family to recruit and build a sales team in a foreign country and help establish a marketing and distribution center with people I've only talked with on the phone. By myself?

For something that we've been working on for what seems like forever, things seem to now be moving at the speed of light.

After days spent working to secure a notarized copy of my birth certificate, traveling several hours to handle the paperwork for my passport, filling out work visas to enter Australia, and handling all the many other things required to travel, we finally await the arrival of my documents in the mail. We change our phone coverage to include cheaper international rates. We buy luggage. We shop at the discount clothing outlet to buy some suitable clothes; not only are the prices better, but we can find out-of-season options that will be appropriate for the weather in Australia. We study up on international travel. We learn what can be packed in my suitcases to fly. We research lodging options. We desperately try to understand the currency exchange systems and the differences in prices for everything. We are on a steep learning curve, finding out just how naive we are when it comes to international travel.

We are financing this trip and our future on credit cards because we have long since run out of extra cash. We are thrilled and terrified all at the same time. If this falls through, we will lose everything.

We made the decision the previous year to sell our first home and rent a condo so that we could use the equity to pay down credit card debt and continue this venture. We don't have any assets left. We have had delays and setbacks, and even the threat of the entire deal collapsing with our Australian investors. Our nerves are frayed. We don't even know anyone who has traveled internationally, much less anyone who has built a business in another country. This is different from anything we have ever done, but we are still hopeful.

"How am I supposed to talk to all these people?" I ask Debbie. "Remember when I started in this business several years ago? I'm the introverted guy who couldn't even stand up and introduce himself to a small room of people. How am I going to make this work?"

She encourages me. "Babe, you must remember why you are doing this. You know you can go back and get a regular job at a grocery store if this business doesn't work out for us. You did that for 17 years. You have skills."

Yep, I have skills alright. Working 80-hour work weeks, every other Sunday off, always exhausted, feeling so stressed that I considered a few trips to the emergency room with chest pains, missing family events and holidays, missing time with my little boy…

"And I can go back and get a job if I have to," she adds.

"No way," I tell her. "You are not going back into industrial sales, not on my watch. I don't think I can deal with more of the abuse and harassment you had to deal with in your last job."

"Do you really want to go back to how things were if we have a chance of making this work?" she asks. "You made a promise to Dany Jr."

She is seriously getting to me now. This is so true. I promised myself and my firstborn son that I would be an involved dad, not one who just sent a check to his mother every month. I'm going to stay involved in his life!

The lyrics from The *Cat's in the Cradle* play in my head.

I don't want to be the guy who never has time for his son while he is growing up, only for him to be too busy for me after he is grown.

"You can do this," Debbie says encouragingly. "I believe in you and I'm here to handle things at home while you're gone."

And then I'm landing in Sydney, Australia.

Even in coach, international flights are kinda cool; there are TV screens in front of every seat. And they have real silverware and complete hot meals! Wow!! How fancy.

With a stamp on my shiny new passport, I get some Australian currency at the airport currency exchange. Not the best place to do it, I learn later, but what do I know? Money in hand, I walk outside to find a ride to the hotel with all my new luggage. I've not been in more than a couple of cabs in my entire life, and never by myself, but I finally work out how to flag one down.

They drive on the wrong side of the road! I didn't know the steering wheel was on the right side of the car here. I am so glad I'm not driving. And how odd is it to do the 'right, left, right' looks before stepping off the curb? Totally opposite to how it is at home. I hope I don't get run over by a bus while I'm here! How would Debbie even know what happened to me?

I finally make my way to my hotel, somewhere in the middle of this huge city, and get to my room. I've been traveling for over 30 hours and am exhausted. I have no idea how a plane can stay in the sky for so long.

I've never felt jet lag before, but I'm not liking it so far. I just want to find some food, get back to my room, and collapse into bed.

I grab a cab in front of the hotel, since I'm a pro at that now. I'm not a very adventurous eater, so I'm hoping I can find something quick for dinner that's not too different or disgusting to me. This is an English-speaking country, but I don't understand half of what people say to me, confused by their accents and all the funny slang words they use. I ask the driver to just drive around and when I see something that looks good to eat, I will let him know. After driving around for almost 20 minutes, I discovered a restaurant that might work. I spot a sign for wood-fired pizza.

That sounds good. I can do pizza!

After eating a very different but delicious pizza, I'm ready to get back to my room and go to bed. I have no idea where I am in this huge, concrete metropolis. I flag a cab in front of the restaurant. "I need to go to the Marriott at Hyde Park, please."

As I start to get into the back seat, the cabbie starts laughing.

What now?

He points out of his front window towards a tall building. "Sir, are you sure you need a cab? The Hyde Park Marriott is right there! A 30-second walk."

I look at him and we both laugh. "Good night," I tell him. "Thanks for not taking advantage of a lost foreigner."

We end up making three more trips to Australia over the next several months before everything is finalized to officially open the country for business, and then we can finally begin making some type of income from this venture we are so heavily invested in. Despite every attempt to avoid it, we are forced to file bankruptcy during this time, but we don't give up hope. We have faith in ourselves, our company, and its leaders, and we believe in our Juice Plus+ concept of fruits and veggies in a capsule and in the Juice Plus+ Virtual Franchise business model. Whole food supplementation is a huge hit with the health-conscious population of Australia. We begin building a massive team of excited people, including major sport professionals, and start a crazy and exciting new journey.

We have since enjoyed over 40 trips to Australia and New Zealand, filled up multiple passports, taken the entire family and made lifelong friends across the world. We have climbed the Sydney Harbour Bridge and dived the Great Barrier Reef, petted kangaroos, and held a koala. We have helped coach over 50 of our Australian/New Zealand leaders to our company's top position and helped thousands of partners enjoy a better life. The personal growth and leadership skills that we knew would be required in the beginning of this journey were developed and continue to be refined as we move forward.

Spring, 2022

"I'm out!" Dany Jr. calls as he lays his winning hand of cards onto the table for us all to see.

"Dang it," Devan laughs. "I just needed one more card to go out."

I lost again on this hand, but it doesn't matter. I'm just enjoying spending time with my family. With everyone's busy lives, it's always an accomplishment to get all of us together. It's nice for Debbie and me to have the flexibility to clear our calendars on a moment's notice and take off when Dany Jr., his wife Lindsi, and our youngest son Devan get some time to be together.

"One more hand," I call out. "Then it's time for the real games to begin!"

We will be heading out for a competitive round of golf. The boys do enjoy their trash talk on the course. Since moving a couple of years ago to a beautiful home overlooking the island green in our golf and country club community, we have all been able to work a little more on our golf game. Debbie has even begun playing so she can join us and not just ride along in the cart.

The steaks are marinating for later. We can't wait to fire up the grill. I can hear Dany Jr. and Devan already challenging each other to see who will best the other on the links. For 16 years apart, they have a wonderful relationship. We all have fun being together.

As of This Writing

I think of my wife, our two grown sons, and our daughter-in-law with a heart full of gratitude. I reflect over the last 30+ years and am amazed at how life can expand when you follow your heart, trust in God's guidance, and listen to the gentle nudges of 'what if?'

Our company has become a multibillion-dollar leader in the whole food-based nutrition industry and provided the opportunity for millions across the globe to take control of their health and well-being. In fact, because of its success with the Juice Plus+

product line, the company officially changed its name in early 2000 to The Juice Plus+ Company. Juice Plus+ has become the number one selling encapsulated whole food-based product in the world and is also the most thoroughly researched nutritional product in the world. The company has continued to thrive under our founder, Jay Martin, and our company continues to build for the future with the next generation of management and leaders.

When Debbie and I made our first trip to the company's global headquarters in Memphis, Tennessee, decades ago, we were deeply touched by Jay's mission statement, written when he started the company and etched onto a plaque at the front entrance. It read, "To build a stable and lasting company that will help as many people as possible realize their dreams." Since Juice Plus+ has come along, a few words have been added to that statement. Those words are: "By inspiring healthy living around the world." This mission statement continues to hold true to this day.

Early in our marriage, Debbie and I were like many others in our society. We believed that if we found a good job that paid well, worked hard, and followed the rules, we would be successful and happy. We got up early, drove into rush-hour traffic daily, and prayed for a decent, drama-free workday. We took our two weeks' vacation each year and arranged schedules for personal appointments when needed, but also missed out on important events in our lives, because that's just the way it was.

Over the years, we determined that success looks different to every individual. We made decisions along the way to find better balance in our work life and family life. It was important to us to be available to our parents in their advancing years and to our children in their formative years. Everyone has a personal set of fears, values, and dreams. We all have different risk and reward levels. We decided early on to expand our risk tolerance and practice what we preach. Coming from very conservative and modest backgrounds, each of us had to work at defining our own personal success and being okay with moving out of the box of 'normal' behavior. Maybe along the way, we became 'abnormal' to some.

We have a nice house, drive luxury cars, and travel the world. In most people's eyes, these things are universally recognized as markers of success, and these things are great, but for us, true success is more than that. Success without fulfillment is the ultimate failure.

As we look around us, we know we are covered in success. Dany Jr. is happily married, and he and his wife Lindsi have multiple successful businesses with lots of flexibility. This has given them the opportunity to open their home to five young men who needed a safe place to live and flourish and to be shown a different path in life than what they were being brought up in in the inner-city. They are making a difference in other people's lives and giving back in huge ways to their community.

Our youngest son, Devan, will be finishing up his college career in the next couple of years, playing collegiate golf and pursuing his dream of continuing to play after college. His huge servant-heart calls him each summer to volunteer his time to minister to junior high and high school-aged youth through his church summer camps.

To know that we have played a part in raising these amazing young men and helping to change the trajectory of not only their lives, but also the lives of future generations, is a huge mark of success to us.

So, to us, in our mind, yes, we have been successful. It has not always been easy, but it has always been worth it.

There are no excuses, only priorities!

CHAPTER 11

Keep punching

Kerry & Mickey Daigle

"Kerry, he's here again!" shouted one of the paralegals.

This was week number six and Emile was back at my office again; he came every day to have me look at this environmental company, selling water and air filtration products through something called 'network marketing.'

I guess I lived in a bubble because I had never heard of network marketing. Who hasn't? I mean, everyone knows about Amway. Guess what? Not me.

My wife, Mickey, and I were newlyweds and had been married four weeks. Everything was going well! A happy couple, or so I thought. She brought her 10 year old son Cliff into our marriage, and I was a new dad right off the bat. It was very different for me; I was 36 years old and had no kids from a previous marriage. The year was 1989—a year I will never forget.

I loved what I was doing, promoting live nationally televised shows in professional boxing and working with some of the biggest names in boxing promotions across the world. Why the paralegals? No, I am not an attorney. Far from it. Just a high school kid with average grades who had a hunger for success. I was bartering skills with two attorneys. I would teach the law firm how to promote their business nationally, and they would handle all the legal and contractual work I needed for the fight game. A great way to barter that worked exceptionally well.

Let's rewind a few years first. From 1970 to 1981, I had built a business that offered me the opportunity to travel the world, promoting fighters and working from Madison Square Garden in New York to some of the most prestigious venues across the globe. Visiting and working in Las Vegas and other prominent cities was a dream come true for an average kid with a limited education, hailing from a small town of 15,000 in Louisiana. I had also developed a few other businesses in my hometown that were doing quite well.

In 1981, the unexpected happened. The bank where I had my largest line of credit for my businesses was shut down by the FDIC. I started making terrible decisions trying to survive. I filed for bankruptcy, which took four years to complete due to my stubbornness to make a point that 'nothing' was my fault. My ego took over. Lesson learned. I lost everything—my business, my home, my self-confidence. I hid from everyone for years. I was back to square one. Overnight, I returned to being the broke kid out of high school.

In 1985, as I began to regain confidence, I started rebuilding my boxing business. Things were looking up. I was back in love with the sport of boxing and had married the woman who would, in 1989, change my life. Little did I know that this little lady, Mickey, would be the difference maker in our success.

The paralegals yelled back, "Do we tell Emile you are here?"

I could tell they were getting agitated with hiding me and not telling Emile the truth. Instead of following a pattern, this time I had a great idea. Mickey was having a birthday party for our son and kids were all over the house. Mickey was very direct in delivering her messages and I figured this was the best time to send Emile over to meet my newlywed wife.

"Emile, you know how busy I am," I said, "but I have a suggestion for you. Mickey is home right now. Go visit her and if she shows an interest and wants to join you in your business I will assist her;

however, if she shows no interest, then the conversations about this will stop. Okay?"

Bam! I had him. I just knew that she was so busy that day that she'd send Emile home kicking and screaming, and I fully expected he would be totally upset. I had it figured out. In fact, Mickey was my 'out'. I was smiling inside. I was going to get off the hook and I could blame Mickey for it... and Emile would understand and remain my friend, thanks to Mickey's rejection of his idea.

Expect the unexpected.

Mickey sat with Emile for two hours, and within a week, she quit her job as Admissions Director of a proprietary college and signed up with a company called NSA (now called Juice Plus+). All this one month after our marriage. Scared me to death! I had waited until I was 36 years old to marry the 'right' woman'—not for her money, but she had a great job and paid her own bills, car note, clothes for her and our child, meaning that I could continue to build my 'fun' business without any financial interruptions.

I couldn't understand what had happened. This had not gone as planned. What I didn't know was that Mickey was totally unhappy with her job. I had no idea. She never talked about anything negative.

"Mickey, what happened?" I asked, confused. "What are you doing? Where is your mindset? Why did you give notice at work to quit your job?" We'd only been married for one month, and this was not how I anticipated things happening.

The answer she gave me left me spinning.

"All your life, Kerry Daigle," Mickey said, "you have said to follow people more successful than you. Now, how long have you known Emile?"

"Since I was 18 years old," I replied.

"Has he been successful?"

Of course he's been successful, and I knew that. He lived in a beautiful antebellum home, was a multimillionaire, drove

$100,000+ cars, wore $40,000 Rolex watches, and was always dressed impeccably.

Here came lesson number one in our marriage.

"Yes, Mickey, Emile has been very successful," I said.

Mickey fired back "Are you a multimillionaire?"

"Well, no, you know I'm not."

"I have watched and admired you as you have over and over again taught others that to be successful, you have to listen to mentors who are highly successful and learn from them," she continued. "So I'm curious why you didn't listen to him."

With a very kind smile, she turned around and walked out of my home office.

I went from six feet tall to four-foot-one. I sat in silence for 30 minutes.

I was so busy trying to stay alive financially that I hadn't listened to my own teachings. I knew all about having the right mentors in my life. I was always saying, "You can't have somebody making $35,000 a year teach you how to make $100,000, and you can't have someone making $100,000 a year to teach you how to make $500,000 a year."

The next day, true to my word, I became Mickey's first distributor/partner.

Within the next two weeks, Mickey dragged me to a conference for her new business in Memphis, Tennessee. I left heel marks from Louisiana to Tennessee. I wasn't ready to go to a conference to get educated on water and air filtration. My skills as a handyman were not good.

I sat in the front row with Mickey and her guests on wooden pull-out bleachers. People crossed a stage, each telling their stories of how they built their business. They spoke of the top position and the huge benefit package that came with it. That caught my attention immediately. Then came the closure. A young lady from the Atlanta area walked on stage and said she had a high school education, was a dog groomer, cleaned houses, and her husband was a sheetrock contractor—and had reached the top position in the company. That blew me away... and Mickey as well, as I watched her mouth drop open!

Mickey and her guests kept hounding me about the speakers and their stories. I got annoyed and moved away to the top of the bleachers, by myself. Everyone thought I was angry and agitated, which was far from the truth. I was absorbing the information and didn't want anyone to interfere with my 'hearing'.

Once back home, we decided if we were going to go full blast. Our first three years, we struggled. Network marketing was confusing to us at the beginning, but we made the position of QNMD, the second highest position in the marketing plan. We weren't moving extra fast but working slowly and building a solid foundation. Studying network marketing was all about consumable products creating a supplemental income. Air filters and water filters lasted three years and were far from consumable. The positions on the comp plan were very difficult to reach while climbing the ladder to higher positions. Regardless, we believed in the president and founder, Jay Martin. In meeting him, we knew he was ethical and loved his distributors (partners) in the field. Watching Jay closely, you could tell his vision was to create a team of distributors that could make above average incomes regardless of their backgrounds.

As we continued to learn, before we knew it 1993 was on us. Jay had found a new product in the whole food industry that was very unique: raw fruits and vegetables in a gelcap.

Juice Plus+ was born.

Through a distributor who is sadly no longer with us, we were introduced to Barry, an ophthalmologist, who took a look at these fruits and vegetables in a pill. Barry was very conservative and very well known in the city of Lafayette, Louisiana. Without any proof of these pills really being effective, Barry immediately said, "I can't put my medical profession on the line as an MD to endorse this, Kerry. This really sounds kinda crazy, and this network marketing thing... what are my colleagues going to think?"

He kept talking, though, and asking questions. I knew people well enough that when a customer says "no", everything kind of just stops. Barry said no, but then he didn't stop. You could feel a sense of curiosity. He kept leaning forward and staring right into my eyes.

Barry then asked me, "Kerry, why are you so sold on this?"

I was always taught by my mentors that those who keep asking questions always want to learn more, that it wasn't a negative incident but rather a 'learning' one. Barry was a very intelligent individual, and I was following my instincts.

"Barry," I said, "I am following my beliefs as an entrepreneur, as well as what my mentors have shown me about how business owners think and create opportunities. Why would Jay Martin, the president and founder of a billion-dollar sales company, want to invest millions of dollars into this product unless he knew something we don't know? Also, Barry, fruits and vegetables never killed anyone, to my knowledge, and it's a pretty neat concept. It's not a fad product. Fruits and vegetables have been around since Genesis in the Bible. I am going to run with it. I would love for you to join us."

Barry jumped in and became the first medical doctor to achieve the highest position in Juice Plus+, National Marketing Director. The years 1993 and 1994 were interesting. Barry and I traveled the country talking about Juice Plus+ and the business behind it. It's funny how things turned out.

We then had a really humorous but creative idea. There were no published studies at the time on Juice Plus+. We put our minds together and wrote a book. Each chapter had information on each fruit and vegetable in the Juice Plus+ product, and we had to come up with a 'catchy' title. *Two MDs and a Pharmacist Ask, "Are You Getting It Five Times a Day?"* was born. The 'official' authors were exactly that: two MDs and a pharmacist. We started doing events promoting the book locally since all three authors were well known in south Louisiana. We were renting restaurants and drawing 200–300 people to dinners at night. Doctors from various backgrounds joined us, and we had five to six different local MDs speaking on the benefits of raw fruits and veggies. We then recommended the 'next best thing' Juice Plus+.

The history continues...

Within a year of Juice Plus+, Mickey and I both made NMD, the highest position in the company at the time! We also promoted ten more individuals to reach that same position within a few miles of our home.

From that moment, a young girl from India with multiple degrees in science entered our lives, joining our community and creating an audio that went viral on Juice Plus+. Mickey ordered hundreds of audios, and the movement started. Records were broken. Physicians, nurses, engineers, moms, dads, and college students joined from across the country. The business of Juice Plus+ was exploding. At the time, the company field representatives were 95% male. Things started changing as more and more women were recruited to join us. Now, the company is over 90% female. I have to give credit to Mickey for being a large part of that movement at the beginning.

Change, of course, can be confusing for many. The problem is, we never know if change is going to be positive or negative. People love positive change. The problem seems to arise when many individuals assume that change will be negative most of the time. Smart and positive thinkers, however, assume that positive or negative change will benefit them in one way or another.

I believe it was Jim Rohn who said, "For the timid and shy in our world, change can be scary. For those who are very comfortable in where they are, change can be threatening; however, for those who are very confident, change is a positive opportunity."

Mickey and I had eight top leaders in the company above us that quit (due to the shift from environmental products to Juice Plus+) and went to other companies. Through something called 'compression', which Jeff, the number one income earner with our company, explains, those who remained were the winners. Jeff was right. We rolled up directly to him—the top producer across the globe—and started learning the lessons of 'network marketing success', which was life changing. Isn't it funny how things work out? Interestingly, the top leaders that left us are no longer with their companies due to poor leadership or poor pay plans. Many of those companies were forced out of business

What do we learn from change? Change brings opportunity.

Change for us was a huge opportunity. An unexpected one. From a boxing promoter and private business owner of a franchise, among other businesses, to becoming bankrupt and then achieving extraordinary success in a distribution system called 'network marketing'.

Who would have thought?

From a single mom to marrying a boxing promoter, Mickey's friends and families thought—"Wow! Is this really happening for her? What was she thinking?" Some of her peers joined her business; others didn't. Mickey was not moved by others' opinions and had vision.

"I had enough of Corporate America," she explained. "I struggled as a single mom. I wanted our marriage to be different. I wanted free time to be with my husband and our son, Cliff. I just want to be a success. I told Kerry with emotion and cracked my words a little. I'm sick and tired of working hard for someone else. I want a lifestyle like you have in boxing. Free and independent. I want to give my husband and son the things they deserve... trips and time with me. I wanted time and creativity and control and wanted to be a pioneer. This is my shot."

I could hear Emile's voice saying, "Change teaches us new things... We start learning and getting wise. We become more confident, which is a priceless asset. It opens our mind to be good listeners. Good listeners are usually the most successful in the crowd."

Our lifestyle had changed drastically. We started owning every minute of our lives. No one person or time clock or boss controlled us. Mickey would look at her watch and say, "Kerry, we own every minute on this watch. We make our own path. Who would have thought that the power of a supplemental income would put us in that position?"

Talking about positive change... let's look at 1999.

Through the power of our business, another change in our lives occurred. A six year old girl without a home came to us during a phone call while we were at a conference in California for Juice Plus+. We returned home to meet Angela and saw an opportunity to give her a better life. We adopted Angela and were gifted with not only a beautiful daughter but also someone we could give a great life to.

Within the first week she moved in, we brought her to Canada and stayed at the Chateau Frontenac. Angela, who had never traveled out of the town we lived in, was now in a castle for a week. It was a true Cinderella story. Watching her eyes go as big as saucers is something we still remember today. Our lifestyle of time flexibility to spend with Angela allowed her to chase her dream of fashion merchandising and work with some of the most recognized fashion designers globally. We could spend time with her and bring her to all the necessary classes and shows to learn more and excel.

Our business allowed us to go to Los Angeles and find her a beautiful apartment in the financial district downtown. None of that would have been possible without the business we built utilizing the system designed by Juice Plus+. Our time flexibility was invaluable.

Today, Angela is married to her high school sweetheart, Christopher. Our business is wrapped around Angela and Chris, along with our son, Cliff, our daughter-in-law, Nicole, and our grandchildren, Keri, Ali, and C.J. We couldn't have painted a prettier picture, and we thank God every day for these 'changes.' Our business gives us the opportunity to be an important part of our family's lives and to make memories daily.

Cliff today holds an executive position as a production supervisor at the world's largest nitrogen-based plant, CF Industries, based in Donaldsonville, Louisiana. He had the opportunity to watch us work through our company, to meet extraordinary entrepreneurs, and to watch their work ethic, which gave him the desire to do the same for himself and his family. We were blessed with our business to create the time to be available for him and allow him to excel in his profession. Giving our time to our children has been priceless.

None of this would have been possible without our business.

Priceless.

I know we hear that money can't buy happiness. But I do know one thing: supplemental income from hard work and following a good business plan CAN BUY HAPPINESS because it buys the most precious commodity on this earth—TIME.

Now people ask Mickey and me all the time. What do you do? Are you retired?

The answer is simple!

Our answer is usually the same. Sometimes it changes, but most of the time it goes like this. Mickey says, "We are teachers. I'm a teacher and Kerry is an author and mental fitness coach. We teach people how to be successful and own their time and achieve dreams and goals." She usually adds, "We have made an incredible difference in thousands of people's lives. So, what is your purpose in life?"

What about retirement?

The business has allowed us to 'retire into our business,' not OUT of our business. We don't see this as work. We love what we do.

Let's visit 2012.

People always ask me about my grandparents, Maw Maw and Paw Paw Daigle. Not many people had the opportunity to meet them, as they passed away many years before we joined this incredible company. In our speaking engagements, I would always mention Maw Maw Daigle's famous quote: "When you see someone without a smile, give them yours. You could change their entire day."

Maw Maw and Paw Paw couldn't speak English and couldn't read or write. Although they weren't educated in the traditional sense, they were always positive and believed in the 'impossible' being 'possible'. That was instilled in me from a young age. They brought me into their lives when I was three years old and became my 'official parents'. Through a positive mindset, and them believing I could be as successful as I wanted to be, I ended up owning my first home-based business at the age of 13, selling used toys and comic books to the neighbors' kids on the weekend. That helped with Maw Maw's grocery bill and was the start of understanding the value of making a profit instead of a wage. Although the house we lived in was a shotgun house without hot water or air conditioning, it was HOME. We did our best to keep it a happy home.

That led me to writing a book entitled *Dreams, Fairy Tales and Miracles: Things I Learned About Success From Maw Maw and Paw Paw Daigle That You Won't Learn at Harvard or Yale*. This book continues to sell across the world. The wisdom of Maw Maw and Paw Paw is something thousands of individuals have enjoyed.

Thank you, Maw Maw and Paw Paw, for teaching me in those early years that anyone can do or be whatever they want to be and that success is about making a decision.

I always get asked, "What are the secrets to success in direct sales and network marketing with Juice Plus+?"

You would expect an answer that would be pages long, but that's not really the case.

At first, I was so confused. Mickey kept telling me to keep things simple. That led me to sit with our sponsor, Jeff, who had achieved ultimate success. Jeff implanted a lesson that changed everything and made me understand how different this business is... and how to create success.

Jeff looked at me directly and said, "The first thing to learn is that our product is not the only key to success. You have to realize that you are just as important as the products you represent. In fact, YOU are a major part of the equation, and you are ALSO the product. Juice Plus+ happens to be the mechanism that makes this business work. Work on being the best product you can personally be." Jeff then arranged for me to have a personal lunch with Jim Rohn.

At lunch, Jim said, "Kerry, here are two things that are important for your success. Number one, the books you read. Number two, the people you associate with on a regular basis." Jim then looked right into my eyes and said, "The five people you hang around the most—your income will be based on their average income."

Wow! Interesting analogy. These are some of the lessons that have been proven to be true.

That led me to research the lessons in reading. What I learned was life changing—that if you quit reading, you have just put yourself into the same category as people who cannot read and are illiterate. I had to think about that long and hard. What a lunch lesson from Jim.

That is why I added this quote from Maw Maw Daigle to my book: "If you hang around a shoplifter long enough, Kerry, you will learn how to shoplift; however, if you hang around successful people long enough, you will learn the power and lessons of success."

Thank you, Maw Maw, Jeff, and Jim.

Many mentors, too numerous to mention, changed our lives. Mickey and I have been blessed. Read the stories in this book, meet our peers, and see why we constantly walk around with smiles on our faces. To be involved with all the storytellers in this book is priceless. No amount of money can buy the kind of alliance we have for each other.

I have something to share that cannot be left unsaid. The success of the stories you are reading right now was all possible because someone believed in these writers more than they believed in themselves.

In truth, we worked hard for years building our business so that we could MAKE A LIFE (the title of a great book by one of the authors here). Doing so has allowed Mickey and I to call all the shots with the TIME we have left on this Earth. Of course, as mentioned, we made sacrifices and worked diligently with daily goals to reach to create this lifestyle. Today we live a life most are envious of.

There is a price. Don't fool yourself; it takes consistent effort and hard (but simple) work, but the rewards are worth it.

The best part is that we are now 'paying it forward', because that is how our mentors wanted payment for what they have taught us.

We now work for 'testimonials'... We hope for you to be one.

Visit us on www.keeppunching.com and say hello. Mickey and I are here to help.

The #1 secret... is to always **keep punching.**

CHAPTER 12

What if?

Jennifer Myers

I flick a crusty glop of artichoke dip off of my forest green Houlihan's apron before stepping into our tiny apartment off the Country Club Plaza in Kansas City. My husband, Sean, greets me warmly as he looks up from his stack of papers on the table.

"How was your shift?" I wish I had a better answer for Sean's familiar question. His curiosity mostly has to do with the amount of my tips.

"Not great. Today was super slow... I only made $35."

The corner of his mouth dips and his eyes go back to his papers. "Hmm... Tomorrow will be better."

I walk over to our makeshift night stand, just a gray, two-drawer cardboard box, and pull out the novel. I neatly tuck the bills in a white envelope, holding my treasure of tips for an extra beat before closing the cover and returning it to its hiding place. I shimmy out of my shoes and fall on the mattress on the floor.

If I could work the dinner shifts it would help, but we only have one car and the walk home is too dangerous. Our apartment isn't in the ghetto, but it's not far from it.

I look around our bargain apartment with gratitude. By anyone else's standards, it is pretty rough, but to us, at $280 a month, it feels like a palace after living in and out of a tent for a year on our backpacking trip. A smile spreads across my face remembering the first time my dad visited. He was dead serious when he made me promise not to sit in the northeast corner of our apartment after assessing the shoddy concrete patching on the outside of our brick fourplex. He legitimately was concerned that the whole corner of the building might separate.

Most of our furniture is borrowed from my friend, Kim. What a Godsend. Dinner, however, requires some coordination, since her chairs are on casters and slide away from the table on our slightly tilted floor.

"How was the job search?" I inquire.

"Tough." Sean's sigh tells me everything.

I catch sight of our beat-up backpacks shoved into the corner of our teeny tiny closet. Exciting memories flash through my mind.

After graduating from KU with business degrees, we took off around the world, into the unknown, for a yearlong adventure with a tent, sleeping bags, a little camping stove, and whatever clothes would fit in our hot rod REI packs. Our 'around the world' plane ticket allowed as many stops as we wanted as long as we traveled in the same direction. We covered 24 countries, visiting places we didn't know existed.

The adventures were monumental, as were the lessons in grit. We faced tough challenges and endured some pretty awful youth hostels, campgrounds, and tent-cities, while keeping our heads on straight in some difficult situations. Our trip was packed with fun and wonder as we discovered sailing, history, life experience, and incredible people. We learned that a smile is a smile no matter what country you're in.

I hold the memories close, but now it's time to get seriously focused, finding our 'real' jobs in one of the worst times possible. The economy and stock market have plummeted over the last two years, and Sean is interviewing against a multitude of people who have more experience. I am waitressing, waiting for him to find employment so I can find mine in whichever city we land in.

Then our friend, Pat, introduces us to an interesting opportunity. He provides a water filter for Sean and I to try. Sean likes the water enough to stop drinking Dr. Pepper but is skeptical of the business.

The following week, while Sean is out of town interviewing, Pat arrives to chauffeur me to a presentation about the water filter business. He looks professional in his crisp khaki pants and freshly pressed shirt, which is quite a step up from his attire at KU.

"Wow, very impressive! What happened to you?" I ask with a glint of amusement in my eye, trying to make myself feel better because my faded jeans and pink and gray striped top is the best I can do. I am hopeful if I keep my left arm down no one will notice the hole in the side seam.

The office space on College Boulevard is beautiful. As I fully focus on the presentation and possibilities, my excitement builds. I like the idea of sharing a product that will help others live healthier lives. I could sell a water filter and make more than my waitressing shift!

Sean and I sold books door to door our last two summers at KU to earn the money for our backpacking trip. We already adopted a 'work hard play hard' mindset, and I know if I could do that, I can certainly do this.

I turn to Pat and say, "How do I sign up? I want to do it." An extra $200 or $300 a month will be life changing and help us through this season when every other meal is spaghetti.

I patiently wait on our borrowed couch for Sean to return from interviewing to share my exciting news. After hearing my pitch, he looks at me dismissively. "I cannot believe you are going to do this. Seriously, it sounds like a scam."

"Well, I am," I shoot back, trying to convey my resolve but also hope. "If it doesn't work, it doesn't work. I want to try it, and I think I can do it."

The next week I drag Sean to a meeting where he is able to hear the same presentation and meet the community. We both realize very quickly that this is an amazing company with a track record of success. We can see there is a system in place, and we like the people we meet, especially Nila Mason, who takes us under her wing. She not only teaches us the basics of the business but also routinely takes Sean to Wendy's salad bar to meet new prospects. She helps Sean with all kinds of 'life' suggestions, including needed advice on buying business attire and his first pair of leather shoes, and that women like flowers.

After one of our weekly meetings, Sean catches the vision. My resolve and excitement have been contagious. I recognize his hope for potential and possibilities when he asks, "What if we treat this like a business? Maybe we won't have to get real jobs."

It is a great vision and decision. We have very few contacts, but we are determined. Even though it entails crawling under sinks to install water filters, I am comfortable retailing our products while Sean figures out team building. It is very much a 'man's business' and culture at this time.

Sean has a rough start and doesn't recruit anyone during his first six months. His belief wavers, but through perseverance and personal growth, he breaks through his blocks and the team starts growing. Within a year and a half, he reaches the top of our pay plan, National Marketing Director (NMD). I have taken a full-time job selling computers to help cover bills, but as I watch Sean growing as a person, traveling and creating success, I decide to join him. I enjoy retailing and sharing the business but mostly become Sean's helper behind the scenes.

Our momentum continues and we get my position to National Marketing Director about a year and a half later. We are in our twenties with an incredible income, full-time benefits, travel, excitement, and success.

We decide to celebrate that success and buy a Morgan 43' sailboat and live on it just off the coast of South Beach, FL, in Miami. After our serious focus and hard work, it's time for some 'play hard', and Sean's love of sailing is ignited. It is truly amazing that we are able to wrap our business around dreams and adventures. We have an office in the World Trade Center in Miami and have plenty of fun when we pull in the lines and the sails fill, eagerly pushing us to a new destination to explore.

It's the best of both worlds, but Sean knows what it takes to create a larger team, and speaking together to larger groups is critical. I love what we are creating together, but have zero interest in the limelight. Not many things make me angry, but whenever Sean asks me to go on stage and just say my name, my blood pressure soars. I have a ridiculous fear of public speaking.

Breaking Through

Despite all of Sean's brilliance, there were some tough circumstances we couldn't control. A company shift from water filters to Juice Plus+, as well as changes in our compensation plan, created a mass exodus in the distributor base about five years previous. We were some of the few leaders who survive, hanging on by a fingernail. It was brutal, and we thought long and hard but decided to stay because of our loyalty to our president, Jay Martin. His vision, his integrity, and his actions through that difficult time had our hearts and earned our loyalty, so we stayed and were rebuilding, which is not for the faint of heart. It required grit, and shortly after that decision, my commitment to personal growth was tested.

I seriously cannot believe I said yes to this.

Sean and I completed the Landmark Communications course together a couple of weeks prior, and in the heat of a personal growth moment I declared that I wanted to overcome my fear of public speaking. Sean, who had grown to become my greatest coach and cheerleader, pounced on that in one second. He said, "I'm scheduled to be the Regional Speaker in Grand Rapids, MI, next weekend. Come with me and we can present together!"

I wanted to be brave and I wanted to break through. I wrote my 20-minute presentation on "Harvest Time" and I practiced, memorizing it word for word. I so wished I could be like Sean, breezing through any topic, inspiring any crowd at a moment's notice.

Instead, I find myself disoriented, staring at an audience of hundreds, unable to read their expressions. The lights are nearly blinding as I gather my thoughts. *Oh, my gosh, what am I doing up here? How bad is my voice cracking? Why did I choose this silk blouse?*

I can feel sweat slowly streaming from my armpits to my waist and hope no one notices.

My rhythm is fast but the words thankfully come; the sleepless night of practice is paying off. *Okay, I made it through that point. Just follow the talk, Jennifer. "Harvest Time" is a good topic.*

I gather a little bit of confidence as I continue with a topic I know well. *Why did I say yes to this misery? I'm almost done. Just get through the close and off this stage.*

I reach for the finish line as my mind strains for my carefully memorized close to stick the landing. I vacillate between feeling proud of myself for conquering my biggest fear and also humbled due to my inexperience. My hand is still shaky and I am drenched, but relief washes over me.

As I exit the stage, I can't wait to tell Sean that I was right. I do not belong on this stage or any stage—it just isn't me. I check-marked my biggest fear and I will never have to do this again! My mind is made up and my resolve is strong.

Out of the Shadows

Rebuilding was going well despite figuring out an entirely new product and approach. We had our first Juice Plus+ National Marketing Director, with more coming, when we had a second devastating shock to our business. The number two earner in the company, who lived in the next city and had been training in front of our Colorado team for several years, decided to jump ship into a hot new travel deal. It was devastating to watch gullible leaders jump ship with him, and the disruption wiped out most of the rest of our team. That was before the auto-ship program, so losing distributors meant losing all of their customers as well. The lesson that 'this is a volunteer army' was never so apparent. People don't sign up for drama, and they didn't stick around to see how this chapter would play out. The hot new deal only lasted about nine months. It was a tough time, full of lessons, and personal growth and soul searching was a must. I thank God that faith in our products, the leaders of our company, and our abilities won the debate again.

The beautiful little French restaurant in downtown Memphis is lovely. My eyes appreciate and take in the blue, yellow, and white French Country table linens and décor. It is a great place for a date night, except this isn't a date. We are at our National Conference, two years after so many jumped ship, and are in disbelief that we have time to go to dinner by ourselves—but, unfortunately, we have so few people attending. I look at my knight in shining armor with eyes as big as my dinner plate, which holds small piles of delicious delicacies begging me to taste them.

"Honey, this is built for you." Sean looks me directly in the eyes, always confident, his tone convincing. My mind is racing in the lull of the conversation, mulling over and over if I am willing to commit myself and my word. "You love nutrition. You love Juice Plus+. You can do this."

I know in my heart and soul that I can and should be stepping out from behind the scenes of our business to the front lines and carefully weigh it out.

Can I step it up into recruiting and serious team building? Can I lead and step out of Sean's shadow?

He is brilliant in our business, and his broad-shouldered shadow is a cozy place for me to be.

These mushrooms are delicious. I savor the first bite but can't quite put my finger on the seasoning I taste. How do the French master these delicacies with the same ingredients that all the rest of us can buy? Do they have special, hidden, reserved for French-only grocery stores?

I also can't quite identify the waves of emotion washing over me. Is it the deliciousness of my dinner, the upset at having almost no one at the conference, or the recognition that I'm actually having niggling thoughts that maybe I really could step up to another level, out of the giant shadow and onto the front lines?

"Okay," I say softly. "I'm ready. I think I can do it, too."

Am I committing? What about that pesky public speaking thing? Whatever am I going to do about that?

By now, I have a couple of little kids, and life is a whirlwind with all the delights and challenges of family life and building a loving, nurturing, fun-filled home. I love being a mom, and we are blessed with two amazing children, Mikaela and Jake. Our house is a constant buzz of activity with two very active toddlers.

I am also in love with our business. Sean was correct; it is truly made for me. I enjoy soaking up education on nutrition from some of the most brilliant and forward-thinking medical professionals brave enough to share the power of fruits and vegetables in these little capsules, despite a skeptical and difficult peer group. Study after study unfolded on the power of Juice Plus+, and my nutrition knowledge grew which was empowering but also created a conundrum for our ever challenging nightly routine called dinner. Cooking is not my greatest skill. Sean likes my cooking and it's good, but I need to figure something out.

I had embraced my commitment at the French restaurant full on. Our team of amazing, mostly part-time mommies were growing teams of their own and blossoming. I wanted to spend more time building our team. I loved it. Except for dinner. How do mommies pull off being a mom while sneaking in three-way calls, conference calls, events, AND dinner? I clearly needed new skills, so I made one of the best decisions of my life and hired a coach. Christen and I met at a networking group and had an instant connection. Her process of identifying priorities, eliminating tolerations, and making a plan to reach goals was exactly what I needed.

During one of our hour-long sessions, I am working on my bed, propped up with pillows, trying to find some peace and quiet in our busy house.

"Jennifer, let's look at the top three things you are tolerating in your life."

Uh-oh. I think this is it. It's time to tackle that lurking fear of public speaking. I was at least a little relieved to learn that this was the number one fear people had in life, including death. Apparently, this is a worldwide issue, and Christen encouraged me to join a group called Toastmasters International.

Seriously? Was I going to subject myself to voice cracking, hand shaking, sweating misery every week and pay for it? That's exactly what I did and was relieved that as I made my way through the ten required speeches, judging, and impromptu table topics exercises, speaking got easier as the weeks passed. I actually started gaining confidence and enjoyed the breakthroughs in this supportive space in some surprising way. Fears can either push you forward or hold you back... I let mine push me.

Next, I created a 20-minute health and nutrition talk using colored and laminated 17" × 11" boards I carried in my little fruit and veggie bag, and I booked myself at Rotary and Kiwani clubs, MOPS groups, churches, and any group I could get in front of. These were friendly audiences, and I was always thrilled when people asked questions and wanted more information for their battle with their latest chronic illness.

Our team was growing, and they started booking me all over Denver in rec centers, schools, hotels, club houses, and wherever we could gather people. Our team kept growing, and the momentum was contagious. It was so contagious that we won our company's very first award for "The Largest Income and Sales Growth of a 39 Club Member" at the very first Elton Awards gala. I say 'we,' not as a reference to Sean and I, even though we were handed the beautiful award. This represented what our team of mommies created. It was one of the highlights of my life as it represented these beautiful, mission-driven women that I loved and respected, as we all learned new skills and pushed through personal growth. This award mostly represented breaking through fear. We all have our own to get through, whether it is picking up the 500-pound telephone, inviting our first guest to an event, or sweating through a blouse in someone's living room, sharing the importance of eating more fruits and vegetables. It was a moment of shock and joy that I will never forget.

Following Dreams and Moonbeams

"Hey honey, do you have a minute?"

Sean waits patiently for me to get off the phone in my very familiar position in my office, which I affectionately call "Command Center One."

"I've been doing the six-month goal planning session and I'm working on how to create more time in the game with our kids. You know we tried to pull off having a mountain place and we were only able to go one weekend the entire summer. The problem isn't our schedule, it's more our kids' schedules. So I came up with an idea." After a pregnant pause, he continues, "I think we should sail around the world."

Okay, wow! I recognize the look in his eye. Sean is the furthest thing from an insincere, "Let's do lunch" kind of guy. One of the many things I respect immensely is that he says what he means, and means what he says... always. I take a deep breath, considering the possibility of taking our children out of school and sailing away to distant lands.

It sounds amazing. Our backpacking trip gave us the travel bug, and thanks to our personal franchise with Juice Plus+, we have had the freedom to travel to some of the most sacred and interesting places on the planet. Our kids are five and eight, and it's been a while.

"Look, I don't know how long it takes. I don't know how much it costs. I don't know any details. Let me do some research and get back."

I surprise myself by responding, "Anything we do has to be on a catamaran." I much prefer sailing flat rather than heeling on a monohull where everything slides from side to side.

Sean spends two weeks researching what it takes to sail around the world and comes back with his best pitch. "It takes three years and about a million dollars to get the right boat."

There is an interminably long pause... 20 seconds... 30 seconds. My mind races at the possibilities, but three years? We can't be away from school, our life, and business for that long.

"I'll give you a year."

Sean designs the coolest trip we can pull off in a year.

Our kids are eight and ten when we depart. We sail, explore, discover, and home-school through the Caribbean necklace of islands, through the Panama Canal and Galapagos Islands, and island hop through the South Pacific Islands to Australia. We lovingly call it "bobbing along on a white rectangle at half the speed of bike." Our white rectangle is named *Souls Calling*, because it is Sean's soul's calling to do this trip Our adventure takes three years to plan, 15 months to do, and changes all of our lives in more ways than I can imagine.

The flight from Sydney back to Denver is a mixture of emotions. Tears stream down my cheeks, and I don't attempt to stop them. I will miss this sacred family time together, and a sea of memories flash through my mind like a highlight reel. I relive the first time Jake snorkeled in the BVI and his pure joy when he yelled back at Sean, "Dad! You've got to see this! This is AWESOME!" while I happily kicked after him and his trail of a thousand glimmering, silver bubbles.

I think about our incredible family bonding time, games, new discoveries, countries, and people along the way. Mikaela stepped into becoming quite the boat girl and grabbed every experience possible, including basket weaving in Tonga. I relish the memory of rallying 16 Peace Corp members on the island of Western Samoa to paint and transform a school in desperate need of TLC.

I won't, however, miss the fear that crept up as I watched the sun disappear into the ocean, marking the start of an endless night on an overnight passage. Sean and I took turns being 'on watch' throughout those nights. That was pure exhaustion coupled with an indescribable feeling of connection with the oneness of all in the dark, stars twinkling above as we followed the moonbeam to our next island destination.

Flying from Australia, I am thankful for it all because you tend to appreciate the good with the bad, the relaxing with the difficult, the deep and profound with the shallow, the cozy, safe, and warm with the fearful, and the light with the dark. Our sailing trip demonstrated that in spades, and yet, isn't it true in all of life?

Many years later, I am beyond grateful we said yes to an opportunity that has given us a foundation for life beyond my imagination. Where else could we have aligned our time, energy, and caring with people, a product, and a company that is up to changing lives for the better and allowing its partners the freedom to create their soul's calling? The positive ripple effect from Juice Plus+, our team, and this community inspires me, and it is a blessing to wake up with purpose.

I continue to be grateful for all of it and appreciate the challenges and required growth in our business and our life, as the contrast makes the success and freedom all the sweeter. Our breakthroughs and lessons learned have enriched our lives on every level, and it has been worth it.

God has endowed each of us with gifts and skills, and we can use them to help others while we design a life that we love. I believe that is what God has intended for each of us, but it doesn't mean the journey is easy. Luck seems to favor hard work, growth, connecting with your soul's purpose, and, of course, breaking through fear.

We look forward to the future and what life will bring as we continue to share health, hope, and solutions and to empower others to design their future and their happiness.

CHAPTER 13

Believe

Barb Kunst

"Kelly has had a stroke. Can you come?" My friend's cousin, a nurse, delivers the heart-wrenching call, and my mind spins with questions, worries, and thoughts about how to help.

I don't even notice the beautiful red, yellow, and orange leaves that dot the horizon on my four-hour drive. All I can think about is being with my friend, the sister I never had, our many family summers together—if we'll ever have another summer again.

Time stands still on one of the longest drives of my life. With every mile, questions whirl through my mind. *Why is it taking so long? Why didn't I fill up with gas yesterday?* Stopping takes precious time. *Why has my healthy, energetic friend had a stroke? Why, when she was so young? Why, why, why?*

My mind won't stop.

I can feel the devastation in the unit as I walk down the hospital corridors, and I don't know whether to walk fast to get there as soon as I can, or slow to prolong what I imagine waits for me in her room. As I walk, I'm surrounded by the sounds of oxygen machines beeping, nurses bustling, and trolleys clanging as they roll down the halls. The distinctive smell of lunch trays lingers in the air.

All too quickly, I reach Kelly's room. I stare at the door and then open it, slowly, tears stinging my eyes and rolling down my cheeks.

I sit by Kelly's hospital bed, my heart breaking for her as well as her family. I feel so helpless. Her room is so still; I wrap my fingers around her still hand. Everything is quiet aside from the gentle beeping of the machines.

Suddenly, it's like my body is hit by a bolt of lightning, and I tremble as the words *EVERYONE NEEDS A PLAN B IN THEIR LIFE* vibrate throughout my body—a voice from the universe. This life-changing moment is like nothing I have ever experienced.

You never know when life will throw you a curveball, one that can change your life mentally, physically, emotionally, and financially. Forever. *Life is precious—everyone needs a Plan B in their back pocket.*

Eighteen years ago, I was given that opportunity in the form of a box.

*

The box of fruit and veggie capsules is a gift from my mom, well meaning, very thoughtful, but one I don't feel I need.

"I want you to take these," she tells me. "I know they are good for you, and you need them."

Dad's just lost his battle with cancer and Mom needs me to be strong. But I'm emotionally spent; my chest feels like it's being pulled down by 100-pound weights. As exhaustion settles in, I feel like if I close my eyes for a second, I may never open them again. I know Mom's concerned, but eating properly is not my highest priority.

Mom is right, I do need to eat well, I do take those little capsules but the skeptic in me tucks them away in a cupboard so no one sees them. It is my little secret.

Months go by, and I am feeling the amazing power and benefits of good nutrition, it's like my very own little safety net. I love the way I feel! The capsules find their way out of my cupboard and move to a special place on my windowsill.

Maybe it IS time to share my best-kept secret with others.

I am so grateful for the box my mother gave me, for my first experience with fruit and veggie capsules, which have catalyzed my life's purpose and passion.

My next box is due to ship, and my cousin, who sold them to my mom, asks me, "Would you like to sign up for the discount?" My mom secretly knew I also needed the business.

It's a moment in my life that directs my path, a fork in the road. I don't know the journey, but I trust my intuition to make the right choice.

"Well, I guess I could," I say, "but would I actually have to sell anything? I don't really want to have to sell anything!"

"You don't have to sell," she replies. "You can just share your story."

With a sigh, I say, "Alright, sign me up." I quickly fill in the form and hop into the truck, looking forward to our holiday adventure. Out of sight, out of mind.

Upon arriving home, my best friend's completed order leans against the pottery fruit bowl on my table. Choosing fax over snail mail is the quicker of my two options to submit the order; there was no internet, online ordering, or email available 18 years ago. I'm excited for her to get her package.

I think to myself, *okay, well, maybe I CAN do this.* And so it begins...

My cousin says, "Start with two events. Just two, one Friday night and one Saturday morning. Invite your friends. I'll come and help you."

My thoughts drift. *Who am I going to invite? What if no one comes? What do I feed them? Should we sit in the living room or around the kitchen table? I wish I hadn't said yes.*

Friday evening, the day of the event, is sunny and warm. Despite everything being ready—snacks are beautifully prepared and ready to serve, all the chairs sit equally spaced around the table—I'm still stressed.

The doorbell rings; people are arriving. I'm so happy my friends are coming, and I smile as I listen to them chatting and laughing. *It's going to be okay.* My cousin shares 'the presentation', and all but one person fills out the order form. My heart does flip flops thinking about my friends getting to experience what I have been for months.

Along with morning comes a new group of friends arriving. I am feeling confident until my cousin says, "Okay, I did it for you last night; this morning, you get to do the presentation."

I am so nervous I can't sit still; I pace from counter to table, delivering muffins and coffee, checking my notes... My mind is whirling. When I start, the room goes so quiet—no one talks, no one laughs, no one even smiles. Everyone just looks at me.

Oh, my God, what am I doing? Why did I ever say I would do this? No one is ever going to buy. Nobody cares—they only came because I asked them to. How can I change my mind and say I don't want to do this?

Negative thoughts bounce everywhere, like my mind is a tornado spinning. I'm mortified, embarrassed, and just want to crawl deep into a hole, safely hidden from watching eyes.

Then, at last, I finish, and relief sets in. I feel calm; hands have stopped shaking, and at last I can look my friends in the eye. I'm ready to settle in to just visit, to call it a morning, but my cousin is slowly handing out the order forms. I can't help but wonder *why*.

Then I realize I've been too judgmental, thinking that no one is interested, when really, they've just been listening. I can't believe it—every person is filling out the order form.

"You just jumped two levels in the company with these two events," my cousin tells me.

The butterflies start to flutter in my stomach as I realize that this is the first of many, and I immediately start thinking of who else I'm going to share with. As I jot down names on the back of a handy purple envelope, a friend calls and asks, "Can I tell my sister about Juice Plus+? I think she would love it?"

I'm delighted. I really CAN do this!

"Come to the conference with me," my cousin pleads with me later, adding, "People's businesses grow so much faster if they attend conferences."

I'm running out of excuses to say no, and so finally, I say, "Okay, I'll go."

*

Music vibrates through my body, hundreds of people are dancing, visiting, laughing around me. The music and the noise fade away, and the speakers begin... *These are my people; I'm so glad I'm here.*

My cousin and I reflect on our weekend as we sit under swaying palm trees and walk through powdery desert sand. I am thankful for my cousin's persistence; I know I am in the right place.

My business is growing, and I am excited.

My family supports me. One morning, my husband Hank comes into the house, looking so proud. "Come check what I put on your Explorer," he says. And there it is, a bold black and orange license plate that says "Powered by Juice Plus+." He's bolted it right to the front of my car.

"You did that?" I exclaim. "OMG, now everyone will know."

My secret is out. It's a big game changer, a giant step, a conversation starter—I now proudly share that I am part of the Juice Plus+ Company.

More friends want to join my team, and we grow together, riding fun highs and challenging lows on our roller coaster ride. The highs are amazing, and the lows are learning curves, challenging me, making me stronger.

I feel like I'm stuck at Sales Coordinator; despite trying to move forward, it seems to be going so slow until...

Your package has arrived!

The message pops up across my phone, and I rush to pick up the huge box of magic. It's white, shiny, futuristic-looking, with pumps that hum and lights that sparkle. Taking my new Tower Garden slowly out of the box, I reach for the instructions to figure out how to assemble it.

Excitement buzzes through me. What am I going to plant? Lettuce, kale, tomatoes... ooh, maybe something fun and pretty like a flower, for that pop of color.

Soon the tower sits glowing in my kitchen, showing off fresh, green bits of life that make me feel alive. Thoughts pop continuously into my head. *I need to show my mom; I think we could put one in her lodge. And I have a friend who loves to garden that I think would really enjoy this. Oh! And the school— this would be awesome there.*

I breathe in the fresh, clean air of passion as my mind races with excitement, thoughts and ideas of what to do with this new addition constantly bouncing around in my head.

As time goes on, I attract people who are curious and find myself empowering families to take control of their health and wealth.

Visions pop into my mind of healthy grandparents dancing at their grandchildren's weddings; moms at home happily raising their kids; families enjoying a second income; a student making their tuition for university. I see families having fun on holidays together at the beach, living their best lives.

I am empowering women to be authentic, the best version of themselves—to become lighthouses and servant leaders attracting people to their business.

I want success for them, sometimes more than they want or see for themselves.

I have one week to go to reach Senior Sales Coordinator (SSC). *Time to try one of those vision boards...*

I find a piece of cardboard from one of my husband's brand-new blue shirts. It's a little bent, but it will work. Snip, snip, snip—images float to my desk. *There! I'm finished; now let's see if it really works.*

I do reach SSC, although my belief in that little piece of cardboard isn't yet strong.

I want to reach Qualified National Marketing Director (QNMD) in six months, so it's time to try it again. *Can I do it?*

I glue the words "It's in the bag" to the top of my piece of cardboard, along with everything else I'm envisioning. The words and images give me strength and inspire me to reach out to more people and work on my business more diligently. Only my eyes see my vision board—an unspoken goal.

A week before my deadline, one of my sponsors calls me.

"Barb, it's in the bag," he tells me. "Don't worry about it; it's in the bag."

The hair on my arms stands on end and goosebumps prickle my skin. *How did he know? He never saw my vision board!*

Turns out, he's right—it's in the bag.

I now believe in the power of making a decision, of putting in print the vision of what I need and being inspired to do the action. It's magical.

*

Now that I have a vision, I lean in. My goal is to reach National Marketing Director (NMD), the top position in our company, but I have some work to do. I do excellent customer care, attend all events regardless of rain or shine, and bring people with me; my team duplicates the process with their own teams.

My team works tirelessly, and two of them also decide to work on reaching NMD. We work together, known as 'the three amigos'. Event after event, mile after mile—my phone feels like it's attached to my hand like a micro-computer. I just need to finish my structure and have the right volume, and I will be there. I will reach my goal by helping my team reach theirs.

I am obsessed! My husband agrees. Three weeks straight, he asks, "Can you pick up butter on the way home?"

"Oh, for sure," I reply. Every day I forget. I laugh thinking of the silliness of it.

*

NMD—it's worth all the craziness and obsession. I did it. They did it. I feel the adrenaline rush; my heart beats faster, my face flushes. I sigh with relief and shed a few happy tears.

My heart is bursting with pride for the efforts of our entire team. It isn't just a title for me; it represents the work of many. I'm so grateful for all their dedication and persistence in reaching their goals.

I admit one of my fears in reaching NMD is sharing my story on the main stage, in front of thousands of people. A thought crosses my mind—*maybe I'll just skip that conference.*

But I don't. Instead, I think of the logistics. What will my song be for when I walk on stage? *What will I wear? (Probably black.) What am I going to say?*

And finally, when I get up and speak, I'm so grateful I attended and had the opportunity to share my Juice Plus+ journey in front of all those people. What an experience!

After, we celebrate and prepare to attend our first black tie event—'The Eltons.' I am NOT missing out on this experience.

I'm reminded of climbing the Fintry mountain to the falls with my friend Kelly, moving step by step up the rocky, steep, winding path lined with wildflowers nodding and encouraging us. Then we came across a rock in the shape of a foot. I believed it was a sign; I went deep inside and let my mind wander, searching every corner of my being. *What footprint do I want to leave on this earth when I am gone?*

The impact from that rock led me to share about it in my NMD speech.

Life has some crazy turns; I love that I took the right fork in the road.

*

The sun streams into our kitchen this morning as my husband and I share our favorite coffee time.

"When do you think we should retire?" I ask him, wrapping my hands around my mug. "Are we too young? Have we put enough money away?" I sort of chuckle and add, "Guess it depends on how long we live!"

"How am I going to keep myself busy if we retire? Will we stay on the farm?" he asks.

I sip my coffee and say, "Will we travel?"

"Let's just wait until we retire to figure that out," he says, on his way out the door to work.

At one of the highest points in the ebbs and flows of my business, as I ride a wave of success, I am hit with one of the worst points in my personal life that I will ever experience.

I sit in the doctor's office with my husband, listening to the doctor speak.

"I am sorry, sir," the doctor says gently, "but you have prostate cancer. I'm afraid it's too far advanced for some of the more typical treatments." The doctor looks at me and hands me a box of tissues, adding, "I am so sorry, Mrs. Kunst."

That one moment turns our world upside down, stilling our thoughts and forcing us to confront the decision we have to make.

Fears creep in, and my mind is full of questions. *What will happen? Will he have to go through treatment? Can they do surgery? Is he going to die? How will I manage? Will I have to move off the farm? How do we tell our kids? What if he never gets to meet our grandchildren?*

So many what ifs. So many unknowns.

There are not enough tissues in our car for the long, quiet ride home.

This curveball changes our lives and puts a whole new twist on retirement.

The surgery is mostly successful; but the health challenge has made life so much more precious, and once again we are reminded to live life to the fullest, in the moment, as tomorrow is never guaranteed.

Retirement means retiring my husband's pay cheque and our medical benefits. Words can't express how blessed we feel that the little Plan B that I started 18 years ago, without realizing what the future would bring, has become our Plan A, much less that it has grown to an NMD position, giving us a welcome additional income stream and our medical benefits.

BELIEVE is a word that lives in my heart. I live and breathe the belief that "Everything happens for a reason; we just have to believe."

Even when something devastating happens and we wonder why, there is a hidden reason somewhere. Life has a way of working out in the best possible way.

*

I believe this business was destined to find me 18 years ago, but I could never dream of the many ways it has daily changed the path of my life to building a legacy from the heart and making a positive difference in people's lives in so many ways. My purpose in life is to help others build theirs...

Over the years, I am blessed to have many people join my team. Reaching 100 Club is the compound effect of work as our huge team of amazing people grows together; I am grateful every day. The marketing plan changes, we continue to grow, and I am blessed to reach Presidential Marketing Director Plus (PMD+), now the top level of the company; the second woman in Canada to reach this position.

Did I envision at the start that I would ever be at this position? No—at first, I only wanted to sign up for the discount, not to sell anything! And yet, I realize now that being able to drop out of my head and into my heart allows me to share my story and passion and truly care about others. I am gifting hope, not selling a product.

With success come challenges. A path is never from point A to point B; it's a very wiggly line. To reach my goal I must get in line, stay in line, and I will succeed. I watch out for those shiny penny moments, as I call them, or the perception that there is greener grass. They are there to tempt, to pull me from my vision and put me to the back of the line. The people who stay in line in our business have the compassion and heart to share the mission and opportunity and make a difference in the world, leaving a legacy for their families. I AM one of THOSE people.

Riding the ebbs and flows in my business is sometimes rocky and beset with sharp points. As with the weather, people have seasons in their lives that take them down different paths. I experience all the emotions—the joy of watching someone walk the stage as a new NMD in their beautiful dress, telling their story to thousands with tears of happiness in their eyes; the excitement of working with a team member reaching their goal; the happiness of meeting a new friend who joins our team; the sadness for the loss of team members and changes in friendships; to say nothing of annoyance, disbelief, and wonder.

Dealing with these emotions, some painful, gives me my strength to lead as a servant heart with integrity and honesty, while challenging me to focus on working harder, sharing more, and appreciating the people that surround me in my life with love, empathy, and boundaries, all shaping me into the woman I am today. It teaches me the importance of building a strong business characterized by both width and depth.

*

I align with the company with a heart, and it's amazing core values of longevity, authenticity, quality, community, simplicity and being approachable.

The mission statement by Jay Martin, president and founder of the company, states that we strive "To build a stable and lasting company that will help as many people as possible realize their dreams," and this is still a living reality today.

I am so grateful for the people who have crossed my path as mentors and friends, who believe in me more than I do myself and have never ceased to encourage and inspire me to be successful.

I believe in the product, company, and opportunity. It is my home, my people, my purpose, and my passion.

What did it teach me? To dream big and live life in the moment, to its fullest potential.

*

We are snowbirds now.

Our 40' diesel pusher purrs quietly as we glide down the road, in a whole new world of retirement. I am watching the next season of our life unfold as I look through the spotless pane of glass.

I sit in Palm Springs with my computer in front of a beautiful fireplace area, under a massive umbrella; around me, palm trees sway in the breeze, and planters pop with reds, yellows, and purples, the flowers nodding as though saying good morning. The lush, green grass is perfectly manicured.

Hummingbirds buzz happily around the feeder, and a nearby puddle from a recent rain shower sparkles in the sun. People stop to visit as they walk by.

I am at peace as I focus on sharing my mission of health and wellness.

My thoughts wander back to my kids and grandchildren, bringing tears to my eyes. I miss them so much. A memory pops in.

"Oma, I miss you with my whole entire heart," says my three year old grandson.

"Oma, can you play with me?" my six year old asks.

My heart strings are stretching...

FaceTime connects in an instant, and I feel calmer. It takes me back to sitting in their kitchen with those little arms wrapped around my neck, answering the hundreds of questions they ask.

"Mom, it is so cold here," my daughter tells me. "School is closed, and we have so much snow. I got stuck in my driveway!" She turns the camera to show me the snow piled on her deck to the top of her BBQ; the thermometer outside her window shows −40 °C.

"I love you and miss you so much," I say, "but I am really happy we are here where it is warm, and the grass is green."

*

With this amazing business opportunity and supplemental income comes the freedom to choose.

Freedom for me is...

Spending as much time with our kids and grandkids as we like.

Going on a three-week holiday during the summer to my favorite place, where the water is blue, the weather is hot with no mosquitos to be found... and extending our stay to three months because we can.

The financial opportunity to say yes more often to our kids and grandchildren, enjoying trips to Disneyland, where "it's a beautiful world."

Supporting our daughter when she becomes a single mom without child support so she can stay at home and raise her children, our grandchildren.

Investing in a new 41' trailer to nestle on our lot in Palm Springs as our newest adventure.

We feel blessed for our health in being able to continue to do the things we love. Hank at 77 still plays pickleball, hikes, and water skis; I have time to enjoy walks and golfing with friends.

Saying affirmations is my daily habit; two of my favorites are, "I am open to receive abundance in all forms now and always," and "I am energy, I am love, I am at peace."

I live in gratitude; I love living a life of purpose and passion serving others. It is my heart; I am paying it forward, so it never feels like work. I am so grateful for my little Plan B, which just started as a discount. I had no idea it would lead me to a life of success.

Success looks different for everyone. For me, success is being able to do whatever I want, whenever I want, with whomever I want.

I believe I have reached that success!

Thank you, Juice Plus+, for being my Plan B.

CHAPTER 14

What if? How one little question can change the world

Loren Lahav

What if? This question is changing my life. A series of *what ifs* brought me to the level of success I've experienced in my life. I'm not talking about the what ifs that lead us down roads of fear and worry.

I'm talking about the *what ifs* that lead us down the road of *possibilities*. When you start with the *what ifs* of possibility, you begin to realize there's no end to them. For those of us who have ever felt trapped in our circumstances—and let's face it, most of us have at one time or another—the possibilities of what could go wrong tend to be what make the most noise in our heads. But *what if* it all goes exactly right?

It's 5 am on the last day of a 21-day stint on the road when I finally start asking myself the question: *what if my chance to say yes to my life and stop living everyone else's dreams is right now?* I have been going from 5 am to 11 pm every single day. My body feels like a ton of bricks as I try to lift myself out of bed for one last day of an event that I'm doing for Tony Robbins.

To say that I'm exhausted is definitely an understatement; I am physically and emotionally burned out. But it isn't about these three weeks; it is about the years of weeks just like this that I've been putting in.

I've been spending those years saying yes to everyone else's dreams; I know now is the time to start saying yes to my own. I can't keep going like this much longer. A familiar song pops into my head, a song I've heard so many times before. However, this time I'm listening with different ears.

It's *Seasons of Love* from the Tony award-winning musical *Rent*, a song that calls into question society's perceptions of how a life is valued and measured. It so poignantly asks the question: how do you measure a life? There are 525,600 minutes in a year; am I truly spending them in the way that I want to?

"525,600 moments so dear ... How do you measure, measure a year?"

What if our measurements of a life were in moments of love? At this particular time, my life is measured in airports, convention centers, hotel rooms, and events. But this isn't the story of someone who suffered for years in the drudgery and dread of doing something she hates. The truth is, I love what I do! I work with great people, travel the world, and am living my passion. Most importantly, I am helping people who are hungry to take their lives to the next level. Anyone on the outside looking in would say that I am a success.

Who could want anything else?

I do. What I realize, as it takes every ounce of energy to pull my body out of bed at 5 am on this particular morning, is that I feel a bit stuck because I just can't seem to get ahead. I have all of the 'things' that enable me to live a comfortable life, but I am constantly under the pressure of the fact that if I don't work, I also won't get paid.

As I look over to my little girl sleeping beside me and the nanny asleep on the pullout couch, I feel even heavier as I realize the moments that are escaping me while I live the dreams of others. My baby girl is already three months old; this passage of time seems to have happened in a blink—a concept I think only parents can truly understand. The primary thing motivating me on this particular morning is the thought that soon, I'm going to be able to go home to my two boys and my dogs, and sleep in my own bed. I relish in the thought that 24 hours from now, I will be *home*... at least until the next event, which will undoubtedly be right around the corner.

Dreams of Dave & Busters with my kids fill my head as I silently move about the hotel room, getting ready for the day. As I quietly shut the hotel room door behind me, I whisper a promise to my baby girl: "It won't always be this way. I promise. I *promise* you." I walk on swollen feet down the hallway, chanting to myself, "You've got this, Lo; let's do this!" as a way to work through my tiredness for this one last event. As wonderful as this life is, it isn't *my* dream that I'm living; I'm helping to build someone else's legacy.

No, this isn't the story of my suffering. It's the story of someone who decided to dream really big, turn off the noise, and stay focused on the big vision. *This* is what I want you to understand from my story.

"In daylight, in sunsets..."

What if it were possible for me to have it all—to prioritize my business *and* be able to see my children grow up? I ask this question of myself as I go about my work. There's a saying in the event world that you are only as good as your last event... and my events are always *badass!* On this particular day, I feel overwhelmed by the evidence of the impact I'm making on all of the beautiful participants at these events. Shouts of "thank you, Loren," "this was such an awesome week," and "this was the best week of my life," are music to my ears, only made better by the laughs and giggles of each and every participant.

The other part of me—the *mother* part of me—knows that the nanny is doing the things I want to be doing with my daughter: playing with her, exploring with her, shopping with her, spending every precious moment with her.

I feel like I have to work so much because I know I'm hemorrhaging money on babysitters and nannies, as well as funding the brand I'm building; no amount of money affords me the opportunity to have more time at home with the people I love the most, and opportunities keep showing up for me left and right.

I know I want to leave a legacy, and an international one at that. I know in my heart and soul that this is possible for me. But I'm grappling with so much noise in my head about how great my life is. Who am I to want anything more? Who am I to want to do my own things?

Then a quiet voice, the voice I know to be that of my own truth, comes forward with the question: *What if* I'm actually *meant* for that 'more'?

It's not lost on me that I'm functioning like an addict; I'm addicted to the rush of all of the events I do. Because I go from event to event, I'm also missing out on a crucial part of the human experience: connection. It's dawning on me that I haven't been able to follow up with people after events; I haven't been able to keep them plugged into the community. I know that me being pulled in so many directions at such a rapid pace means that I'm not giving anyone my very best, least of all myself.

I'm to the point where I want to teach these awesome events because *I want to*, not because I *have to*. At an event where I'm educating primarily on health cleanses and nutrition, my friend Jeff Roberti—the #1 person in the history of network marketing— pulls me aside during the break.

He can see the layers beneath my happy exterior; he can see my longing for a way to unify my family and my business, to get out of the rut of constantly being on the road.

He tells me about Juice Plus+, a vitamin and supplement company that helps people to lead healthier lives. I wish I could say that I immediately see this as the opportunity he does.

Instead, my blood boils and my arrogance kicks in. How dare he try and educate me about this? I've been teaching health cleanses and nutrition for years. I've literally helped *thousands* of people with my knowledge!

"Just come to this conference," he insists. "Then you can officially tell me no."

I enthusiastically go to the conference he invites me to because I am so excited to finally get him off my back about this company!

I eventually say yes to Juice Plus+... and that changes everything for me.

"In laughter, in strife..."

It only takes me 17 years to say yes to Juice Plus+; this is the first time I actually listen to and am receptive to what Jeff has been trying to tell me all along. Why did I say no for so long? The truth is that I was scared. I am one of those people who is all in or all out. I knew things would have to change. Change is scary; it's human nature to cling to what we know, even if what we know isn't working. The noise holding me back was trying to convince me that this didn't work, that the people around me didn't actually want to help me.

Except they do. They truly do.

Juice Plus+ offered me another revenue stream, which eventually allows me more freedom in my time. But first—I have to get to work! I don't want to work with Jeff because I'm afraid it's going to affect our friendship if I don't do well. When he says he has a mentor for me—someone to team me up with as I embark on this adventure—I roll my eyes and think, *okay, fine; let's do this.* I'm as surrendered to the process as I can possibly be.

Jeff sets me up with a woman named Cheryl. I'm not going to lie; I have so many doubts heading into this. But I push past the noise in my head and get on the phone with her. A sweet Southern accent greets me on the other end of the line.

Oh, crap. Jeff's set me up with a sweet, prissy lady; how am I going to get out of this one? This isn't going to work for me!

Then I meet her in person at a conference. She is a gorgeous badass! She is this poised, polished, eloquent woman who glides through the space she's in, engulfed in the energy of elegance and grace. She doesn't have to say anything; she just owns the room with her energy, which just lights up the space. For this reason, she's called the Velvet Hammer—equal parts badass and grace.

Our eyes meet, and I just know that I finally have a running partner. My body surges with certainty. In one glance, I know we are going to blow the lid off this thing.

"Your first assignment," Cheryl says to me, "is to write a list of 15 people you know, love, and care about."

Because I don't do *anything* half you-know-what, I write out a list of 56 people.

At that point, Cheryl decides to come out and work with me. We hunker down for two weeks getting everything set up. After weeks of going from 6 am to 11 pm, I finally feel like I'm getting out of this addiction to events.

I begin to wonder…

What if this is the thing that will give me the flexibility that I crave so that I can not only be the business badass I want to be, but also the *mother* I want to be?

I have never been more certain in my life; at this moment, it's abundantly clear that my mission is to change the world for mothers everywhere. I'm going to help each and every woman who wants to create lives where they would be able to stay home with their kids. My opportunity to put my money where my mouth was comes to me fairly quickly when Linda, a distributor for Juice Plus+ based in Australia, begins having doubts about renewing her distributorship.

I know Linda's potential; I know that she's the exact right person who can really launch Australia. She just needs to get inspired again. I just *know* I have to get her to a conference here in the United States, but the flight is $2000. I look in my bank account to confirm what I already know; I don't have the money. My heart aches, hanging heavy and contracted in my chest. My stomach and mind churn as I consider my options. I finally decide that I need to borrow the money from a friend.

My friend willingly gives the money, with one caveat: I need to have the money back by the 1st of the month. She is *insistent* on this point. I make sure to pay her back by the agreed upon date. She doesn't tell me until years later the reason why she needed it back so quickly.

"I borrowed the money," she confesses. "I knew how important it was for you to get Linda here. So I borrowed the money so that you could borrow the money."

My jaw drops to the floor. I'd known that my friend was going through a divorce, but I didn't know the specifics of her money situation. I'm so grateful that I have so many people in my life who are willing to take this kind of chance on me.

Now, I get to do the same for others.

It occurs to me that I have an opportunity to do with Linda what Cheryl did for me. If I can just get Linda into the environment of a conference, so that she can see the impact this business has, then she'll see the truth that she's not doing it all alone! She just needs a little reminder of the vision she saw in the first place.

Sure enough, Linda is reinspired at the conference. We repaint the vision for her and she flies back to Australia ready to go! As I fly to Australia to do for Linda what Cheryl had done for me, I am excited beyond belief.

Shock doesn't begin to cover how I feel walking into Linda's apartment. It's a dark, dank, and moldy two-bedroom, with mold in the bathroom as well. We buckle down in a room that shares her son's crib. I become more determined to help Linda when I get there; I need to help her get to a place where she can get out of this terrible apartment.

When I say we got to work, I mean it! We do events all over Australia. We network until we finally meet two other people who also share our vision and purpose. Before my eyes, I see the beautiful trickle down of success that results from choosing not to listen to the noise of all the reasons why things won't work out. From there, thousands and thousands of lives have been transformed because of Linda's decision to renew her distributorship for Juice Plus+.

It all starts with one courageous yes. I begin to wonder:

What if each and every woman on the planet gets to have it all?

"How about love?"

We only have one life, and it comes with many different layers. What I understand is that there is no such thing as work–life balance. Work doesn't fit into neat 50/50 buckets. It can get a bit messy, but there's so much beauty in the mess. We're not going to get it right all of the time, but that's part of being human. The habit I've created around navigating work and life so that I can get it right more often is just asking the question: will I feel bad if I miss this?

Here's the thing—no one will ever remember the business meetings that you miss, but your family will remember the precious moments that you're there for. I live a life of no regrets now because of just asking myself this simple question. With this business I've created, I've found I can do it all my own way; I can write my own rules rather than follow the rules of others. Okay, so I had to listen to Jeff and Cheryl for a bit... but once I learned the ropes, I can and do write my own rules!

I am helping others to do the same. This is my north star. Motherhood can be hard work. I see so many women trying to smile through it all while trying to do it all. I think what every parent can identify with is those moments when all is calm and your children are content in the space you've created for them. Seeing your children healthy, happy, and loved—that's also another area where you feel success and fulfillment. Over time, I've seen so many women start in this business who are now mothers living their lives with complete freedom. I tear up every time I think about it because all of these mothers have an opportunity that I didn't have with my own baby girl; they have the beautiful opportunity to be with their babies.

My story is a story of success in the way that the world measures it, and in the measurement of love. There is so much reward that comes in moments—moments measured in love: love for myself, love for my children, and love for every person on this planet who is meant to be impacted by my work and the legacy I'll leave.

By the way, I still do events for Tony Robbins. But now I do them because I want to do them, not because I have to do them.

What if it were all possible for you too? It *is*. It absolutely is.

"Measure your life in seasons of love..."

CHAPTER 15

Finding purpose

Ali Schneider

"When do you think you can get your stuff out?" my boss asks delicately. He knows I'm struggling with this transition.

"I'll do it," I tell him—the man I'm committing the rest of my life to.

Sitting at my desk, which is rightfully no longer mine, in an office that is also no longer mine, I know I have to get my belongings out. My heart feels like it is breaking and swelling with love at the same time. I don't even know how that is possible. My fiancé, Brandon, is tiptoeing around my feelings because he loves me, but he also needs me to get out of this office so his new assistant can move in. We have made the right decision. Even though I don't feel like I am ready to close the chapter on my coaching career, this is truly what I want. Brandon will continue to grow in his coaching career, and I get to marry the love of my life, have kids, and find a career that will allow me to be unapologetically present in their lives.

I am 28 years old and leaving a career that has only just started. I'm leaving a sport that has been a huge part of my identity since childhood. I should be feeling total excitement. Brandon and I made this decision together as a team so that we can get married and start a family. Raising kids the way we envision would be nearly impossible with two college coaches with the stress levels and schedules that come along with that would be nearly impossible to raise kids the way we would like to.

"Do you think you can get it out today?" Brandon asks. "Jory needs to get his stuff in here."

His voice is softer than usual, but there is also a sense of urgency about him. To an outsider, there is nothing special about this small corner office, which has no windows and shares one wall with the head track and field coach and another with the assistant men's basketball coach. There is definitely no quiet or privacy unless it's late at night. But to me, it represents so much. This is the space that I got to call my own when I got my first coaching job. The hard metal chair in front of me is the spot where our players come to sit throughout the day to talk about everything but basketball. The candy jar that I keep on the corner of my desk ensures they all stop in at least once a day. The candy jar was left by the coach before me, and I plan to leave it for the new coach moving in. I'm going to miss these relationships the most. I'm going to miss the daily interaction with our athletes on a personal level. I know I will still be part of it as the coach's wife, but that is such a different role and a new identity, one that I'm not sure how to embrace yet. Maybe once I'm Brandon's wife, it will feel like an easier transition.

"Yeah. I'll do it."

I can't stop the tears so I just shut the door. I have so many mixed emotions around this move that I'm struggling with how I feel. Boxes have been sitting behind my desk for over a week, and it's time I pack them up and move my things out of this office. As I begin putting the pictures of my family and friends into the boxes, I try to focus on the future—the excitement of marrying Brandon and starting our family. I am ready for my next journey. *Our* next journey. I'm ready to start a family and find a career that will allow me to be all the things I need to be as a wife and, hopefully, a mom. But right now, at this moment, as I close this delicately short chapter in my life, I am lost. I feel like I'm losing part of myself. Basketball has been my life and identity for so long. I know my identity is so much more than a sport, but I don't know where this next chapter will lead me. I don't know if I will ever find another career that brings me as much joy as coaching. I will miss this.

*

The energy in the event center is electric. There are 8,000 chairs set up, and everywhere I look I am greeted by smiles and hugs. People are nearly breaking down the doors to get in and get a seat, like at a rock concert with open seating. The music is loud and on point, almost forcing people to stay up and move their bodies. The flashing red, green, and purple lights illuminate big, decorative balls hanging from the ceiling. The clock on the big screen is counting down the minutes and seconds until the morning session of the international conference gets started. The itinerary says they will be kicking off the morning with new National Marketing Director speeches, and I am here for it. My kids are also here for it, because that's just how I roll right now. My husband is on the road recruiting, so my options were to bring the kids or not come. Like I said, I'm here for it, and so are they.

"Ladies and gentlemen, please welcome to the stage new National Marketing Director..."

Those words, arcing out over the busy room, stir up a sense of excitement, awe, and admiration. This is my favorite part. I love listening to the new National Marketing Directors share their stories. I have been part of the Juice Plus+ Company for a few years now and I love coming to conferences for this experience right here—listening to the success stories of everyone who has made it to the top position in the company. Hearing their stories wakes up the athlete in me. It makes me feel like I can do it. They have all been through their own struggles and prevailed.

When I gave up my career as a college basketball coach, I dipped my toes into everything health and fitness related. I started by teaching health classes at the university and quickly knew that was not for me. I moved on to managing a fitness center, offering personal training and teaching group fitness classes. I loved the work but had no control of my own time, and as soon as our first son was born, I knew once again that it was not for me.

The first day I took my son to daycare, I left feeling like I had been punched in the gut. As I carried my three-month-old baby through the doors of his classroom, I was immediately met by the amazing teacher's assistant, who already had her hands full with another child. She placed the other child in a baby swing and turned back to me with outstretched arms, to take Cash away from me for the first time. She graciously and patiently smiled and listened as I went through the list of his needs, likes, dislikes, eating schedule, sleeping habits, and last dirty diaper. When I couldn't think of anything else to say, it was time to leave. As I reluctantly walked out of the building and back to my car, I told myself that the tears slowly dripping down my cheeks were because of my hormones. Deep down, I knew that was not the case. Deep down, I knew that leaving my baby at daycare was not how I had envisioned my life. I think the Juice Plus+ company might be the answer to my prayers, but I haven't committed enough to find out.

Now, I stand on the sidelines against a wall, making sure the stroller tray stays full of snacks so that my boys will be quiet long enough for me to soak this part in. Cash just turned four years old and Cole is three. Every second they're occupied allows me to soak up each new story. Stories get me! These people figured out how to maximize this opportunity and have just made it happen. It's like winning a conference championship with a basketball team. Everyone on the team must be on the same page, going after the same goal with passion and purpose. I know how to do that.

One of my mentors, Doug, comes up next to me. "You know," he said, nodding at another of my mentors, Joy, "she has you pegged for the podium."

"I know." It's all I can respond because right now I want to hear these stories and not talk about my own struggles. At the same time, that's all I need to hear. I know that my sponsor believes in me more than anything. I know that she is holding a vision of me making it up to that stage. I know that she is probably not so patiently waiting on me to decide that I am ready to build this business. That's one of the greatest things about this business: people believe in you before you believe in yourself.

"Well," he replies, "you know you can only lead a horse to water." It's his way of telling me it's time for me to show up. And as much as I want to keep living my comfortable life, I know that he is right. It is my time. I can see it now. I can do this business with my kids. My husband is beyond supportive of anything I want to pursue. After winning a national championship a few years ago, he's killing it in the coaching world with his new job. With the grueling schedule of a college basketball coach, he is not around much to provide extra help or hands for support in that way, but his unwavering emotional support, belief, and encouragement for me to go after whatever I want provides me with the peace and confidence to know that I can do this for our family.

"So," Doug asks as Joy appears beside us, her hands full of beautiful flower arrangements, "are you ready to build this business?"

Joy has team members walking the stage with big promotions this morning, and she ALWAYS has the biggest smile on her face. She radiates light and energy as she cheers for every person who crosses the stage, always the first and last to lead the audience in clapping and cheering. As I watch her celebrate everyone's success, I feel a deep longing for more. For the first time since getting out of coaching, I feel fire igniting in my belly—that feeling before games of pure excitement mixed with a touch of nerves, a strong dose of confidence, and laser focus on the goal of winning.

I know the first step in building this business is to find some buddies to join me, to start putting my team together. I also know just the people I'm starting with. AJ isn't at the conference with me, so as soon as I get home and have a conversation with Brandon, she's first on my list. I know if Brandon and AJ are both on board, it will be game on.

★

"Mic her up. She's on in 10 minutes." The barked command comes from a small man backstage, who appears to be the one in charge of all the moving pieces.

The poor gentleman trying like hell to find a place on my stage-ready outfit to clip the microphone flinches. "I'm working on it," he murmurs.

"Just do whatever you need to get it clipped," I reassure him as he hesitantly feels around an outfit with no logical place to pin a mic or clip the receiver. I'm in my zone right now and don't need a microphone malfunction to break my focus. *Thunderstruck* by AC/DC blares from my air pods, blocking out all distractions backstage and raising my energy level to the ideal place for inspiring and holding the attention of approximately 10,000 passionate business partners, without being over the top, and at the same time leaving them with some education. "Seriously," I tell the audio guy. "Just unzip it and clip the mic to the inside of the waistline." My royal blue, open back, halter top jumpsuit might not have been the wisest choice when it comes to finding a place to clip a mic, but it's the perfect choice for the stage.

And then I hear, "Please help me welcome to the stage National Marketing Director, Ali Schneider!"

Being introduced as a National Marketing Director is something that I'm accustomed to now, but I'll never forget the day I got the call congratulating me on my promotion to the top position of our company. I had my three year old sitting on the counter in front of me, trying to wipe the avocado off his squishy face and hands, and my four year old was running circles around the kitchen counter, chasing the dog, and singing the Mickey Mouse Clubhouse theme song at the top of his lungs. He only has one volume and that is loud.

I saw the number from Collierville, TN, pop up on my phone, and I knew it was the call I had been waiting for since I joined the company. I knew that my business partner, my regional director, and my sponsor would all be on the other end of that call, and there was no way I was going to let some avocado and Mickey Mouse distract me from answering the phone. As I said hello, squeezing my phone between my ear and my shoulder, I had to laugh because this was how I had built my entire business: a baby on my hip, a phone to my ear, superhero masks on my face, hiding in closets to find quiet, snapping my fingers, setting goals with my family, and celebrating wins. My team and I did countless events—sometimes they were awesome, and sometimes nobody showed up. I took my kids on weeklong road trips to visit team members and do events in other states. All of it finally came together at the very moment of that dreamed-about phone call—a phone call that came six chaotic, blurry months after I left the conference that lit my fire.

It's amazing to think about how much life has changed in the two years since that call.

As the Regional Sales Director waits for me to meet him center stage, I take a deep breath. I feel like doing a handstand as I walk onto the stage, but I'm afraid I might have a wardrobe malfunction. Instead, I stick with a powerful walk and a hug for Jason as he hands me the clicker for my slides. I have 27 minutes to spend up on this stage in front of the loving, loyal crowd. No matter what I say, they will clap at the end. But I want to knock their socks off. It's my time to give back to this community all that has been poured into me over the past 11 years. It is my time. These are my people.

As the clock on the floor in front of the stage starts counting down, I settle into my best energy space and deliver the presentation that I was meant to share. I am here because I have worked my butt off to get to this point. I am here because I fought through the challenge of losing myself, and I am emerging as an even better version of me. I am here because I have an amazing team!

The clock hits 26:00 and my right hand, holding the clicker, stops shaking. Because of the spotlight, I can't see very far into the audience, but I *can* see my team and mentors sitting front and center. The main idea of the message I am delivering today is not to give up on people and not to take things personally. This business we're in is all about loving people and being willing to put ourselves on the line for someone else's benefit.

"We all have noise in our lives," I say, projecting from the stage. "Your prospects have noise in their lives. Always offer grace and understanding when following up with your people." The clock continues to tick down; time is racing by and I still have so much I want to say. I want everyone in this exhilarating exhibition hall to realize what a special community we have.

I knew they were going to go crazy at the end. They do it for everyone who takes the stage. In sports, the crowd will either be rooting for you or against you. A room filled with Juice Plus+ partners wants everyone to win!

I take a deep breath and soak this moment in. This is what it feels like to lose yourself, start all over, go through the struggles and successes, and end up on top.

CHAPTER 16

Holding the space for good, to turn to great

Dougie Barlow

1993/94

The lap on the 42-day liner service from North America to South America is just about complete. I feel a sense of great pride, having recently acquired my 1st Assistant Engineer's license with the US Coast Guard.

During the voyage back up north, we have to divert to Bermuda to offload a crew member who's having an alcohol-induced seizure. Although I should have expected it, I'm not prepared for the witch hunt that takes place as a result of this crew member's actions.

The chill of the night air is still evident in the predawn darkness as we tie up to the pier in the ship's home port of Jacksonville, FL. I'm completing my log entries from the last four hours of my watch when the bridge calls to let us know that we need to check in with the Port Captain. I walk into the Chief Engineer's office.

"Hey, Chief, what's up?"

He replies, "Stand by your room and the Port Captain will be by shortly to ask you a few questions."

I can hear the footsteps of the inspection party echoing in the passageway as they make their way towards my state room. I introduce myself as the 2nd Assistant Engineer. After a brief hello, the Port Captain asks, "Do you have any alcohol or illegal contraband in your state room?"

"No, sir!" I reply.

The Port Captain then asks, "Do you mind if we search your room?"

"I don't have anything that you're looking for," I answer, unsure what has prompted this search.

Ignoring my words, he and his assistant start opening and closing drawers on my desk.

"Are you calling me a liar?" I demand. "I told you I don't have anything in my room that's illegal."

He replies, "Well, we're going to take a look anyway!"

I can't believe I'm being treated this way. I feel humiliated. While they come up empty from their search, my pride and integrity are shattered. Is this really the courtesy I am to expect moving forward as a professional maritime engineering officer? Despite the attractive income for only having to work six–eight months of the year, I can no longer subject myself to this kind of humiliation in the work environment.

I've been working in the maritime industry for almost ten years, and I knew from the very beginning that I didn't want to grow old and lonely at sea. Sooner, rather than later, I want to find a loving partner and have a family. I just need a different plan that will allow me to maintain my lifestyle. But how? Where else am I going to make good money and have the free time that this job affords me when I'm on leave? And where can a man find an employment situation where he is acknowledged as an ethical and diligent worker?

I start to reflect.

This isn't the first time I've been forced to leave a job where I wasn't being recognized for my work ethic.

1985

After I graduated from the United State Merchant Marine Academy in 1983, the economy was such that shipping jobs were hard to come by. After biding my time in other exploits, I finally took a job, sailing below my license, as a day-working machinist aboard the SS Mobil *Syosset*. I signed onto the *Syosset* for a six-month stint, with the hope of being hired as a 3rd Assistant Engineer, but by month five, things weren't going exactly as planned.

While I had permission from the 1st Assistant Engineer to go ashore 15 minutes early, to manage a few affairs before the business day ended, I didn't expect to run into the Chief Engineer. He had gone ashore in Port Angeles, WA, to inform his wife that he would be home a few days earlier than expected. Apparently, she had replied, "Great, you'll be able to meet with me and my lawyer. I'm filing for divorce."

So, when I ran into him on the gangway, right after he had gotten this news from his wife, he looked at this watch, noting the time. I still remember his words.

"Pack your bags. You'll be on the beach before the ship sails later tonight."

I immediately went to the captain to plead my case, and he told me, "I can't really dispute the Chief Engineer's decision."

"But I didn't do anything wrong!" I pleaded, aware that my termination had nothing to do with my performance.

The captain ended the conversation with, "While I understand that there may be some injustice here, it's his department, and I don't want to rock the boat."

I packed my sea bag, said my goodbyes, and, with an air of frustration, went down the gangway before the ship weighed anchor and sailed on.

As I dejectedly walked down the gangway of the *Syosset*, I realized I needed to find a place to stay and sort out what my next life move would be. Who did I know that could help? I remembered back to the spring of 1983, when I was in NY, dating a gal who was studying at the Fashion Institute of Technology. My girlfriend's roommate's mother, Sue, was from Bainbridge Island, WA, and had been visiting her daughter in the Big Apple. Sue had treated all of us to a wonderful Broadway show. Before we all said our goodbyes after the show, Sue had extended an open invitation that had stuck in my mind.

"If any of you kids are ever near Bainbridge Island," she told us, "my house is basically empty, and you are more than welcome to visit."

Knowing that everything happens for a reason, her words would eventually lead me to my first shoreside engineering gig on Bainbridge Island.

My desperation after getting kicked off the *Syosset* in Port Angeles, WA, led me to then make a bunch of panicked phone calls that finally got me what I needed: Sue's number on Bainbridge Island. I nervously dialed the number, not exactly sure what I was going to say. The phone rang a few times and eventually a motherly voice picked up.

"Hello, Sue!" I said brightly. "I don't know if you remember me... I used to date your daughter's roommate back in NYC. Do you remember when you came to visit your daughter, and you took a bunch of us to a Broadway show and... any chance you remember me?"

"Um, well, yea... sort of."

In my nervous desperation, I forged ahead, saying, "You said if any of us were ever in the area we should give you a call and..."

After a few minutes of filling in the blanks and listening to my tale of woe, Sue hesitantly said, "Well, if it's just for a few days to get your bearings, I guess it would be okay."

I hung up the phone and let out the biggest sigh of relief!

It took me ten days to buy a car and get my trip back east sorted. During that time, Sue and her husband lent me a sports coat and a pair of slacks. They convinced me to interview with a neighbor of theirs, who was also a Kings Point graduate like me. Turns out that their friend had been a senior partner in a local engineering firm that did shipboard vibration analysis for the US Navy's aircraft carrier fleet. The interview went well, and while they didn't have a position for me, they said they really liked my resumè and wanted to offer me a position when they signed their next contract.

Fine with me, I thought, as I needed to go to my sister's wedding back in NY first anyway.

Before I could complete my road trip to western New York, the engineering firm called back, asking me if I could start three days before Christmas.

1988

I experienced three adventure-filled years, traveling the globe and honing my skills with this engineering firm. I had just returned as a lead engineer from a successful field job overseas and was walking into the office on a Monday morning when I was met by a mid-level managing engineer who said, "Don't get too comfy at your desk; your services will no longer be needed here."

I was flabbergasted. With the two main principals of the company away on vacation, I asked to speak with the junior partner of the company. He said sympathetically, "I understand how you feel, but there is nothing that I can do. All I can say is that I, too, was once too young, too smart, and didn't know when to keep my mouth shut!"

Was he talking about me? I was absolutely gutted.

What was the point of doing your job well? If I saw that things could be done more efficiently, and made a suggestion, was I going to be penalized for attempting to do right by the company? I was very confused and upset, with no idea of how to deal with the fact that I had been let go—for putting forth my best effort.

This was not exactly how I had envisioned my professional career as an engineer. I thought I could sail for ten years, see the world, put some serious money in the bank, and then sort out a career on the beach. Maybe I just wasn't meant to be an engineer?

I did enjoy the challenge of being an operating engineer and appreciated the accumulation of knowledge. But, at times, I wasn't sure that I had what it would take to be in charge.

Water has been a main feature of my entire life. I suppose it started knowing that my mother had been eight months pregnant with me and still sailing on the Niagara River. The engineering part came as a suggestion from my father, but I had been a willing participant. I knew myself to be a social creature, but shipboard life can be very isolating at times. And then there were those moments where I would get off watch, clean up, and go out on deck. The night air on the ocean would be thick with moisture as it caressed my naked skin. The endless horizon of the vast ocean at night. The magical illumination of bioluminescence in the wave-tossed surface of the ocean. No other signs of human existence except the low-frequency rumble of the ship as it plowed through the oceans of the earth. The personal experience of being so connected to source energy has oftentimes been overwhelming, and while I was romanced by the siren call of the sea, something just didn't feel right.

It was a very confusing time for me, as I wasn't really sure what I was supposed to be doing with my life. I enjoyed traveling the world by ship, making a good living wage, and having the free time for personal adventuring. But time away from loved ones, missed holidays and social gatherings, people not able to understand your constant comings and goings—I felt that my life was a Pandora's box of pros and cons that I was really starting to question. Maybe it was just me realizing that life has many twists and turns and that our job is to figure out where we fit in, knowing that there are an infinite number of possibilities for human potential and making a difference.

Back in 1993/94, reflecting on 1979

I have fond memories of being a kid, living at the beach on the Canadian shore of Lake Erie every summer with my parents and sister. When my father asked about post-high school plans, I said, "I'm not really that keen on university, Dad. All I really want to know is where those ships end up after they sail over the horizon."

My dad replied, "Well, son, I believe that you could find out where those ships go and continue your education at the same time!"

Since my father had only received a two-year degree before entering the employment world, he felt it was important for me to continue my education. My father was instrumental in assisting me with the process of applying to a few engineering schools. At the recommendation of a neighbor, I applied to the United States Naval Academy as well. The end result was that I had chosen to attend the US Merchant Marine Academy in Kings Point, NY.

While my father helped me with the next phase of my educational journey, for most of my youth, he had always been at work. My mom had managed my day-to-day affairs for all of my formative years. I remember her saying, "Well, if you really want to participate in ski racing, you are going to have to contribute 15% of the cost. Your father and I can't afford to pay for all of it!"

"How am I going to come up with that kind of money?"

My mom replied, "If you really want to ski badly enough, you can get creative and figure out ways to make money!"

While money appeared to be an issue during my youth, I later realized that it was just an ongoing commentary. The real takeaways from my mother's love and guidance had been developing values such as hard work, being polite, and being self-sufficient. These would serve me well for the next phase of my life—a life beyond being a shipboard engineer.

1994

It's been four months now, and my shoreside engineering job search has me frustrated and a wee bit depressed. Little reminders inspire me to continue my search, like words from a British-educated Egyptian pilot, who once asked me, "What's a guy like you doing in an industry like this? You're wasting your skills, living in subpar conditions here on this ship. You could be living a much higher quality of life and making a real difference in the world!"

I have never forgotten his words.

My biggest concern about leaving the shipboard engineering life is how I'm going to accommodate the current lifestyle that I so appreciate, earning a solid five-figure a month income and, more importantly, the free time to do as I choose and get the most out of what life has to offer. Choosing to change careers after such a lengthy period of investment can be a daunting task, and the anxiety increases with each rejection letter that comes my way.

And then I finally tune into the frequency of life that provides me with the solution that I've been looking for.

1994

My girlfriend and I receive a dinner invitation from a couple we enjoy spending time with. As the meal is winding down, our hosts mention a new concept in whole food plant-based nutrition that they had recently started eating.

The wife says, "As a climber, I know you only pack dehydrated meals. Do you also take fresh fruits and veggies with you? If you did, do you think you would have more energy?"

"It's really just about eating enough calories," I reply.

And then a fascinating conversation ensues. We take home a bright orange box of encapsulated fruit and vegetable powders that night. At 33 years of age, I already sense I will need to pay more attention to my lifestyle habits if I don't want to end up like the average man I see out there. No judgment—I just value my health and all the work that I have done over the years to maintain my well-being. I can't deny that it just makes a ton of sense to get more fruit and vegetable nutrition into my body in order to stay young and healthy.

That night I dream of George Jetson, the futuristic cartoon in which the characters had access to food in capsule form. I freak out—in a good way! I think to myself, "It's 1994, I'm six years ahead of the 21st century, and a friend who I trust has just shared fruit and veg powders in a capsule with me!"

After three nights of this recurring dream, I call my friend and ask, "Doesn't everybody need to eat more fruit and vegetables?"

It occurs to me at this moment that it's the one thing that every medical expert in the world could agree on—if their patients would eat more fruits and vegetables, their health outcomes would improve. I feel all this potential and absolutely no controversy about eating more plants.

I immediately begin thinking about the financial potential that an opportunity like this presents. Then I ask my friend, "If everybody needs more fruits and veg in their diets, could I make money by telling others about this 'amazing lifestyle hack', as you've shared with me?"

She replies, "I'm not really sure, but there is an upcoming event you can attend so that you can get all of your questions answered."

Though I am unable to attend the first couple of events, thankfully my friend keeps the invitations coming, and, eventually, I show up at a presentation. My friend, a biochemist, stands on the stage, speaking about these amazing plant powders. She's got one transparency with multicolored words like "vitamins, minerals, antioxidants, fiber" and so on, on the overhead projector, to highlight how a rainbow diet of fruits and vegetables is paramount to human health. She also shares an independent lab analysis that shows these micronutrients are present and active in the red and green encapsulated plant powders.

I could do that. I could share what she shared!

Then someone else speaks about the company's history, its leadership, and its successful track record as a product introduction company. The final speaker is an out-of-town expert. The guest speaker asks several questions that all feel so personal.

"Are you getting paid what you are worth?"

Absolutely NOT.

"Are you able to work on your own terms?"

Another defiant NO.

And for me, the most important question he asks is, "If you wanted to, you could put this business model into play and compress a lifetime's worth of work into a couple years' worth of effort?" He follows up with, "Now, I don't know about you, but how often does work get in the way of having a good time?"

My mind starts racing at the possibility of retiring by the time I'm 40, or at least creating a life designed on my own terms.

Then the speaker puts the final nail in the coffin for me.

"Do the math!" he says. "How many hours a week will you have to work at your J-O-B, for how many weeks of the year, and for how many more years till you have enough to retire?"

I sadly realize that my parents are still working into their late 70s out of necessity, and if I want to do better, I will need to find a way to work smarter, and not necessarily harder.

Little do I know that my introduction to fruits and vegetables in a capsule is about to change my life for the better, in more ways than I ever thought imaginable. I've always known that "dietary excellence" is a challenge that all humans face, and when I saw this simple solution, I knew it was going to be a game changer.

I immediately start taking action and asking lots of questions. I grab a spare door and put it on two sawhorses for a desk in a spare bedroom. I make a list of all the people I want to share my newfound life hack with. I set up my phone and my fax machine and realize that if I get up at 0600, I can contact people on the east coast. And then at 2200 hours, I could still call AK and HI. My friend and her husband become people who I speak with several times a day.

At first, I'm simply 'ignorance on fire', contacting the communities of people I became a part of over the last 20 years or so. But I have very little direct sales experience or networking skills other than my extroverted personality, a strong work ethic, and excitement to share this new found 'life hack'. So, when the opportunity to attend an event in Portland, OR, shows up, my friend's husband encourages us to make the investment and increase our belief, our confidence, our skills, and our vision of where this could take us.

My friend and sponsor in the business gives me the details for the upcoming training event in Portland. Neither of us drives a very nice car, so her husband recommends that we rent a nicer car to arrive fresh for the meeting in Portland and be able to get the most out of it. This is good advice, as it turns out.

I have never sat in on a meeting like this before. The inspiration, the education, and the systems shared by others who are having success with this business model are amazing. While we are at the event, everyone is talking about attending the upcoming national conference, which is going to cost valuable funds that I don't feel I can spend.

I wonder why I need to attend another training session after I just got so much out of this one. How can I keep growing my business if I'm spending time, money, and energy on attending yet another conference?

Hesitating, I ask my sponsor, "Are you going to go to New Orleans? Can't we just implement what we learned and be successful?"

Neither of us see the need, and we leave Portland with a much larger vision and belief in what we are taking on.

A few weeks later, my friend suddenly calls and says, "I've decided that I'm going to attend the upcoming extravaganza in New Orleans in three weeks' time."

I can feel the anxiety building as I don't really think it's necessary to attend since I'm still on a high from our time in Portland. And besides, my first commission check was only $37.84. I can't afford it.

My friend then says, "Well, you don't have to go, but if you don't, there is no way that you'll ever catch me in this business."

The FOMO I feel in that moment is intense.

"I'll think about it and get back to you."

She replies, "Okay, but don't wait too long. It's only a few weeks away."

Being new to the entrepreneurial mindset, I'm terrified at the prospect of spending money that I don't think I can spare, to keep investing in an opportunity that isn't really making any real money yet. Nonetheless, I do the homework from Portland, which is to set some immediate short-term goals and a few long-term goals. Since I made a promise to myself to not end up back on the ship, my immediate concerns are my mortgage, car payment, and food on the table. The reality is that I have money in the bank, but I am very uncomfortable with dipping into my savings as an investment in my future.

The choice to go full time into this business is not for everyone. I have nightmares about forgoing a 15-year investment of time and energy in an industry that I know, for something that sounds good but that I have no personal experience in. Having always been a wage earner, I have to learn to be accountable to myself. I have to take advantage of the knowledge of other people in the organization, and they are more than willing to validate my position. The learning curve relating to how to be one's own boss is challenging and, at times, overwhelming. The opportunity for constant and never-ending improvement is real.

With great trepidation, I finally tell my friend that I will be attending the New Orleans event. It's another important step in the process to making it big in an industry I know very little about.

As my knowledge and understanding of this newfound career path grows, so does the anxiety around my personal life. It's been about five months of reaching out, following up, and sorting out who my next team member is going to be.

Then my dad calls. He asks, "Is everything going okay?"

I cringe on the other end of the phone. "Yup, everything is fine."

But as I listen to myself lie, I can feel the stress and pressure of my unresolved issues rising dramatically. My safety valve of emotional inflammation is about to release. I burst into tears and list off a half a dozen concerns that I don't know how to resolve. I'll never forget this moment. The most endearing feature that my father possessed is to make everyone around him feel at ease. I also realize that I know very little about my father, since he worked long hours to support us and didn't share a lot of personal information about himself. I share my personal concerns about a few physical issues I have from abusing my knees over the years. A doctor even told me that I should either pull back from my adventures in the mountains or lessen the impact of working on the ship. I tell my father that I have a daughter I haven't told them about because I was afraid of the way my mom would react. And, finally, I share that I'm not sure that my abilities in the world of improving people's health by using food as medicine will allow me to fulfill my life's goals and dreams.

My dad provides me with invaluable insight into each of my concerns. He reminds me that my body wants to heal and just needs the proper resources and time. He understands my trepidation about revealing the fact that I have a daughter to my mom, and says, "While your mom can be a tough egg at times, I believe you will feel a lot better if you let her know of the situation and allow her to react in a positive manner."

And then he moves on to address my biggest fear, which is to allow myself the opportunity to succeed in this newfound venture that I'm also having so much fun with. Informed by his own challenges of having to figure out a forced career change in his mid-50s, my father says, "I can see the passion and enthusiasm you have for this venture. I mean, after all, I'm one of your first customers. Tell me, though, what is the worst thing that could happen if you invest your time, spend all of your money, and fail?"

The silence is deafening as I contemplate his question.

I slowly let the air out of my lungs and I quietly hear myself say, "I suppose that I could always go back to shipping and pick up where I left off."

In that instant, my dad gives me permission to put my best effort into my newfound passion.

Twenty-eight years later, I still hold that moment with my now-departed father dear to my heart, as the moment my journey really began. And that biochemist gal, who first shared this amazing life hack with me, has become my best friend and partner in life. Through life's twists and turns, we eventually married and raised three amazing daughters together. Of course, that is another book unto itself.

I am so grateful to all the people who willingly shared their experiences and knowledge for our benefit. It has allowed us to pay it forward for the next generation of leadership and those who feel called to make a difference, seeking the best that life and science has to offer.

CHAPTER 17

You have to give up something

Ilona Morrison

—⁓⁓•⁓⁓—

My stomach clenches as I hear the question, "How is your Wee Piggies franchise business going? Are you actually making any money with it?"

I am taken aback by the question. The heat of embarrassment floods my face as she asks, with complete sincerity, like any friend would. I am not good at keeping track of monthly expenses or revenue, but I do know I am not making much. My side hobby costs more in time and expenses than I make per month, but I keep trying anyway because there was a bigger mission I am trying to accomplish.

I want to be home with my kids; however, this is the most unappreciated job there is, and being home all day is mentally exhausting. They need my attention all day and sometimes even during the night. I glance at the clock, eagerly fantasizing 6:00 pm while I stir the spaghetti; unfortunately, it's only 5:00 pm. The countdown for my husband Jon to get home is on. My son is hanging off my leg, wanting to be picked up; this is when he gets tired, and I need to keep him up until dinner, which is not an easy task. I am so looking forward to some alone time in peace to gather myself.

But this was what I had signed up for, right?

I catch myself and refocus on my conversation with my lifetime friend Sarah.

"How are you doing health wise and with eating your fruits and veggies?" she asks.

I answer firmly and quickly, hoping she can't hear my bluff. "Pretty good! I eat lots of fruits and vegetables."

Even though most days I only eat whatever is left on the kids' plates, with a baby on my nipple and a toddler attached to my hip.

She continues to quiz me. "How are you feeling overall?"

I break, honesty flowing from my lips, vulnerability sweeping over me. "I am really constipated," I blurt out, "sick a few times a year, exhausted and napping every afternoon before picking up the kids with coffee in hand, not sure how I am going to make it through the day."

"Oh my gosh, I am so sorry to hear that," she says. "I think you should try this amazing Shred 10 program. Could be a great way to kickstart your health and give you back your energy. You already love and trust your kids on the fruit and veggie chewables; all we have to do is get the capsules and shakes for yourself and you are ready to start."

This is exactly what I have been looking for. I don't look at the research or watch any of the videos she graciously sends me. I trust her and value her opinion. I am ready to do whatever it takes to get my energy and self-confidence back.

"Let's do it," I say with confidence. "I'll get the capsules and shakes and start next week. I am so excited and ready to start feeling better."

"Loneski," Sarah says, "I think you should sign up and get a rebate back on all the products you use. It's only $52 per year, and you'll get that back and more just on this order alone." She's enthusiastic as she explains, hoping that this time the timing will be right and I will say yes. It's been four years since I ordered the kids the chewables, and she has been telling me about the business side of things since then, waiting for it to be the right time for me.

I consider it seriously before saying, "Okay, let's do it, just for the rebate."

She screams loudly into the phone. "Yes!! Awesome!"

She has been waiting for the day when I finally join her on this journey. Her Juice Plus+ business was growing in stolen moments while raising her three active boys. This supplemental income was really helping her to have the life of her dreams of being a present mom and taking as much time off as possible to spend with the kids. She takes several vacations per year, and her Juice Plus+ business allows her flexibility to take time off more often.

I want that. I need it. For me. For my family.

I love traveling and sharing experiences with my kids, but every time we go on vacation, I lose money with my Wee Piggies business. I still have to pay the monthly franchise fee, and when I don't see customers, I don't get paid. The number of customers that pile up while I am away and need to be booked in upon my return is overwhelming.

Sarah starts to paint a picture of what the Juice Plus+ business could do for me and how I could start earning some supplemental income instead of trading my time for money—how I could be my own boss, make my own flexible hours, create a better life and say Yes more often.

"Thanks for all that info, Sarah," I tell her, "but I am not interested in doing this as a business. I am so busy running the Wee Piggies business and with my job." In addition to my Wee Piggies business, I work part-time as a chiropractic office administrator. "I do not need, and cannot take on, a third job. I don't have any time as it is. All I want is to do is get a discount back on my products."

She understands and we go ahead with the sign up as I reassure her once I again that I am **never** doing this as a business.

Network marketing is something I have heard of, but it's definitely not something I want to be known to be a part of. I am actually not too sure what it is, only that my friends who are with other companies are self-motivated and self-driven. They get paid for how hard they work, don't have a boss, and make their own hours. Secretly, I envy them.

I, on the other hand, am someone who needs consistency in paychecks. The thought of not knowing what I'll be making month to month makes my stomach churn. Uncertainty is the fear that held me captive for years.

I am not feeling confident in my abilities to do much with this business, but when Sarah asks if I can think of other moms who could use some help with their health, I light up and start writing down names. Despite my reservations, it is so exciting; I am smiling ear to ear, imagining how much this program can help my friends without me feeling like I'm a sleazy salesperson.

I begin stepping out of my comfort zone. I share about Juice Plus+ on social media, getting over my fears of what people think of me and how they will judge me. I do everything exactly as Sarah tells me to do, with some hesitation and pushback, but I know and feel she wants this for me as much as I want it—maybe even more so.

Goals are not something I set, because I don't want to be disappointed if I don't hit them. It's easier to not bother and to avoid feeling like a failure. Feeling like a failure is not something I want to experience again. I sit with the mentality that I will just keep working, and if I hit the next rank I will, but if not, that's okay, too.

I rise in the ranks to Qualifying Sales Coordinator (QSC) and get my QSC bonus. I did it!!! I am so proud of this achievement, and I can feel the love from my upline Sarah. She is over the moon and so proud of me. She believes in me more than I believe in myself; she sees my strengths when all I see are my weaknesses. I get a handwritten card in the mail with a gift and am acknowledged on the team call as well as in the monthly newsletter. This is the best day ever!

QSC is just the beginning, and there are many levels above it. Maybe, I think, I can try for the next level. I can set this goal and hit it. Let's try for Sales Coordinator (SC)!

*

"You have to give up something!" My husband, Jon, is frustrated and finding it hard to support my Juice Plus+ business, which isn't going well.

The warm sun I was enjoying moments ago suddenly feels hot on the back of my neck, and little beads of sweat form, running down my back.

This 'meeting' I planned between us is squeezed in between his meetings and my lunch break. I've been nervously anticipating this for days, and the butterflies in the pit of my stomach are indicative of the tension I feel, wondering what he will say. It isn't normal for me to have a voice in our marriage, because he is amazing, capable, and I trust him. I feel so taken care of that I often lack the confidence to speak my mind.

Am I just worried that I won't get my way? Or am I truly afraid that he's right and things just aren't working in this business?

I grab my usual decaf coconut milk latte and a hot chocolate for him. The metal chair is hot on my bare legs, but it is a nice break from the chilly, air-conditioned office.

"I hear you and your frustration, but you know I have been working so much that I feel like I can't keep up and I'm drowning," I say. "I feel like I'm half-assing everything I do."

Being home with my now six year old and a nine year old, running the Wee Piggies business, and working at an office part time, plus doing Juice Plus+, has left my plate fuller than ever. I am being pulled in all directions, all at once, and feel too inadequate to complete anything.

I used to contribute financially, having money of my own, but since becoming a stay-at-home mom I lack that confidence of self-worth. I decided that my worth was determined by how busy I was since I could no longer financially contribute what I used to.

Jon goes to work every day to provide for us while I spend all of the money on the kids' necessities and groceries. This makes me feel more like a burden on him than a contributor, so I worked harder to show my appreciation.

Despite trying to sell my Wee Piggies home-based business, which we bought for $17,000, so I could be home with the kids, I know something else has to go until it sells. I am trading my time for money. The enjoyment I get out of sharing Juice Plus+ with the people I care about on my lunch break and in stolen moments outweighs the joy I get from working at an office and building someone else's business.

"Are you going to stop doing Juice Plus+?" he asks without hesitation.

His question makes my heart skip a beat. My throat feels like it is closing in; I can hardly get the words out. I sit up straight and muster up the words in a strong, convincing voice. "No, I am going to quit my office job."

He looks at me, dumbfounded. I can tell he is processing for a few seconds, not understanding why I would want to give up a stable income when my Juice Plus+ pay check was just barely covering the cost of our products. Financially, this doesn't make sense, but in my heart it does.

After a long deafening silence, he says, "Okay. Just make up the money you are letting go of at the office."

I am so happy to hear this and also a bit worried about how I am going to make this happen. I will get to work on my Juice Plus+ business; I don't want to face the alternative of possibly having to go back to another office job. I accept his challenge; I always work so much better under pressure.

Going to bed that night, I know in my heart this is the right move. I know it because I will soon be able to give the answer my son wants to his daily question: "Are you picking me up today after school?"

Andras asks me this daily, but like most days, it isn't happening today, either. His tiny arms hug me tight as I say goodbye and wish him a good day. "No buddy, not today," I answer, then bow my head down, my body tightening.

I walk away with heaviness in my heart, feeling like a failure as a parent because I won't be there to grab him and he will have to go to after-school care. I carry his sadness with me all day. The drive to work feels longer than usual. Although disappointment and dread fill my body, there is a glimmer of hope just a few more weeks away. I am determined to make this work.

I dread the goodbyes on the days they go to after-school care. But my son's tiny voice in my head pushes me to work harder at my Juice Plus+ business. Once I make up the money, I can quit my day job, and I am hoping soon that my home-based business will find a new owner as well.

Daycare days don't just mean not being home; it means a sink full of dirty dishes, clean dishes on the drying rack, bathrooms messy from getting ready, laundry piled up, a dog begging to be walked, and no dinner magically made. The kids need to be picked up at after-school care, and one of us needs to be there on time; it's usually me, as my job isn't as demanding. Not to mention the demand for attention and time from the kids once they are back home. Everyone is affected by this, and I know this rat race isn't for me. I need time, freedom. I need to be the mom I always wanted to be.

*

Pinching myself as I write this chapter after seven and a half years of ups and downs, the day of me sharing my story is so surreal. I have always wanted to write a book, and here I am doing just that. Never could I have imagined where these years would have taken me.

I am just finishing another live stream on Facebook, followed by recording a video that I can use for reels and TikTok later. My creative juices are flowing as I am batch creating content, swapping outfits, and really finding my voice in the world.

Speaking on camera to my followers is such an incredible feeling and so freeing. These people are interested in what I have to say and in what I do daily. Here I am, making my mark on the world.

It's definitely not always glamorous. I sit here with no makeup on and hair in a bun. I share the importance of practicing gratitude in one of my lives on Facebook, not worrying about being judged, because I know they are relating to me being natural. Gratitude is what helps me see the good in every situation in my life, even if things aren't going the way I planned.

Speaking of going off plan, it was a beautiful day in the Okanagan when I decided to veer off track yet again, this time for something fun to add to my wish list of dreams.

"Zsofi, you wanna go test drive vehicles again?" I ask with excitement in my voice.

Zsofi eagerly decides to join me for a little mother–daughter bonding I always have time for. I test drive SUV after SUV. None of them impress me. As we browse through the vehicles outside, soaking up the sunshine, a white, fully loaded 2019 Jeep Wrangler catches my attention. I feel a spark of excitement. Zsofi keeps harassing me to test-drive a Jeep, but I thought I was more of a luxury SUV kind of girl, until I lay eyes on this beauty of a vehicle.

It has heated black leather seats, black rims, a rocking sound system, and even Bluetooth, which beats the CD player in my minivan.

"How was it?" my friend Jayson eagerly asks after my return.

Stepping down out of the Jeep with the biggest smile on my face, hardly containing my excitement, I answer, "OMG, it was amazing!"

"This is it. This is your vehicle," he responds without missing a beat.

But here I am already allowing my inner critic to speak for me, talking myself out of buying the Jeep and coming up with every reason in the book as to why I don't need a new car. As I ramble off my weak excuses, my daughter comes up with solutions for all the objections I throw at her. Eventually, she looks right into my eyes, holds me close and affirms me.

"Mom, don't settle for a less expensive vehicle that you don't love," she says firmly. "Get something you will love to drive. You work hard and you deserve a new vehicle."

When did my little girl become so wise and well spoken?

My eyes start to fill with tears; I'm so grateful to have her with me to experience this breakthrough together, so proud of her, and I know she is right. I am worthy and I do deserve this. We head off to make the decision—this Jeep is for me!

Eagerly cleaning out my minivan, I decide to share this moment with my Facebook followers and friends. I push the live button, and as I get the few first words out, I burst into tears. I don't know why I'm so emotional. It's an old, dirty, scratched up minivan I'm getting rid of.

I ramble on about how long I have had my minivan for 12 years, and then it hits me—this isn't about the minivan. This is starting a new chapter in my life, our life.

As the end of the month approaches, my kids ask, as they do every month: "Mommy, how close are you to hitting National Marketing Director (NMD)?"

I love that they are watching me and are interested in seeing how my business is doing. I answer them honestly, but with no guilt or self-judgment because I know they hold the vision with me and are my guiding stars to my dreams.

"Not there yet, but I am getting closer," I say with a smile.

It gets hard, hearing the same thing repeated month after month. Their enthusiasm, encouragement to keep going, and cheering me on are all that motivate me some days when I see my team's overall volume dropping. I stay positive, as I know that just as quickly as it's dropping, it will also go back up. Now is the time to hold that vision, keeping it crystal clear and allowing it to guide me and my team.

Giving up is not an option. I have come to terms with the fact that NMD will come when I am ready for it and when it's supposed to be mine! I am focused on my goals and work towards it daily without feeling like a failure. Let's be honest—building a business, changing lives, and creating a legacy is not an easy uphill battle. I am enjoying the journey, driving in my Jeep, my Juice Plus+ business, and showing my kids that I am never giving up on my dreams.

I do this for them, I do this for me, and I do this for our amazing community. Dreaming has become my reality thanks to Juice Plus+.

CHAPTER 18

Radka Prusha

1985

I am on a plane from Prague to Cuba. A breathtaking sunrise welcomes me to Canada—a new life in a free country ahead of me. I am both excited and scared. My mind is spinning. Will I see my beautiful Mom again? What about my sister and her family? Will I ever swim in Lake Lipno again and stay in our family's extraordinary lake house?

Radka, you will be fine. Be strong and courageous. You have to get out. You have to do this; the communist regime is killing you. This is your only chance.

I am trying not to pay attention to two men, obviously secret police, watching me and my then-husband, Vladimir, very closely. We are trying to be calm, relaxed, and pretend to be looking forward to a dream vacation in tropical Cuba. We play the part, as our luggage is filled with summer clothes, snorkeling gear, and flip-flops. We had heard from others that one route of escaping communist Czech Republic was to book a flight to the allowed country of Cuba, knowing that the plane refuels in Montreal and passengers have to disembark. The only money we have is 100 dollars in our shoes.

We are now landing in Montreal. The plane is refueling, making our escape possible. Now is our moment! My heart is racing; my hands are sweating. We are doing it. As we walk through an empty corridor, leaving secret police behind us, an airport employee in uniform greets us. We grab her hand and ask her to protect us. We are escaping a communist country, and we tell her we are seeking asylum.

Her smile melts my worries. She puts her arms around our shoulders and walks us to the refugee office.

My head is spinning. My heart is in my throat. Vladimir is doing all the talking. The only thing I see is a TV playing an ad for Toyota where people are jumping out with glee, exclaiming *Toyota!* This is the happy, freeing feeling I am experiencing. Welcome to Canada! Welcome to freedom!

Everyone in my Czech family is, or was, a scientist. My incredible scientist dad, a brilliant innovator, died of cancer when I was 23. He was only 60. This makes me determined to work in cancer research and to try to be part of a team that will find the 'magic bullet,' if that exists. With divine intervention and my own determination, I end up at McGill University, in Montreal, working in the breast cancer and bone marrow transplant clinic as a research assistant.

1988, Montreal

McGill University is an English-speaking university, a foreign language to me. I am thrown into a new language and I have to learn English as fast as possible. Nights in the classroom learning English and in the library reading papers. I feel unstoppable. I hardly see my beautiful baby, Eva. She is my big reason for persevering. I want her to be proud of me, just as I am of my incredible parents.

I learn much about human strength, courage, hope, and suffering at the clinic. With everything that I have witnessed, I realize that there is a lot that I do not know or understand about cancer. Why do some people get it? Why do some survive? Why do some die? Is it as random as it seems, or are there avenues for prevention? I am determined to answer these questions. I start taking courses in immunology, virology, and environmental science while at McGill.

In my lab, I grow human cells in petri dishes, both stem cells and cancer cells that have been harvested from the patient's marrow in order to better understand the cancer cell's sensitivity to chemotherapy. This means that I have to give the cells nutrients, proper temperature, and CO_2. The goal is to keep the stem cells alive and kill off the cancer cells in order for that particular patient to survive autologous bone marrow transplant after their chemotherapy ends. What I find astonishing is how resilient the cancer cells are compared to the stem cells. This marks my eureka moment and transition from disease research to focusing more on prevention and wellness as the path forward.

While working at McGill University, I meet my current husband, Paul. He is a highly talented artist studying comparative religion, mathematics, and fine art at Concordia University. When our son, Lukas, is one year old, we pack our car, in the middle of the cold east coast winter, and drive to the west coast of Canada.

1996, Salt Spring Island, British Columbia

I love working at the cute naturopathic clinic. I love the smell of herbs, tinctures, and Weleda products. I love the people I work with. I learn that our body can heal itself if we give it what it needs. This is something I never heard discussed while working at McGill Cancer Research. I find it fascinating to learn about homeopathy, hydrotherapy, ozone therapy, and so much more. I strive to know more about the power that nutrition and lifestyle have on human health.

While working in the naturopathic clinic, I hear of an upcoming lecture by Dr. Jeffrey Bland, PhD, about the science of epigenetics. He is known as the "father of functional medicine", and I know I have to go. I find myself in a room filled with healthcare professionals who, like me, are hungry to learn more about the science of epigenetics. I am enthralled by the presentation; the words of Dr. Jeffrey Bland strike a chord with me. He says, "Your genes are not your destiny. They are the canvas. Your lifestyle and behaviors are the paint and design. The whole of the painting is the art of your life."

Fascinating! Could this be what I was looking for all those years ago in the labs at McGill?

I want to know more and decide to sign up for the Master of Nutrition program. Driven by the same desire to be successful in my children's' eyes, I am again determined to learn, grow, and serve as a healthcare professional with a Canadian diploma.

Unfortunately, the situation at the clinic changes. I am feeling overworked, constantly tired, and not fulfilled by my work. Also, my boss feels threatened by me gaining more knowledge in the field of nutrition. With full support from my family, I quit.

Now I am a stay-at-home mom with my beautiful kids, supported by my husband, studying nutrition, and taking public speaking classes at the University of Victoria. I begin to pursue my dream of opening my own nutritional practice, be a public speaker, and be my own boss. To do what I love, have autonomy, and serve others.

2000, Victoria, British Columbia.

I am with my seven year old son Lukas in the pediatrician's office. He has dark circles under his eyes and is trying not to cough. In my mind, I am questioning, *Why are we here? What am I expecting?* The pediatrician's verdict is that Lukas has pre-asthmatic condition, and the only recommendation that I receive is to get him an inhaler. The doctor places the puffer in front of Lukas' face, making him cry.

I am furious. Why is he not addressing possible allergies and food sensitivities that might be causing these symptoms? Is the only answer drugs? I know too much about the potential side effects. And I promised Lukas beforehand that we would not use drugs. I am trembling inside and trying to control my disappointment and anger.

I say, "Thank you, but that's not what we're going to do." The doctor is furious.

We steam out of the clinic, and all the eyes in the waiting room follow us. What a scene! As we drive home, Lukas is still sobbing. I look at him and try to comfort him. "Lukas, we will find a solution. You will be well again."

But my mind is wondering, what am I going to do? He can't stand the noise in the gym because his upper respiratory system is inflamed and every little noise irritates him. I tried everything I learned over the years, from an elimination diet (no gluten, no dairy, no sweets, no artificial coloring), to many different supplements, B12 shots, hydrotherapy, homeopathy, and, much to his dismay, no Halloween treats. That didn't make me a very popular mother. But none of these things made a lasting change. My heart is sinking.

That evening, while praying with my husband about this situation, I suddenly remember the colorful brochure a patient on Salt Spring Island gave me a year ago—a straightforward concept of fruits and vegetables in a capsule. I call my friend out of desperation. "Hey, Frances, are you still using the fruits and veggie capsules?"

She replies, "Oh yes, I'll never be without them."

The scientist in me asks, "Do they have any clinical studies?"

"Yes! Studies show that adding Juice Plus+ capsules to your diet can have a positive impact on a variety of health related areas, including cardiovascular wellness, immune function, DNA protection, and many others."

Bingo! This is what I need for Lukey! The following day, I jump in the car and drive to Frances' house. I ask her for some to give to Lukas today and place my order for my own box of Juice Plus+. On the way home, I pray these capsules would be the catalyst to help Lukas.

Within two months, I'm signing him up to karate classes! Soon after, he gets very good at gymnastics and soccer.

Fast forward 22 years, and Lukas is now living in Vancouver, working as a talented software engineer, and loves to scuba dive, bike, and go rock climbing. He never stopped taking his Juice Plus+.

Can colleagues be best friends?

It is June 2001, and I am falling in love with the Juice Plus+ Company, its people, and the products. I am in a packed conference room at the stunning Tigh Na Mara Seaside Resort on beautiful Vancouver Island with my friend Fiona, my very first business partner in my new adventure as a representative with the company, Juice Plus+ Global. Looking around, I see happy, friendly, and excited people. Everybody is so lovely to me, and they congratulate me on deciding to become a partner with the company. I am now part of a healthy, vibrant Juice Plus+ family, striving for the coveted network marketing professional designation.

I have never, in my past professions, been around colleagues who actually want me to succeed. Honestly, at first, I thought, *Why are they so nice to me? What do they want from me? This seems too good to be true.*

Anybody that presents on-stage at these events is super successful. I meet Dr. Mitra Ray, PhD, for the first time. Her brilliant presentation on the science of Juice Plus+ is fascinating. I am more than impressed by what is going into the manufacturing of Juice Plus+, the research, and the academic caliber of training.

In my mind, I think: *I am not an entrepreneur. I hate selling, but I love the product and I want to share it with the world. Remember that girl who got on the plane to escape communism. No challenge is too big. You can do this!*

I feel inspired, and the spark is catching—I'm ready to share my passion for wellness and entrepreneurial freedom.

October 2002

I am with my beautiful daughter Eva at the epic Peabody Hotel in Memphis, attending my first International Juice Plus+ Conference. This year's theme is 'The Science of Juice Plus+'. I am awestruck at the academic level of the scientists who are researching Juice Plus+. When Dr. Lovell A. Jones enters the stage, tears start to roll down my cheeks. My scientist hero is here! And he is conducting research on fruits and vegetables in a capsule and protein shake. I know him from many brilliant studies on breast cancer. Now, he is on stage in front of me, describing the randomized parallel-group dietary study for stages II–IV ovarian cancer survivors at MD Anderson Research Center; the study was published in 2011 in the *Journal of Gynecological Oncology*.

Also at the same conference, I listen to powerful and inspiring National Marketing Directors' stories. With my eyes closed, and with the inspiration I've been witnessing, my mind wanders and I see myself on the stage, courageously sharing my story too.

A few years later...

I am one of the speakers at the West Coast Women's Show in Nanaimo, British Columbia. I present on one of my favorite topics, a presentation called "Thyroid Self-Care". Afterwards, our Juice Plus+ booth ends up packed with curious folks. It is during this time that I meet Roxanne P. for the first time. Meeting her is one of the critical moments in my business. She ends up becoming my Gemini soul sister.

Four months later...

I am back in Nanaimo, BC, in a bright, beautiful room at their new conference center. I am a host for a health education presentation with Dr. Frank Englesson, a prestigious dentist from Texas. Guests are entering the room. Suddenly I see my dear customer, Kate, at the door. *Is this the same Kate I met four months ago at the West Coast Women Show? I hardly recognize her! I see her transformation. I realize that on my quest for wellness and health, I have found that Juice Plus+ can be a catalyst to propel people into pursuing healthier lives.* Her skin is glowing, her hair looks so healthy, and her smile is radiant. What a difference! Later on, Kate and I spend the evening together at an all-friends event she organizes where ten new customers sign up on the spot. We're both so excited!

The same show, a few years later...

The West Coast Women's Show in March 2012 is a turning point in my business. I introduce the Tower Garden, a growing aeroponic system that our company brought onto the market this year. I am doing a PowerPoint presentation and everyone is asking where the Tower Garden is. "It's coming to Canada in one month," I say. I am thrilled to see the incredible, vibrant, and always-smiling Roxanne S. enter the room. I know she is a fantastic gardener, and my mind is spinning. *I would love to have you on my team, girl.* For the past seven years, I have broached the subject of her working with Juice Plus+, but I always get the same answer: "I am trying something else right now."

One week later, my phone rings. "Hi, this is Roxanne. I would love to get a Tower Garden." My heart does a backflip and I follow it up with a happy dance. My song was, fittingly, *Happy* by Pharrell. I've since learned it's an uplifting song on any day!

Later that year...

It is a warm June evening and the room at Tigh Na Mara is packed with guests. Handsome triathlete Dr. David Phillips, is our healthcare professional presenter. One of my guests, Roxanne S., introduces me to her friend Megan. Another gorgeous lady, but I can't help but notice that her complexion is so gray.

One week later, the three of us are sitting on Megan's deck at her breathtaking coastal resort. The ocean is blue, glittering in the sunlight, eagles gliding above our heads, and I feel I am in west coast heaven. Megan is a very busy owner of the resort and a natural entrepreneur. She loves people, being healthy and vibrant, and having fun serving others. Juice Plus+ is a perfect fit for her wellness goals.

Two months later, we host our first ever Wine and Wellness event on her deck—the first of many to come. I watch Megan share her recent health transitions with others and how she is taking control of her own health; part of this change is taking Juice Plus+. My heart is singing, *Look at her! She looks so healthy, her skin is glowing, and her gorgeous curly hair is shining.*

I love my 'job' and helping people gain more control over their health, many of whom I am privileged to call my best friends. And because we are all a team, I get the double bonus of working with them, too. I think back to the lab at McGill, or even the naturopathy clinic on Salt Spring Island, and just how different this working experience is compared to those places.

Family life meets business life, and it works!

In 2005, Lukas, who is now 12 years old, and I are on our way to Whitehorse, Yukon. We are flying above an endless chain of coastal mountains covered with bright white glaciers. What breathtaking beauty and wilderness. My friend has invited me to do a health education seminar introducing Juice Plus+ at a sports complex. I love that my business allows me to mix family adventures and share my passion for health and wellness with others. I am interviewed at a local radio station, and I feel Lukas is very proud of me.

On the evening of the presentation, Lukas greets guests at the door. I can't believe how charming, chatty, and handsome my son is. Later that night, he tells me, "Mom, great job. I am very proud of you for what you do."

This trip is a turning point in our relationship. We are both Gemini, and we used to disagree about almost everything. During this trip, we both gain respect and appreciation for each other. Now, he is singing Czech songs with me to scare grizzly bears as we mountain bike through remote mountain trails.

Sometimes it takes a village to make a son proud of his mother. Sometimes it takes a journey to create a mother even more proud of her son.

In 2010, I find myself at the spring conference and I reach QNMD, the second highest position in the company. I take the bonus that I receive to make our dream of going to Hawaii a reality. I call my husband. "Paul, can you book tickets? We are going!"

While in Hawaii, bubbles from my son's diving gear appear in front of my snorkeling goggles. Lukas is putting in diving hours to earn his dive master certification; this is my boy who had difficulty breathing when he was seven. My heart is so full. We will never forget the ten days in paradise we spent with all the young, adventurous divers. My vision board picture of me snorkeling and swimming with turtles is now a sweet reality.

My mom Mila has been a big fan of Juice Plus+ from day one. She is a brilliant microbiologist and gets the concept right way. She is my cheerleader and supporter. Every time I visit, at least once a year, I bring her Juice Plus+ as it is not yet in the Czech Republic. I pray that one day that will happen, and it does in 2022. I am blessed that I don't have to ask my boss if I can go see her when I need to.

My mom was 91 when she peacefully passed away. She was a family rock, always getting everybody together, arranging trips, and opening doors for my kids. We all have many extraordinary memories with her here in Canada and the Czech Republic.

It's 2013 and my dream to get to NMD has come true.

Everything happened so fast for me. At the beginning of April, I achieved my goal and received a promotion to the highest leadership level, national marketing director. In a whirlwind of events, I've received an invitation for our elite 39 club company retreat. Quickly changing my flight, in a few days I find myself at the gorgeous resort at stunning Huntington Beach, California. While I should be feeling on top of the world, I find myself hesitating. I feel out of place and intimidated by fearless leaders who have known each other for years. I want to be with my special team, but they are not here with me.

As usual, my escape is nature; the blue ocean with endless sandy beaches is where I find my peace.

At the resort, I rent a cute blue hippie bicycle. I pack the front basket with a picnic, towel, bikini, and print-out of my NMD speech, which I will share in a few days in front of thousands of people on the main stage. I can't concentrate on anything else. *No time for celebration for me yet. I have to first survive that stage.*

A long bike ride around the roaring ocean calms me down. Swimming in big waves gives me back my confidence. I am strong and courageous; I can do this.

No one is around me; it's just me, the ocean, the beach, and my speech. I am in my zone, lying on my towel in a bikini with no sunscreen! Hey, who needs sunscreen in April? I'm a Canadian west coast girl. The ocean breeze is cooling my slowly burning skin. It's time to head back to the hotel.

In my beautiful ocean-view room, I look in the mirror and I look like a lobster. I am taking a cold shower. I realize I overstayed my welcome in the sun. But I thought I would be just fine. As I put on my dinner dress and swallow tons of Juice Plus+ capsules, my gut tells me I'll be paying for my stupidity very soon. Probably that sunscreen would have been a good idea.

I have a multi-course dinner with California pairing wines that my sponsors organized. After a beautiful sip of red wine, I feel as if my body is on fire inside out.

Excusing myself, I run into the resort store and grab aspirin and the last bottle of aloe.

Back in my room, I try to relieve the burning pain in the cold bathtub and eventually fall asleep on the bed with a soaked bathrobe on me.

The next day I am finally with my fantastic team—Roxanne P., Megan, Roxanne S., and Robyn. They take a look at me and immediately move into nurse mode. They soak me in the bathtub with tea bags, ice, and bags of oatmeal, slapping me from head to toe with the lotion.

At the Canadian reception, everyone hugs and congratulates me. Oh, what a celebration! Yes, we are the Juice Plus+ family. But the hugs are a little bit intense. I have tears in my eyes, not from emotions, but from pain. I feel blood on my beautiful black dress as my skin cracks. The fear of having to speak is replaced by pain from third degree burns. If I survive this, I can survive anything!

And you know what? My speech is a hit anyway.

2017

We are empty nesters, camping with our one year old black lab Ruby Roo on the pristine lake on remote Quadra Island. One night Paul asks, "What about we go to the Czech Republic for Christmas and stay for three months? We can both work remotely. We can be global digital nomads."

There are a lot of Evas in my family, and my sister is one of them. I call her and ask "Hey Eva, what do you think if we came with Ruby Roo for three months?"

She answers, "That would be superb!" I love my sister's sense of adventure.

While preparing for this trip, I spend a lot of time figuring out how to travel internationally with a dog; I could write an entire book about it now. Finally, we are all together around the Christmas tree singing carols. I had no idea it would be the last time I would be cross-country skiing and skating on the frozen Lipno lake at our beautiful family lake house, with my sister. Two years later, on March 11, 2020, she lost her battle with pancreatic cancer. On the same day, the WHO declared the COVID-19 pandemic and the whole world shut down. I am very grateful I was able to spend three incredible months with her.

Present day

It is a warm summer morning, and I'm on the patio of our beautiful heritage dream home on Vancouver Island.

The sunshine is shining on my yoga mat. The water in the swimming pool is blue and I am jumping in. The sweet fragrance from flowers is in the air. My eyes are kissing all the colors and admiring nature's beauty.

Fresh raspberries from our garden melt in my mouth as I take a few steps into my office. Our resident hummingbird is drinking from the flowers on our patio Tower Gardens.

I take a deep breath; my heart is filled with joy, gratitude, and love.

Yes, this is where I was dreaming of being when I arrived in this country with 100 dollars in my shoe.

CHAPTER 19

Nicole Scott

"I am not interested, Mom!" I yelled through the phone.

Why does she keep pushing her snake oil pills on me when I've already told her NO for months? Plus, it's a network marketing company, and she knows I would never dare join after watching her fail in six different NWMs. No, thank you!!

She didn't get it. I was a nutritionist and already ate well. I didn't need her fruit and veggie pills. I ate my fruit and veg; I knew better!

Although I was sure I didn't need help with my diet, my reaction came from deep within. I could feel a lump in my throat, and the tension behind my eyes threatening that tears were about to break through. *Strong girls don't cry. Suck it up.* My trembling voice betrayed me and the tears started to flow. "Mom, I feel so lost. I am dealing with another breast infection, the baby is hungry, the house is a mess, and Ella is screaming in pain with another ear infection..." The cordless phone pressed to my ear, I paced along the cold hardwood floor in the living room, nursing Sydney and keeping an eye on Ella as she sat on the couch, gazing at the TV. "Mom, I am exhausted." I never thought motherhood would be so hard. "I miss you, Mom. I wish you lived closer, so you could help me."

I knew she had no idea how I'd been feeling and what I'd been going through. But now the dam wall was broken, and there was no stopping me.

I cried, "I need you. I have no energy to be a mom anymore. How did you ever survive raising four kids as a single mom?"

Mom listened quietly as I continued. "I miss my work, my friends, my old life. I dream of getting out of the house, blasting music in the car on the way to work. I miss my freedom and having my own money. I miss dressing up and feeling confident." I said all this as I stared at my reflection in the window, noticing my stained, worn-out pajamas and realizing I also really needed a shower. "I feel trapped and I find it hard to breathe. Will it get better, Mom?"

*

"Mommy, mommy, mommy!" Ella screamed in the middle of the night.

I winced. *Dear God, please not another ear infection.*

This would be the fifth ear infection in months, entailing more antibiotics and sleepless nights, and requiring more patience than I had. *Enough is enough.*

Off we went for another trip to the pediatrician for more drugs. There has to be a better way. *This can't be normal.* My mommy intuition and a friend's referral desperately led me to a local naturopath doctor for a second opinion.

This is going to be a waste of my time and just an expensive appointment, I thought as I sat impatiently in the waiting room, trying to entertain a nine month old Ella in her car seat.

Finally, the ND turned to address my nervous anticipation after all the tests. "Ella has approximately 75 food and environmental allergies, which are caused by a leaky gut, and she is immune compromised."

"What?" I gasped. "75—are you kidding me?"

My body felt heavy, my heart was pounding, and the room got hot all of a sudden. I felt sick to my stomach and just wanted to cry. What had I done wrong? "Why didn't our family pediatrician catch this? What the heck is a leaky gut? Immune compromised? Really? Is that even a thing? Can we fix her? Will she ever get better? What does all this even mean?"

I felt my head spinning out of control; I could barely catch my breath. Panic started to set in. I was angry and wanted answers.

What happened to her body? What could I have done differently?

Mommy guilt was sinking in fast. I blamed myself for her state of health.

With baby number two coming in less than seven months, I needed to find answers—I could not handle another sick child.

Reluctantly, I snuck back to my corporate sales job in the food industry for six months, right after we received Ella's diagnosis, so I could secure another year of maternity leave.

"You did what?!" my shocked husband said when I told him I'd registered for a 12-week night course to learn more about nutrition and cooking healthy food for our family. "How can you possibly add one more thing to your plate? You're uncomfortably pregnant, you're working full time, you have a big commute, we have baby Ella, and you're completely exhausted."

Secretly, I knew he was right, but I was a mom on a mission...

I was now cooking scratch meals and eating very clean and healthy. We were making some progress with Ella's health, but we stood out among our friends and family.

"I just want to fit in," I said to my husband. "Why does this have to be so hard? Why can't she just eat the damn birthday cake and candy like all the other kids? I feel so bad for her."

Ella, put those candies down; you can't have them.

Over and over again I said the same things, like a broken record, and felt like such a bad mom. I wanted her to feel normal like the other kids.

Why does eating differently feel so uncomfortable?

I really cared what people thought. I did not want to stand out. I did not like all the extra attention and the questions. Over the years, the struggle was real. I was juggling two babies and a new way of feeding my family. I was exhausted but highly committed to helping Ella become healthy again.

"You signed up for a two-year nutrition school program on your second maternity leave?" My husband gave a resigned sigh. "I'll support you if you really want this, but it will be a lot of work. Are you sure you're ready?"

At home, on my knees with my hands in prayer position, I looked up and asked God...

Why me?

Why Ella?

Why this hard life?

Please, guide me on what I need to do next...

"My mom is coming, my mom is coming!" I shouted out loud. She was arriving within a week to help us and attend my graduation from nutrition school. Yippee!

Prayers answered... *Thank you, God.*

All I could think of was the extra sleep, helping hands for the kids, and all the home-cooked meals she would make for our family. I could already taste her hearty chicken noodle soup hitting my lips and nourishing my deficient, tired body.

The babysitter arrived and we headed to my grad.

They called my name and I anxiously went on stage, reached out with my hands trembling, and accepted my two-year nutrition diploma with honors.

Now what?

What will my future hold?

Will I ever make a corporate salary again?

Will people actually pay me for my nutrition advice? Me?

Can I make this work? How do I make this work? Or will I have to go back to my corporate grind?

I am scared!

*

As I sat peacefully nursing Sydney on the couch in the basement, I watched my mom sneak the DVD in the player. *Really, Mom?* I gave her a big eye roll. I knew this was going to be a Juice Plus+ pitch again; she was determined. My sneaky mom was getting me to watch a sales pitch while breastfeeding.

I only half-watched it, ready to unleash my criticism, but no words came as I became engrossed in the video. I was impressed by the famous Dr. Sears reviewing the research and hearing the stories of the impact Juice Plus+ had on children. It took me by surprise, and I gave myself permission to wonder—could this be the answer to my prayers to help Ella's health?

*

My heart racing and self-doubt flooding my brain, there I was, sitting in the boardroom of the Canadian Juice Plus+ office with my mom, signing the franchise partner agreement together.

Nicole, what are you doing? You promised yourself you would never sign up with one of those companies.

I was 100% skeptical about network marketing but really curious about the product and what it might do for our family.

Without my mom knowing, I called my best friend Anita, who was a holistic nutritionist, to test my daughters and me through live blood analysis before we added the Juice Plus+ capsules to our day.

We were back in Anita's office four months later, waiting anxiously to see the results. Secretly, I wanted her to tell me this was a waste of my money, but that was not the case. My mom was right.

"OMG, Nicole, check out your results," she said excitedly. "Everything is improving, including Ella's immune markers. This is great news. How are you feeling?"

I told her I had more energy. I had let my healthy lifestyle slip over the years, so now that I had that back, and had added the extra nutritional support, I was staying up longer, running again, and the kids had fewer sick days. I was starting to feel like myself again and had hope for the first time in a long time.

Anita was so impressed she signed up as my first franchise partner, and my new business was born.

Where would it go? I had no idea.

All I knew was that I wanted to help my friend Anita WIN in this business, so I was open to learning how to build our franchise.

*

I was starting to *win* in my NWM business, but I knew it was not enough to keep me home. I used to bring home so much more as a corporate woman. I was so grateful for my $2500 a month residual income, but it was not going to cut it in order to keep up with our lifestyle.

My frustration grew in the business and I got stuck at the same level for four years. I felt paralyzed and embarrassed by the debt I was building.

I knew I was playing small in my business by not showing up consistently, and I was scared to lead a team. What if I failed my team? It was easier to avoid them than to try and help them. I listened to top leaders preach about the importance of investing in yourself and showing up to events, conferences—to be loud and proud! I used every excuse: I'm too busy, my kids are too young, I don't have enough money to attend events, and secretly, I just thought I was just too cool for this business model. I was holding myself back and I knew it.

*

"Bye, girls," I said, and then kissed my daughters' cheeks as they anxiously walked onto the bus headed to their new school. My first chapter of parenthood was closing. They both would be in school full time and I would have the day to myself. That reflection of now what was building in my heart. Holding back the tears as the lump in my throat grew, I waved goodbye. Their little heads stared out the window, their faces unsure and scared. I turned my head and started walking up the long country driveway towards the house so they couldn't see the tears pouring down my face.

Why is it so hard to let them go?

I dreamed of this day for years, to have all day to do what I wanted, but I was so sad and empty. *Now what?* I thought again, and again. *What should, could, would I do to stay home and still make enough money to support our family's future?*

A week after school started, the dreaded conversation with my husband finally happened.

"Nicole, you've got a year to pay your $20,000 debt and show me you can make something out of this NWM, or you're going to have to go back to your corporate job," said my frustrated husband.

I understood his frustration, and it was go-time. I needed to do this for my family and, most importantly, to prove to myself I was worthy of success again. I was in love with the results it provided for my customers and my team was amazing; it was just me holding back my own success. I knew it was time to level up and do the high-paying activity, because there was no way I was going back to my corporate job.

*

Six years after I started my NWM business, I found myself sitting at a conference on a Saturday morning with my family, head pounding, mouth dry and pasty, nursing a hangover. My amazing team was sitting in the audience, waiting to cheer me on, and I wanted so badly to make them proud. I was so grateful so many had flown to the USA from Canada to support me. I heard my name being called from the main stage.

Sweating profusely, heart thumping, I wanted to run away. It was my turn to walk on stage and tell my story about how I got to a top leader position, and I just didn't feel ready. *I'm so scared I will screw up and embarrass myself,* I thought as I forced myself to get up on stage.

What could have been the happiest moment in my career felt like deception and deep sadness. Behind the scenes, my marriage was crumbling, my drinking was out of control, and I was broken. I did not feel like a great leader, and surely, I was not worthy of this new title.

A year earlier, desperately trying to save my marriage, I lay in bed after another big fight that led me to contemplate taking my own life. My dark thoughts rolled over and over through my confused head. Again, I found myself on my knees asking for God to show me a sign. My body lit up in gold and the warmth of God's love poured over me, something I had never seen or felt. I was bawling my eyes out and in shock and questioning what just happened. Yet the message was loud and clear; I had more work to do in this lifetime.

*

"Here you go, Ms. Scott. Congratulations on your purchase of your new town house; here are your keys."

It was a cold December afternoon when the movers pulled up, along with my two best friends to help me settle into our new home. My new single life was about to begin, and I had so many questions running through my insecure brain.

Will I ever find love again? Will my kids ever forgive me for leaving? What's next?

I knew something had to change or my money was going to run out fast. I still didn't have a big enough paycheck to cover all the bills.

Lying on the couch Christmas morning, kids dropped off at their dad's, the house was empty and cold. I already missed the noise, the coziness, my children, Christmas as I always knew it to be. The big questions began swirling in my head again. *Did I make the right choice?* I no longer have little girls' voices in the background. No little feet running up and down the stairs, no "Hey, Mom can you come here?" It was just me and my thoughts and my self-doubt... Now what?

That first year was an exhausting blur of emotions. Their broken hearts were part of my broken heart. My pain was my nudge, and I knew that I wanted it to be different. *Enough is enough, Nicole... I need to seek help.*

I picked up the heavy phone and heard my mentor's voice answer. "Hello, Mitra," I said. "I am ready to take my business to the next level so I don't have to go back to my corporate job. I need help. I need this to work."

She asked me, "What is your why?"

I gazed out the window at the townhouses around me, contemplating this question. "My mom was a single mom with four kids and we struggled hard, and even had to use the foodbank at times. We didn't have much and I heard NO a lot when I grew up, and I did not want that life or that cycle to repeat."

I went on to tell her that I was willing to do what it took to earn an aspirational income. I knew that I wanted to raise my girls on my terms and wanted to say YES more often. I was done living paycheck to paycheck. I wanted to have extra in the bank so I could start traveling more out west to see my family who I missed so much. I wanted to contribute to others in need. "I am ready and hungry to become the leader I am meant to be," I said, adding, "I just need guidance." It was a relief to say out loud what I'd been holding inside for so long.

Mitra paused and then said in a gentle voice, "Nicole, take a deep breath, close your eyes, and imagine what you want your life to look like, to feel like. Stay with me... Keep breathing deep and really feel it. Who is Nicole? What does she look like? How does she show up for herself? Her kids? Her team? Her community?

Where are you living? How often do you travel to see your family out west? How many customers do you have? How big is your team? What do your holidays look like? Are you single or with a loving partner? Are you happy? How much money do you see yourself making? What will you do with this money to serve others?"

Tears of hope filled my Kleenex for the first time as I sat with her over the phone in a meditative state, connecting to my 'why' and what my future could look like. I felt excited and could really see and feel what was possible if I truly started to work.

"Nicole, I believe in you, and you need to start believing in yourself," said Mitra. "This is your time. I want you to work on yourself every day. Personal development is the difference between great and mediocre leaders. If you invest in yourself daily, your business will start to grow. Promise me that self-care will be your top priority, because then you will have the energy to take care of the daily tasks of building your franchise. Deal?"

"Deal," I said confidently.

Mitra planted a seed in me that day that started to grow...

It was go-time! More self-development was required. I was going to prove to myself and to my girls that this momma bear was worthy of a life of freedom and achieving her dreams. I knew I wanted to impact more families with better health and help more women make supplemental income to help them achieve their dreams. I went to work. I showed up. I got brave and focused on having a helper's heart.

*

It was a rainy Friday morning when I got the news from corporate that our team had achieved our big, audacious goal. The first person I called was my BFF and top leader, Melissa Hyde. She answered the phone, and I screamed out, "OMG, we did it!! The team hit PMD+—thank you so much!"

We giggled and screamed over the phone together, like little kids winning a race. "Remember when you started working with me, and we used to say 'what if' a lot? What if we could make enough to pay for a car payment? What if we could get a free trip? What if we could pay our mortgage? What if we could afford a trip for our family?" Melissa remembered and celebrated with me. "Melissa, our dreams, our what ifs, are coming true. Thank you, friend, for trusting in me and believing in my leadership. I can't wait to help you keep growing and help you achieve more of your goals. We are just getting started."

I hung up the phone and ran upstairs to share the news with my love, Brad, and my girls, that this momma bear had achieved her goal. Jumping up and down, we hugged and danced in the hallway, celebrating together the pure joy of hitting such a huge goal.

*

I sat alone on the plane and gazed out the window at the cold winter in Toronto, headed to Mexico to visit my mom and bonus dad Jim for six weeks.

Pinch me.

I reflected on my new life—my dreams were coming true! A huge smile spread across my face. *Wow, Nicole, you are only 51, and now you have the freedom to play in this big, beautiful world. This is my dream board incarnate. I did it!*

I was able to take six weeks off to hang out with my parents and shop for a vacation property in Mexico, all because I finally listened to my mom and did not quit on myself. Mitra was right. Daily personal development was the key to breaking through fears and believing in myself again. My seven years post-divorce were a painful exploration of darkness that was necessary to go through to explode into the light. The butterfly emerged and proved she could accomplish that which she believed in. Was it hard? Yes. Was it worth it? Heck YEAH!

As my plane was about to land in Mexico, I finished up my PowerPoint presentation about my journey to the top. My final slide was pictures of my new life, including my blended family of seven, the new adventures we had taken, my new book about going grey, and the new condo we were planning to buy in Mexico, all because I said YES to NWM.

"Mom, Mom!" I shouted in the hot Mexico airport, waving my hands in delight as I spotted her signature silver hair and purple streaks sparkling in the sunlight. I ran to her, full of kid-like energy, and gave her the biggest hug.

I whispered in her ear, "Thank you, Mom, for being brave and sharing the Juice Plus+ business. Who would have thought that network marketing would change our lives forever? I can't believe you finally bought your dream home in Mexico, and to think we both considered quitting when it got hard. I can't wait to see your home and shop for my dream vacation property with you. I get six weeks to play with you in Mexico. What a gift! What a dream we have created."

Mom just smiled and squeezed me even tighter. "I knew you could do it," she said. "Now, let's go for a swim in the ocean."

CHAPTER 20

Love lifted me

Wendy Stewart

He's gone. My husband Mike is gone.

My best friend and Mike's boss knocked on the door what seemed like minutes after I had kissed Mike goodbye.

"I'm sorry, Wendy, but a crane has fallen on Mike at work and he passed away," he said, before pulling me into a comforting hug.

My nine month old, Michael, cried out. I immediately ran to his crib to pick him up. *He will never know his daddy.*

My house instantly filled with people. I didn't know them, but they seemed to care. I was in a daze. My happy life had changed in a minute. Mike and I had so many dreams. We thought we had found the answer to them; it was called Amway. Mike drew circles to share the business at night and I shared our products during the day. We had hope.

I took Michael and moved from Odessa to Dallas, Texas. I never heard from my support team again. I quit! I was a mess and needed help with just living day to day, needlessly trying to build a home-based business with no help. I quit dreaming of more and concentrated on my little boy.

Weighing now just a little over 90 pounds, there was an urgency for desperate change. To escape the solace of my unbearable grief, I needed an out. The local pub was where I landed. It was there I met Bobby. Bobby was a distraction that I let direct me to where and when I went next.

We moved to Waco and started an electrical business. Naturally, I was still grieving Mike's passing. I was just going through the motions of living. During the mid-1980s, the economy took a downward spiral, taking us with it. The contractors running the jobs we had invested in filed bankruptcy; our bank called our notes due. Making money as we knew it was over, and surprise! I was pregnant.

Landon was born July 30, 1986. He brought so much joy and happiness to an awful life.

Michael was thrilled to have a baby brother.

A couple of years after Landon was born, we were still financially in a mess. I had yard sales weekly and sold anything I thought we could live without to survive. We filed bankruptcy, owed the IRS $100,000, all our bills were due, and we didn't have a clue where to turn.

A business acquaintance named Gene Dalton called and asked if he could drop by with something to show us.

I welcomed him with open arms but knew I only had two hundred dollars and that I had to pay the electric bill and buy groceries. As he was leaving, he asked me, "Do you know anyone that would be interested in earning an extra five hundred dollars a month?"

I answered, "I'd like more information," and he left me with a two-hour long video.

I watched it several times and liked what I saw. One woman, Sue Burdick, caught my attention with all she had done prior to making money. I thought to myself, "If she can do it, so can I!" She said she was earning $10,000 a month, and that really caught my attention.

Today, with modern technology, we have tools that we didn't have when I started. It is so much easier to build. Gene and Audrey Dalton were the sweetest couple and made a decision to invest in me to help me get started. I made my list, joined arms with them, and we went to work! This was January 1988. I knew there had to be someone just like me, who needed money and was willing to work. I had been praying for answers to help us financially and heal my sadness.

It felt like God joined my mission, and several joined my team. We were having some fun and making money. The company was called National Safety Associates (NSA) and was based in Memphis, TN. I made a commitment with myself to try to build my business within a two-hour radius of Waco, and that worked with having two young boys. I would pick the boys up from school, help with homework in the car on our way to an event, feed them dinner when the event was over, and they would bunker down in the car to sleep on our drive home. We did the same routine at least two nights weekly. My days were spent working with my partners. I tried to focus with face-to-face meetings, having lunch, or meeting for coffee. One of my objectives was to meet more people to share my story in hopes it would increase my team. I made the top position of national marketing director (NMD) in 1990. I was proud and felt successful.

I helped build four national marketing directors in the Waco area. We had built a CO-OP in a beautiful building with four offices and enough space to seat one hundred guests. I was dreaming again!

With a loud knock on the door at 5 am, the IRS raised their heads with both our vehicles on tow trucks. They wanted to make an example of us, and we had no idea what the future held.

I was making money and excited—I knew God had answered my prayer. Then the IRS raised their heads again and levied my largest check of $22,000. There was no question what to do next. We hired an attorney to help us set up a payment plan, and I continued to work my NSA business and started paying some bills. Change is something I've learned to deal with over the years.

When payroll ran the next month, I decided to drive to NSA in Memphis, TN, to pick up my check the minute it was printed and cash it at their bank. It was only nine hours from Waco. I continued picking up my check monthly and started making that nine hour drive pay for itself by taking potential partners with me to go through a tour of NSA, showing the potential of National Safety Associates. It was a $5,000 buy-in to join at the level where you could start making money with NSA when I started. I started with a few water filters and four distributor kits in 1988.

I learned quickly how to make money with my new business and began sharing it with others. I was having success!

Now, it's 1993 and NSA has a new consumable product we are introducing to the market. It's called Juice Plus+. Since Juice Plus+ products are consumable, the marketing plan was changed. A few of my leaders decided it wasn't for them and moved on, but I stayed put. I continued taking trips to Memphis. I decided to start over when everything changed with NSA. I decided to play devil's advocate by purchasing $5,000 of Juice Plus+, which gave me exactly 72 two-packs of Juice Plus+. I was paying all my bills in person with cash and began to carry a four-month supply with me. And, as I had hoped, people started paying attention to me and asking what I was carrying with me all the time. I sold all my products in just two weeks. I proved to myself I could do business with Juice Plus+. Fortunately, it's so much easier today to build our business. Our company, the Juice Plus+ Company, does all the work except finding the customers and partners. Once we find a potential person, we have our own website and the new prospect can go and place their order and or sign to be a partner. It's amazing!!

In January 1995, Bobby and I finally divorced. At this point in time, though my divorce was final, new problems started to arise… my health. Amidst all these health complications, I continued sharing our products. My house sold, so Landon and I moved in with my sister, Joy, and her husband Randy. It was supposed to be a couple of months until I was back on my feet, but because of trouble with my surgery, it felt never-ending for all of us. I can never repay my sister and brother-in-law for their kindness and the love they showed for my sons and me. My surgery was scheduled for July 6, 1996, and even though my health wasn't good, I continued to push myself. My doctors gave me medication to help with my heart function, but the meds were a temporary fix.

In the spring of 1996, I was asked by Sean Hopkins and Gail Bosclair (both worked for Paul in the Canadian office) if I would fill in for a cancellation at an event in Vancouver and Victoria, BC. I said yes. Being new to Canada, Gail said Paul Stewart, President of National Safety Associates Canada, would pick me up at the airport. I had met Paul in passing at the Crowne Plaza Hotel in Memphis at our conference in October 1995. He had a beautiful smile and I was interested in learning more about him. Paul began working for National Safety Associates Canada in the mid-1990s when the company was buying back product distributors had purchased and stacked in their garages instead of working their business and selling the product to the end consumer. It wasn't a fun time to work with NSA, but for those of us that stayed through the buybacks and introducing Juice Plus+ to the market, it has paid off. I can't see myself being with any other company ever! Paul started working as the president as an employee in the beginning, but an opportunity opened for him to buy shares and partner with three others; at that time, Juice Plus+ was the focus, making Paul the president and CEO for Juice Plus+ Canada. He and his staff worked tirelessly with partners in the field to turn a company that was in the red to one that was doing seven figures plus a month.

After getting to know Paul in BC, we began talking two and three times a day. Thank God for cell phones, or we wouldn't have gotten any work done. We started meeting every two weeks; Bobby had Landon every other weekend, and I was free to go. Paul and I were getting pretty close. In June of 1996, Landon, Michael, and I went to Paul's for a visit. I wanted Paul to know my great kids and the boys to get to know Paul. We had never been to Canada to actually see it, and I wanted us to experience it together. We stayed a month.

The kids and I drove back to Texas just in time for me to check into the hospital for my previously scheduled surgery. I cried a lot on that trip back. I didn't know what the outcome would be. I knew God was in control but wasn't sure we were on the same page.

On July 5, 1996, I checked into the hospital with Paul and my family surrounding me. Surgery was scheduled for the next morning. My surgeon, Dr. Pepper, came out from surgery drinking a Dr. Pepper and told Paul it hadn't gone as planned. The valve was replaced, but he was working in such a small space he had accidentally cut a thoracic duct and didn't know how to repair it. Once they found a surgeon, they would have it repaired.

The doctor released me from the hospital, but after just a week at home with my sister, she took me in for a follow-up and I began having problems at the doctor's office. They rushed me to the hospital.

After a month, my kidneys failed and my liver hemorrhaged, which forced the doctor to find help, and they rushed me by ambulance to Dallas for three more surgeries.

I was doing all I knew to be healthy again. I wanted my life back. I'd been in my sister's home a year and knew they probably wanted their life back as well. I felt like my hands were tied with my health being so unstable.

I started trying to make some serious decisions. I had an 18 year old in his own apartment and knew moving back with Mom wasn't what he wanted. I also knew Paul and I had become really close. I'd been looking at buying, renting, or possibly moving to Paul's home in Toronto, Canada.

In December 1996, Landon and I moved to Canada and cohabitated with Paul and his nine year old daughter, Victoria, in an adult lifestyle condominium. I'm pretty sure Landon and Victoria broke every rule the condo board had. We enjoyed living in the condo but knew we would have to make a better choice once we were married.

In the meantime, Paul hired a sweet woman to help with the kids and I. I was still healing from the surgeries and couldn't do the simple things it took to keep a house running.

Not long after I moved to Toronto, my support team, Gene and Audrey, moved to Tennessee. It wasn't long after Gene and Audrey moved that I received a call from Elton Dubois, former VP of Internal Affairs. He made the suggestion that my team and I work under the Daigle Team. They lived close to my Texas team and would be a valuable asset if the need arose. I spoke to Paul about it, and it was a unanimous yes.

Despite joining the Daigle team, Audrey and I stayed in touch. Gene passed away a few years after from Alzheimer's. Audrey passed away on June 7 this year, just one day before what would have been her and Gene's 71st wedding anniversary. Her son said it was the most beautiful passing he had ever witnessed. Audrey was always so uplifting when we talked and God's word was a part of who she was. They are both missed. I will never forget how hard we worked together to build our NSA business and the friendship we felt regarding each other. My children even commented that Gene and Audrey felt like our grandparents.

She was so appreciative of the succession plan they received and thanked me for my part in that; I told her I just worked. But, deep down, my heart is blessed with the small part I might have played. With feeling more secure about my Juice Plus+ business, and my health now on the mend, I realized my heart now had room for more. Paul and I bought a house in Cheltenham, a small community with a school, church, country store, and golf course. Just the right place to raise two kids.

We got married in our backyard with about 50 friends and family. It was lovely! Our home was surrounded by one hundred acres and we were able to cross-country ski, snowmobile, ice skate, play ice hockey, and more. I couldn't wait until I could set up the house with my personal belongings.

My friend and one of my NMDs, Steve Monson, rented a U-Haul and met my son Michael at the storage locker where everything I owned was stored and drove it from Waco, Texas, to Cheltenham, ON, Canada. I was so appreciative. I will never forget Steve calling me from the Canadian border, needing me to meet him so they would let him crossover. I had to prove it was all my furnishings. Needless to say, he flew back to Texas. Steve Monson was a great guy!

Unfortunately, Steve passed away a couple of years after, as did another one of my good friends and NMDs, Kathy Logan. Like I said, change is one thing you can count on. It's just how you deal with it that matters. I work even today with both Steve and Kathy's teams, and I appreciate their commitment and the love they had toward their business.

In August 2022, I asked Paul for 50 years of marriage when we said our first I Do's. We will be married 25 years on the thirtieth of this month. Nothing is perfect, and I found that, being married to the president and CEO of Juice Plus+ Canada, I was the president's wife instead of Wendy Stewart, NMD.

I have struggled building my business for that reason. Paul asks me all the time, "If you could change anything, what would it be?" My honest answer would be not one thing. I'm very happy being married to Paul. I have great respect for my husband. Since his retirement, we've worked out a great plan and bought a house in Waco to be south in the winter so we get the best of both worlds. Our kids live in Texas as well as our five grandchildren. The holidays are amazing. Lots of love and food!

Paul enjoyed his success with NSA/Juice Plus+ Canada. He took over a company that was overstaffed and too large a space with partners lined up down the street to sell their water filters back to NSA. After he hired a new office team and moved the office to cut costs, business began to turn around for the Canadian office. He spent many years running Juice Plus+ Canada with success. Once Paul retired, it seemed I found my footing again with Juice Plus+. I'm Wendy Stewart, PMD, and Mrs. Paul Stewart. I work with my team almost daily, scheduling zoom and three-way calls. I've added to my team in Canada and the USA. I look forward to Monday morning zooms and seeing my Juice Plus+ community. I've been seeing this community on Mondays for several years. Training from the Freedom Revolution, Juice Plus+ Insights, and now the HUB.

I will continue to share Juice Plus+ as the great product it is and will still look for partners through my journey of life.

AUTHORS

Ali Schneider

"Say yes and figure it out"

Email alischneider34@gmail.com
IG @ali_schneider34   **FB** @ali.schneider2

My desire is to inspire other people (specifically women) that they can build a business with the Juice Plus+ Company, no matter what else they have going on. To a fault, I am the epitome of busy and over scheduled. I am the wife of a Division I Head Basketball Coach. I am a homeschooling mom. My husband and I have two boys (ages 12 and 11). We have too many pets to count, yet I do count them because I also find myself in charge of keeping them alive. I coach and run a youth basketball program. We live on 11 acres of awesomeness that also translates to time and work. My philosophy in building a Juice Plus+ business has always been, "Say yes and figure out the details later."

With a Masters Degree in Health, Physical Education, and Recreation, my passion has always been helping people and educating people on living a healthy lifestyle. I have worn many different hats in the health and fitness industry, including college professor, personal trainer, group fitness instructor, manager of a fitness center, nutrition counselor, and coach. My role as an Executive Marketing Director with The Juice Plus+ Company allows me to fuel my passion of helping others get healthy while providing our family with a life changing income stream.

My goal is to model, motivate, and help lay a path for other busy people who desire to live a healthy lifestyle and/or build a business with The Juice Plus+ Company.

Barb Kunst

Email barbkunst.juiceplus@gmail.com
Web bkunst.juiceplus.com
IG @barbkunst **FB** @barb.kunst

As a Presidential Marketing Director Plus (PMD+) with the Juice Plus+ Company I live the mission of 'Inspiring Healthy Living Around the World'. The power of making a decision to change the world is magical.

I believe everything happens for a reason; the Juice Plus+ business was destined to find me 18 years ago, so I could leave my footprint on this earth making a difference.

Success has challenges, the ebbs and flows of life have given me my greatest strength to lead with a servant heart gifting hope, living my purpose and passion with integrity, honesty, and loyalty; challenging me to become focussed, share more, and appreciate the people that surround me in my life with love, empathy, and boundaries shaping me into the woman I am today.

My husband Hank and I reside in a farming community in Alberta, Canada. I'm a mom to our daughter Karyn, son Michel; and Oma to two grandsons, Boston and Olson. They are my life, and the reason for my passion as I leave my legacy...

Everyone needs a plan B in their life. If my story inspires you to have a Plan B and leave your legacy, I welcome you to join my team and help share the 'Gift of Health'.

Bob & Sue Burdick

"You can make the bed, or you can make a fortune"

Email Sue@BurdickEnterprises.com
IG @sueburdick   **FB** @SueBurdick

I built a business as a busy mother of five without an education or budget. I have spent the last 35 years teaching others to set goals and establish a daily method of operation. One of my greatest joys is to watch other women achieve and blossom into the people they were always meant to be.

I feel the most significant advantage I provide is experience. This is a road I have traveled many times over and my experience with struggles and obstacles helps me identify pitfalls, while developing strategies to overcome those hurdles.

As a high school dropout, house cleaner, dog groomer, aerobics teacher, and construction worker, I tried many ways to earn money for my family of five teenage boys before coming across a system of earning money while helping people that changed my perspective, helped me experience personal growth, and changed the trajectory of my family.

Since 1987, we have built a business that spans 28 countries and traveled around the world dozens of times teaching people how to master their own future and develop their own version of success and happiness.

In 1999, my husband and I became the third recipients of the prestigious Founders Award, given by our parent company for the work we did building our team, traveling millions of miles around the world teaching partners from the entire company the techniques to find our own success.

Curt & Lori Beavers

Email curt@makealife.com
Web MakeALife.com

I love life! Lori and I have a passion to help people make the life they desire. The solution starts with understanding your purpose, and then building a business that allows you to pursue that to the fullest. We can do that together. God has a unique plan for each of us!

Actually, I wrote a book (MakeALife.com) about this very thing. I believe that everyone deserves to make a life, not just a living. Helping people see their potential through an abundance mindset is truly rewarding.

This business has given us choices, and choices are the thing in life that makes you rich. We love our church, Bible study, and lots of great ministries. This business has allowed me to serve on many boards, write two books, and spend time with my amazing family and friends. I love the outdoors. Hunting, fishing, skiing, lake-life, boats, golf and more. Time on my tractor at the farm is a blast too. I've even done a zoom call from my tractor mentoring a new team member. Life is FUN!

Lori and I have 3 adult kids (all married to amazing spouses) and 3 grandchildren. I have degrees from Emory University, Georgia Tech, and a Masters in Biblical Studies from Logos University. Our business is in over 25 countries and all 50 states.

Find God's unique and perfect purpose for your life. Then, build a business that becomes the foundation to pursue it. I would love to do this with you!

Dany & Debbie Martin

"There are no excuses, only priorities"

Email dany@cox.net **Web** danymartin.com
IG @danymartinsr **FB** @dany.martin.980

Growing up in very modest circumstances in Baton Rouge, LA, we both believed hard work and loyalty are vital to success. We also learned in our early careers that it is important to discover joy and fulfillment in your work. Doing something you love every day and bringing value to others is the way to build a career that doesn't simply focus on paying the bills.

Now residing in Gonzales, Louisiana, we have been married since April, 1989 and are the proud parents of two sons, Devan and Dany Jr., married to Lindsi. We love being involved in our church and community activities and organizations.

Starting our Virtual Franchise with The Juice Plus+ Company in February 1990, we have been able to build a better life consisting of time freedom and family choices. We enjoy an international business and the recognition as leaders in our company.

Surrounding ourselves with amazing mentors over the years, we have learned the skills, knowledge, and wisdom to coach business strategies and self-development to thousands of others around the world. We have also raised our boys with these life-lessons. Touching and changing lives for the better is a rewarding experience. Life takes fortitude and resilience, but living well can bring gratitude and joy.

We KNOW the Juice Plus+ Virtual Franchise Business Model has been life changing for many families around the world.

Dougie Barlow

Citizen of Earth, Agent for Change, RLT
"If you are not living on the edge, chances are
you are taking up too much space"

Email dougbarlow@ssintl.org
IG @itsmedougieb
Co-founder Shiningstarinternational.com

Yo Yo, it's me, Dougie B. I grew up enjoying the snow belt of Western NY and the Canadian shore of Lake Erie. These two environments have offered me a lifetime's worth of outdoor adventure as an avid backcountry skier and competitive sailor. With an affinity for all forms of water I wound up at the United States Merchant Marine Academy where I earned a Bachelor's of Science in Marine Engineering Systems and a 3rd Assistant Engineer's license with the United States Coast Guard. Shipboard life gave me the opportunity to travel the world and brought me to the Pacific NW in my early 20s.

After a productive ten years in the maritime industry I needed a change. Life was good on the ship, but I wanted great! How was I to know that a casual dinner invitation would lead to a career as a successful affiliate with a world leader in the functional food arena? Since 1994 I have enjoyed helping people who are willing to change, improve their relationship to health span and free time. I was having so much fun with the woman who brought me this wonderful business opportunity that we chose to be life partners as well. Dr. Mitra Ray and I currently live on the shores of the Salish Sea in Northwestern WA state, and we are the proud parents of three wonderful adult daughters.

Harriet Sulcer

"Tenacity In the middle of the mess"

Web harrietsulcer.com

Almost thirty five years ago, I became a National Marketing Director with the Juice Plus+ Company. Through the years it's been my mission to Help Families Thrive.

As a member of the prestigious Founders Club, I am invested in developing leaders. My passion is mentoring women by inspiring and equipping them to reach their full potential.

For four decades, I have enjoyed serving as a women's Bible study teacher. It was a privilege to be featured on the 700 Club as well as several appearances on Atlanta Live.

My book, Promise Point, has brought encouragement and hope to many families in crisis. Dr. Gerald Harris, past editor of The Christian Index makes this statement in his endorsement, "In her book, Harriet takes us on a journey from the valley of despair to the pinnacle of blessing and the journey is nothing less than a modern day Pilgrim's Progress."

Although my residence is in Atlanta, home to me is Promise Point, the mountain lodge my husband and I built in the Blue Ridge Mountains. My greatest joy is having all my children and grandchildren gathered there to make lifelong memories.

It's then I'm reminded that this dream became a reality because of the opportunity I was given with the Juice Plus+ Company.

Ilona Morrison

Email ilonamorrison@gmail.com
IG @ilonainkelowna

I am a wife to my husband Jon and a mom to my daughter Zsofia and my son Andras. I live in Kelowna, BC, Canada. People know me as Ilona from Kelowna :-)

I was born in Budapest, Hungary, lived there until I was 9 years old, moved to Germany for 4.5 years and landed in Mississauga, Ontario at 14.5 years old. Without any language skills I learnt to adapt and fit in into a new country and culture.

I graduated from Georgian College with a Business Administration/ Human Resources Diploma. Hoping to work somewhere where I can help people. After working at many jobs I am so glad 7.5 years ago I joined the Juice Plus+ Company where I can work on my own terms and authentically help people on their health and wealth journey.

Helping other moms that have lost themselves, forgot how to have fun, have no self worth, and who are ready for a change brings me so much joy. I can relate, I have been there, I have gone through it and I can show them how to live their best life every single day confidently.

Helping people grow their own food with the tower garden is another huge passion of mine. Everyone should have the ability to grow their own food.

I wake up everyday with my passion in mind and ready to help whoever wants to make a change in their life. Connect with me—I love meeting new friends and business partners.

Janice Neigum

"Own my impact"

Email janiceneigum@gmail.com **Web** earth.canada.juiceplus.ca
IG @neigumjanice **FB** @Janice Neigum

I have been on an unexpected, wonderful & messy journey with the Juicplus+ Company for 17 years this October. I am a woman of passion and when I believe in making a difference I use my heart to guide me. I turn 70 years young this September and this company has allowed me to live with passion and realise my dreams.

My husband and I recently celebrated 30 years together, married 28. Loving 16 grandchildren requires extra income so we can enjoy adventures together.

We currently sponsor 5 children with different charities and in different countries. My husband & I volunteer with "The Refuge of Hope". My husband assisted in wiring the building where the children are fed delicious, healthy meals, educated and made to feel loved and included! The best part is this is all free to the parents whose children are in need. We are currently working with a family whose 10 year old son requires surgery for his club foot. The process began when our daughter Nicole said, how can we help? The rest on the story is nothing short of a miracle.

Life became a daily miracle when I believed I came here for the bigger purpose of raising others up! Some days it is as simple as a smile or a compliment from the heart.

The icing on the cake was when our daughter, Nicole Scott, purchased her Dream Vacation Condo in the same city we winter in beautiful, Bucerias, Mexico.

Jeff Roberti

Email jeff@roberti.net
Web roberti.net

Do you know what I love about this business? For the past 36 years, I've been blessed with the opportunity to mentor and inspire others on a daily basis while creating a lifestyle that I never dreamed possible when I first began in Network Marketing. What has really been powerful is that over the last three decades, I've been able to witness countless people improve their health, improve their lives, and build a business of their own. For me, that is the definition of fulfillment.

My wish for you is that you pursue your own dreams of greatness. There is greatness in every single one of you. If I can do it, YOU can do it! It hasn't always been easy, but it's been worth it!

One of my mottos is that "No dream is possible unless it's greater than your biggest obstacles in life." As I shared in my story, the bigger the problem, the bigger the paycheck, and I've embraced the challenge of every big problem I've encountered! For me, it's like, "BRING IT ON!"

Have the mindset that every obstacle can be overcome – you just have to be resourceful and confident (bring in that Certainty I talked about), knowing that you have the power to tackle anything that comes your way. And with a bit of ingenuity and a lot of hard work, you'll be reaching your dreams and inspiring others to live theirs'. You got this... and you have my support all the way!

Jennifer Myers

Email jennifer@myers.bz
IG @jennifermyers10   FB @Jennifer Myers

I am all about living a life well-designed and on purpose while empowering others to do the same. With a Bachelor of Business from the University of Kansas, my husband and I began our 33 year career with the Juice Plus+ Company. Meeting people where they are, while inspiring and guiding them to where they want to go, has helped me attain the top position of PMD+ in the company as well as the prestigious Founder's Award.

Coaching people to see past the limitations that hold them back and inspiring them to breakthrough and become more than they had originally thought possible is a focus of my life's work. I love speaking across the country and internationally on health and wellness, as well as training others to build a business and life they love.

Sean and I have lived an extremely adventurous life as we've spent time in over 80 countries. We sailed from the British Virgin Islands to Australia over 15 months while homeschooling our two amazing children, Mikaela and Jake.

With the right discipline, focus, strategy, and mindset anyone can transform from where they are to where they want to be—and have it all. I've become certified in Healing Touch and Reiki and believe that in order to move past current limitations people need a holistic approach to not only their health, but their direction in life.

I look forward to the opportunity to serve, lead and help people find their inner happiness!

Kerry & Mickey Daigle

Web keeppunching.com
Web mickeydaigle.com

I am a proud Cajun from Louisiana who walked into the Juice Plus+ Company with my guard up high, trying to avoid the punch coming right at me. Coming from professional boxing taught me to always avoid taking a punch. That was until my friend, Emile, who I turned down for 6 weeks on a daily basis to look at the business behind Juice Plus+, spoke to my wife, Mickey. She joined the company and I became her first partner. That day she met Emile changed our lives drastically over the next few years.

My profession as an international boxing and concert promoter doing business with all the major networks and cable giants was something I enjoyed. I loved what I was doing although I worked 70 hours a week. Little did I realize Mickey's decision would send me on a different journey.

I started studying network marketing and eventually was chosen to serve on the board of directors of a direct selling organization that worked with over 2000+ network marketing companies. That experience gave me the confidence to help Mickey design a plan to build an international business.

Today I am known as a talent scout and mental fitness coach in both combat sports and the Juice Plus+ Company. Mickey became known as a powerful and empowering leader among women. In 2012 we were both awarded the Founders Award, the highest honor given in all 26+ countries, by the President of Juice Plus+.

Loren Lahav

IG @I AMLORENLAHAV   **FB** @Loren Lahav
Email Loren@lorenlahav.com   **Podcast** THE LOREN LAHAV Podcast

If you want to learn some no-nonsense, proven strategies to manifest your dreams and live YOUR best life, I would be honored to support you. I am living proof of why being True to YOUR style is your secret sauce.

AND I've applied the learnings from 33 years of helping tens of thousands of people around the world get real about what they truly desire, inspiring them to take action to achieve their dreams. I'm not afraid to call you out on what's not working in your life and tell you (with love) to get your as* off the couch and take action: aka GOYA – (Get Off Your As*!).

I've had the honor to meet wonderful people hungry for more happiness in all areas of their lives. As the original facilitator for **Tony Robbins' Life Mastery Program**. I have facilitated 250+ Life Mastery events in Fiji, Europe and the U.S.   I've also been a keynote speaker for audiences of 10,000+ at high profile events for over 2 decades. And had the honor of sharing my message in the five best-selling books that I've authored, which have been translated and distributed all over the world.

And I can help YOU do the same.

I am a **PMD+** with the **Juice Plus+ Company**. We are **YOLO International** with teams of tens of thousands in 20+ countries and over 45 NMDs and above. **Juice Plus+** has enabled us to create a global community.

My greatest joy is being a mama to Jos (26), Quinn (22) and Asher (15). I am bonus mom to Sam (26) and….I met my husband Z at baggage claim.

Remember to Stay True to Who YOU are and OWN YOUR WORTH!!!

Melissa Hyde

Personal Trainer and Network Marketing Trainer/Coach

Email melissaannhyde@gmail.com
Web melissahyde.ca
IG @melissaannhyde   **IG** @your_network_marketing_coach
FB @melissagayowskyhyde   **Podcast** Network Marketing Nuggets

I'm a mind, body, and soul coach and one of my superpowers is being able to help people realize their unique gifts which ignite their life's vision and set their soul on fire.

I've spent my entire life in sports being coached and/or working in a coaching capacity. Still an athlete, Peloton and CrossFit are daily activities. My career as a fitness instructor and personal/team trainer began 35 years ago while obtaining my Kinesiology degree from UWO.

Knowing that a strong mindset is equally as important as physical training, I went back to school and became a Certified rREST Mindset Coach. With this training I can help my clients even more by clearing emotional barriers that hold them back.

15 years ago, in my search for a multi vitamin for my kids, I was introduced to Juice Plus+. It just made sense and the rest is history. I'm an Executive Marketing Director with The Juice Plus+ Company where I continue to live my passion for training and coaching network marketers globally.

I'm super excited to be launching my new podcast entitled Network Marketing Nuggets. And I've also co-created The Menopause Reset. Success in business starts with good health.

If I'm not travelling, you'll find me at my cottage just north of Toronto, Canada with my hubby Rick and our three greatest achievements; Kenzi 26, Maddie 24 and Calvin 22. We are still not empty nesters :)

Nicole Scott

Web nicolescott.online
IG @Gorgeous Grey Movement

I am a mom who cares deeply about others and I am so grateful that I found a passion for helping women feel their best.

I graduated from the University of Calgary with a BA in Psychology and Business minor. I spent ten years in the food manufacturing industry in sales before changing careers after learning my daughter had food allergies. After graduating from the Canadian School of Natural Nutrition, I was blessed to work in a wellness clinic, consulting and teaching nutrition workshops in my community. In 2005, I added Juice Plus+ as a tool in my practice and today I am a top global leader inspiring healthy living around the world.

I am a new author of the Gorgeous Grey Movement and currently working on an upcoming podcast that will focus on having real conversations about aging as a woman. During the pandemic I went back to school to become an rREST Mindset Coach in order to support my clients better. I am also the co-creator of the NEW Menopause Reset 8 week program launching in the Fall of 2022.

I believe every woman deserves to feel their best at any age. Hence why I have dedicated my life to helping women gain confidence in achieving their health and wealth goals.

Nila Mason

Email nila@nilamason.com **Web** nilamason.com
IG @nilamason **FB** @Nila Mason

I enjoy inspiring people to be more, do more, have more, so they may give more. People often settle in life, not recognizing that their untapped talents could make a difference in their own lives as well as others. I show individuals why they are meant for more and how to turn that wish into reality. Good health is the catalyst. When the mind and body function optimally, roadblocks and detours give way to superhighways for happiness.

I own International Marketing, LLC, teaching people how to be healthy and create wealthy lifestyles. I mentor others to create a home-based business around freedom and flexibility that will impact the quality of their life and others worldwide. I have enjoyed speaking throughout the United States, Canada, Puerto Rico and Europe.

I especially enjoy empowering women who perhaps because of a challenge or setback, can now see a path for fulfillment, purpose, dignity and joy.

I have a Bachelor of Arts in English and for ten years taught high school English. I have a Masters Degree in Social Work and was a representative with the United States Chamber of Commerce for six years.

I am a Presidential Marketing Director Plus (PMD+) having been with the Juice Plus+ Company thirty-four years. Combining teaching and people skills, I rewardingly have been able to impact thousands of lives. I look forward to the future.

I reside in Kansas City, Missouri. I especially enjoy traveling, sailing, entertaining, creative writing, and being with my family.

Radka Prusha

Web phytosforlife.com

The direction of my life changed when my father passed away from cancer at an early age. Upon immigrating from Prague, Czech Republic with a Masters in Biology, I became a research scientist at McGill University, working in both the lab and hospital within Breast Cancer and Bone Marrow Transplant sciences. I also spent time in the fields of Neuro Immunology and Virology where my research has been published.

I broadened my education in 2005, receiving the Master's degree in Nutrition. I was drawn to the science of nutrition and its undeniable impact. I recently completed certification as a Certified Holistic Cancer Practitioner (CHCP) in an effort to round out my understanding of the prevention, causes, and treatments.

As a National Marketing Director with the Juice Plus+ Company, I am enjoying sharing the science and simplicity of whole food nutrition, while having fun with a purpose driven community of like-minded people.

I live in our dream home in Brentwood Bay on beautiful Vancouver Island with my family and favorite running partner, black lab Ruby Roo.

Shelly Mackey

Email mackey9124@gmail.com
Web shellymackey.juiceplus.com

I am 61 years old and have been married to Mark Mackey for 33 years. Our family lives outside Kansas City on a working cattle ranch.

I graduated from Kansas State University with a degree in Elementary Education. I taught 3rd grade until becoming a stay at home mommy for 25 years to Morgan, Marisa, Maggie, and Joe-Joe. I became a chauffeur for a gazillion sports, short order cook, maid, and 24/7 on-call nurse… I traded in my uniform from being a college cheerleader at KSU to being the Mackey family cheerleader!!!

I began sharing the mission of "Inspiring Healthy Living in Others Around the World" November 2013. In one year, I made the top level of The Juice Plus+ Company, becoming a National Marketing Director in November 2014. Just ten months later, I promoted two frontline NMD's in two different states, my "Team JCJP+" reached 75 Club (this was my very FIRST attendance to the Elton's) & I was awarded "24 Club Member of the year". The following year our team hit 100 Club in record time & I was "nominated for 39 Club of the Year!" Fall 2021, I was awarded "Resilient Leader" award at the Elton's.

My friends and family call me passionate, energetic and infectious! I feel my true calling from the Lord is to help others in all facets of their life… from their walk with God to their journey of health and everything else in between!

Wendy Campbell

RN, PMD+

Email wendycnmd@gmail.com

I believe God challenged me with the awesome responsibility of not only touching current and future generations with health, but also through authenticity, vulnerability, and empowering others to achieve their full potential to live a truly abundant life.

My husband of over 40 years and two of our three grown children and their families live in the beautiful mountains of Montana where we have horses to ride, cattle to herd, rivers to go tubing and fishing, lakes to enjoy wakeboarding and sailing and golf courses galore.

After graduating from the University of Hawaii School of Nursing, my career path highlights included: Medical, Surgical, Pediatrics, Psychiatric, Gastroenterology Lab, Supervisor E.R. and O.R. and Supervisor for a major Hawaiian Hospital and Clinic.

However, as much as I have loved every nursing position through the years, they all paled in comparison to the personal growth and financial rewards I've been blessed with for over 28 years with The Juice Plus+ Company. As of August 2022, our "Campbell Team" has birthed 175 creative, brilliant and servant hearted "National Marketing Directors" with well over half of them moving to even higher echelons of achievement.

I've had the privilege of speaking throughout the United States, Canada, Germany, Belgium, France, Italy, Australia and the United Kingdom and have been recognized beautifully with special awards throughout the years including: "Elton's 39 Club Duplicator Award", "Elton's Organizational Development" and the most esteemed, "Founder's Award", in 2008.

My motto: "Honor God; Serve People"

Wendy Stewart

Email jpwithwendy@gmail.com
Web wendystewart.juiceplus.com

I was born and raised in Texas in 1955 with a heart defect which affects me today. Learning from my grandparents, I've learned to buy and sell anything from antiques to travel trailers to earn a living. I decorated repossessed houses for one of the largest banks in Waco to update and increase the sale of the properties until the middle eighties when banking and construction took a downward spiral.

I joined National Safety Assoc. in 1988, and have helped introduce several products to the market from water filtration, air filtration, and more. Today I am sharing what I feel is the right product at the right time—Juice Plus+.

I live in Campbellford, On. Canada with my husband Paul six months of the year and we live in our home in Waco, Tx the other six months. We have three children and five grandchildren.

WRITE YOUR OWN BOOK

Have you thought about writing a book?

Do you want to raise your profile, get professional speaking engagements, or charge more for your coaching or consulting?

But you're overwhelmed with where to start…?

Maybe you're worried that you're not a good enough writer or concerned what others will think?

You can write a beautiful book, with the right guidance.

Our aim with book coaching is to provide you with all the guidance and support you need to:

- Get clarity on the exact book idea which will position you as an authority and raise your profile so you can attract high calibre clients and/or opportunities.

- Have a clear map of which steps to take each week through the entire writing and publishing process so you never get overwhelmed wondering what to do next.

- Keep accountable to your writing goals so you can set a launch date and stick to it without feeling like this book is taking over your whole life.

- Get feedback to improve your writing each week so you don't have to worry if your book is any good and just know that you're delivering a high quality product.

- Create a strategy for promoting your book so you can be seen in all the right places by the right people, and ultimately, earn more money.

- Have my team take care of editing, formatting and publishing so that you can just focus on writing your book and doing what you do best!

Please visit www.changeempire.com and schedule a free initial chat about your book idea.

I can't wait to hear from you.

Cathryn Mora

Founder, Head Coach and Publishing Director
Change Empire Books

Instagram   @changeempirebookcoaching
LinkedIn   linkedin.com/in/cathryn-mora/
Email   publisher@changeempire.com